The Homemaker's SAMPLER

A collection of family favorites from Homemakers Extension Association (H.E.A.) members in Macoupin County commemorating their fiftieth year.

Compiled by
The
Macoupon County Homemakers Extension Association
Macoupin County, Illinois
1980

COVER DESIGN BY MRS. DORIS KANALLAKAN LACY

Macoupin County Homemakers Extension Association
210 North Broad Street
Carlinville, Illinois 62626

International Standard Book Number—0-918544-45-9

Printed in the United States of America
Wimmer Brothers Fine Printing & Lithography
Memphis,Tennessee 38118

"Cookbooks of Distinction"™

H.E.A. PIONEER

BERTHA O. ELDRED
1888-1978

Each organization has its champions. Bertha O. Eldred was our champion and founder of HOME BUREAU in Macoupin County. In the early years she traveled miles over roads that were sometimes almost impassable to spread the word of Extension and unite the county for a very worthy cause. Following in the footsteps of her father, founder of the 4-H movement, she gathered homemakers together and after two years of hard work saw a dream become a reality. On October 24, 1930, Macoupin County Home Bureau emerged as the only professional organization for homemakers. Bertha O. Eldred was elected the organization's first president, an office she held for two years.

i

FOREWORD

THE HOMEMAKER'S SAMPLER offers 751 family favorite recipes, old and new, and is submitted by "good cooks" of Macoupin County. The recipes are edited for clarity by the Cookbook Committee.

Good cooking is easy on the taste, but difficult to describe. The language of good eating is found in good recipes and that is the reason why The Homemakers Extension Association (H.E.A.) created THE HOMEMAKER'S SAMPLER as the most fulfilling way to commemorate its Fiftieth Anniversary—1930-1980. A special page is presented in honor of Bertha O. Eldred, its first president.

During its fifty years, H.E.A. kept pace with social, economic, political, and cultural changes. The roots of many of the recipes in the sampler come from the iron kettles on the old kitchen wood-burning stove. These roots have subsequently reached into the saucepans of the gas stove, the pyrex dishes of the electric burner, and are now in microwave cookware.

Cooking today is yet another art form. Good recipes have become as lyrics to song, as paints to art, as scenes to drama. They now charm young and old, men and women, rich and poor. H.E.A. helped make nutritious cooking an art. Its members have drawn from American heritage and from great cooks worldwide to enhance the spirit of loveliness in the eating of good food. The chicken dumpling, the pasta from Italy, the Quiche from France, Pita Bread from Greece . . .

The historians of H.E.A. have carefully recorded its fifty-year history. They moved from the written word of secretary's minutes, to pictures, historical books, photography, tapes, and other media to record its history. These are available to its many publics, and may be found in the Macoupin County Extension Office. Obviously, the depth and length of its fifty-year history, with its many distinguished individual contributions, are too great to be documented in this foreword, however, the compilers would like to focus on a few memories.

The *Thirties* began with an organizational meeting on October 24, 1930, with the required 550 members. [Five hundred twenty-seven were presented; (payment for an additional 32 was advanced from proceeds earned from sales at the County Farm Bureau Picnic)] and a dream became a reality! During the following years, signers found it difficult to be relieved of their commitment to join Home Bureau. Ministers' spouses were accepted as honorary members.

Gertrude Beckman was employed first home adviser; $435 was borrowed from Farm Bureau to purchase a car and pay insurance; a desk was purchased for $10 and a typewriter for $57.50, and the Home Bureau Office was officially opened.

Foods and Nutrition was selected as the first topic of study, followed by sewing and health. Women traveled for miles by wagon and buggy over almost impassable roads, to learn current information provided by the University of Illinois Cooperative Extension Service. Members participated in school diptheria immunizations, and assisted the Red Cross. A county chorus was organized; powder blue and dark blue were chosen county colors, and in 1933, the organization received its "not for profit" charter. Market Days, a lunch program for various events, and unit and individual assessments strengthened the organization financially.

In 1939, the board received a request to petition President Franklin D. Roosevelt that, "We are opposed to sending our boys into foreign countries to fight." This resolution was sent to the State Federation for consideration.

The *Forties* ushered conditions alien to our American scene—gasoline and tire rationing, shortages of sugar and other household items. Unit and other meetings were curtailed. County Home Bureau activities included lard and scrap metal "war effort" collections. It is difficult to realize that "over there" was "over here" to our allies. The Home Bureau Federation collected monies to purchase an ambulance for our military. Macoupin County members did their part on this project. Units also donated to 4-H and to military memorials. Clareta Walker, the then Home Adviser, emphasized that in defense work, the kitchen apron was as important a uniform as the soldier's, if we practiced what we learned.

Programs were planned to keep current with needs and to educate the whole family. Brides were given a six-months free membership. A lap lunch was served at the tenth annual meeting. Lunch stands were set up at corn huskings, and R.E.A. meetings; cookbooks, published by LaSalle County Home Bureau, were sold; and 30¢ per member assessment helped raise funds. Market Days ended in the early forties, and play days were organized.

The last half of the second decade saw adjustments to a peacetime America. Membership growth, unit lessons, work with 4-H, Rural Youth, Young Married Couples, Sports Festival, and physical fitness programs became leading activities.

The 1940's, which started with 312 members, closed with 845.

The *Fifties* showed an all-time high in membership—state honors were awarded for its 20% gain, when its membership reached 1,073. "Ted, the Traveling Rooster," an award for the district showing the highest percentage of increase in membership, was introduced—a traveling gavel was presented to the winning unit. Crafts became an important part of the activities, which included among others, textile painting, glove making, and basket weaving.

4-H membership continued to increase during the late Fifties—and boys continued to join girls' clubs. One thousand dollars, the proceeds from the Macoupin County Fair, was donated to the Western Illinois 4-H Camp.

Delegates to Farm and Home Week at Urbana found new inspirations for programs. Home Bureau members were involved in a county health survey. The Fifties ended with 32 units, and a membership of 700. Assessments were no longer used to raise necessary operating capital. A cookbook, published in 1954, and special tours supplanted assessments.

The *Sixties* brought an end to the name Home Bureau. In 1962, its name was changed to Macoupin County Homemakers Extension Association governed by a thirteen person board more closely aligned with the framework of the University of Illinois Cooperative Extension Service. Membership remained steady, and 33 units were in effect. The health survey was completed and earned national recognition. Pennsylvania Dutch Cookery was the first ethnic foods lesson; hat making was popular. Macoupin County sent its first delegate to the National Extension Homemakers Council meeting, Madison, Wisconsin, and two delegates attended the Triennial Conference of the Associated Country Women of the World in East Lansing, Michigan. Annual meetings became evening events, and 4-H members shared their achievements during the programs. The office relocated at 128½ North Broad, and equipment and furniture were replaced to increase operating efficiency. Cooking schools, fashion shows, as well as a very successful tour program provided some of the required funds.

The *Seventies* began with "The Ruby Years" Celebration. Bertha O. Eldred recalled the early years, charter members and past presidents were honored, and Mrs. Donald Kelly, IHEF President, gave an inspirational talk on "Rubies and Gems" to honor distinguished members and their accomplishments.

In 1975, the office was relocated to its present address, 210 North Broad, Carlinville, Illinois. The county association presented $500 to the County 4-H Federation to erase its debt to National 4-H Foundation.

Activities and events included voluntary action, breast disease screening, and international programs—one of which received state recognition for the program on Poland. Perfect attendance pins and certificates were awarded, and in 1977 the Loyalty Award was started. In 1979, Units participated in the county's Sesquicentennial celebration.

Programs continue to keep pace with the changes, notwithstanding that membership dues remain $5.

The committee has enjoyed working on this project. It is hoped that the recipes will add to your cooking pleasures. The committee warmly thanks its many members and friends for their generous contributions to THE HOMEMAKER'S SAMPLER.

PAST PRESIDENTS

*MRS. M. E. (BERTHA O.) ELDRED	1930-1932
*MRS. CLYDE (LOUISE) LAND	1932-1933
*MRS. BERT (EFFIE) RUYLE	1933-1935
*MRS. A. E. (RUTH) CONLEE	1935-1937
*MRS. ROY (RITA) TALLEY	1937-1939
*MRS. ED (ADA) SNELL	1939-1941
*MRS. OTTO (LYDIA) ARMOUR	1941-1944
MRS. STEVE (MARY) MARKO	1944-1945
MRS. HOWARD (ANNA MAY) LEACH	1945-1948
MRS. JOHN F. (STELLA) GROVES	1948-1951
MRS. ROBERT (JESSE) FENSTERMAN	1951-1954
*MRS. R. W. (HELEN) HANKS	1954-1956
MRS. JOHN (HOPE) CHISM	1956-1958
MRS. FRED (EMMA) NUMRICK	1958-1959
MRS. ELDON (VERDA) ARMOUR	1959-1960
MRS. MILTON (LEA) HEINZ	1960-1962
MRS. PHILLIP (HELEN) CHERRY	1962-1964
MRS. JOHN (HOPE) CHISM	1964-1966
MRS. JOHN F. (STELLA) GROVES	1966-1968
MRS. ARTHUR (JANEVA) CLARK	1968-1970
MRS. HERSCHEL (SYLVIA MAE) FRITZ	1970-1971
*MRS. RALPH (MAE) STIEHL	1971-1974
MRS. EDWARD (MAXINE) TONSOR	1974-1976
MRS. HERSCHEL (SYLVIA MAE) FRITZ	1976-1977
MRS. CHARLES (ELEANOR) ROSS, JR.	1977-1979
MRS. LESTER (MARY) LAWTON	1979-

HOME ADVISERS

GERTRUDE BECKMAN	1930-1934
CLARETA WALKER	1934-1942
MARGARET JONES	1942-1943
*DEBORAH SOLLIDAY	1943-1953
E. NADINE DAMON	1953-1957
**JACQUELINE H. THOMAS	1958-

*Deceased
**Title changed to Extension Adviser, Home Economics in 1967.

BEHIND
THE
SCENES...

Lela Klaus　　　Janeva Clark
Co-Chairmen

Mary Lawton
President

Mary Jane Thomas　　Jacqueline H. Thomas　　Gail Spudich
Typist　　*Extension Home Economist*　　*Extension Secretary*

Jo Maxeiner   Sylvia Fritz   Marian Gwillim

Eleanor Ross   Georgina Blair   Linda Schien

Doris Lacy

Lillian Vanfossen   Alta Florini   Hester Clark
Berna Huhsman   Millie Turner

An Aim
for the Home-Maker

To have the home

Economically sound
Mechanically convenient
Physically healthful
Morally wholesome
Mentally stimulating
Artistically satisfying
Socially responsible
Spiritually inspiring
Founded upon mutual
affection and respect

Juliet Lita Bane

CONTENTS

I didn't have potatoes so I
substituted rice,
I didn't have paprika, so I used
another spice.
I didn't have tomato sauce, so I used
tomato paste.
A whole can, not a half can, I don't
believe in waste.
A friend gave me the recipe, She said
you couldn't beat it.
There must be something wrong
with her—I couldn't even eat it!!!

DRIED APPLE PIES

I loathe, abhor, detest, despise,
Abominate dried-apple pies,
I like good bread, I like good meat,
Or anything that's fit to eat;
But of all poor grub beneath the skies,
The poorest is dried apple pies.
Give me the toothache, or sore eyes,
But don't give me dried apple pies.
The farmer takes his gnarliest fruit,
'Tis wormy, bitter, and hard, to boot;
He leaves the hulls to make us cough,
And don't take half the peeling off.
Then on a dirty cord 'tis strung
And in a garret window hung,
And there it serves as roost for flies,
Until it's made up into pies.
Tread on my corns, or tell me lies,
But don't pass me dried-apple pies.

Unknown

x

APPETIZERS AND BEVERAGES

The First Methodist Church of Carlinville, (South Broad and East First South) was the site of the October 24, 1930, County Home Bureau Organizational meeting. This structure, built in 1881, was replaced by a new church and educational building dedicated February 14, 1971. With nostalgia, members returned to this location on October 24, 1970 for their 40th annual meeting, in the midst of replacing "the old with the new."

Photograph courtesy of F & M Bank

BAGNA CAUDA

1 stick butter
1 2-ounce can anchovies
¼ cup Mazola oil

4 cloves garlic, chopped
½ cup thick cream

Combine all ingredients except cream. Slowly bring to a boil and simmer 20 minutes, stirring often. Slowly add cream and bring to boil. Serve immediately with celery sticks; cabbage, cooked or raw; peppers, raw or canned; lettuce; Italian bread. Makes 2 or 3 servings.

DELLA WARGO   DO MORE UNIT

CHEESE BALL

2 8-ounce packages cream
cheese
1 2-ounce package blue
cheese

1 8-ounce package sharp
Cheddar cheese, grated
Garlic to taste

Mix ingredients together. Form into ball and roll in crushed pecans. Refrigerate.

IDA MAE LEACH   BIRD UNIT

CHEESE BALL

1 garlic bud
1 3-ounce package Roquefort
cheese
¼ pound blue cheese
1 small jar Old English
cheese spread

8 ounces or more cream cheese
1 small onion, grated
½ teaspoon salt
Parsley, chopped fine
Ground walnuts or pecans

Mash chopped garlic. Add softened cheeses. Grate onion and add salt. Mix all ingredients together except parsley and nuts. Shape into ball; let chill. Cut parsley very fine. Roll cheese ball in parsley and then in ground nuts. Excellent served with wheat Triscuits or any snack cracker.

LINDA WATTLES   GILLESPIE NIGHT UNIT

FLAKY CHEESE PUFFS

1 cup flour
¼ cup (½ stick) butter
2 cups (8 ounces) shredded
  Cheddar cheese at room
  temperature

½ teaspoon Worcestershire
  sauce
⅛ teaspoon salt
Dash cayenne pepper

Combine butter, cheese, salt and pepper. Beat until well blended. Gradually add flour. Mix well. Shape dough into ¾ inch balls. Place on lightly greased cookie sheets. Cover and refrigerate until ready to bake. Bake at 350° for 16 to 18 minutes or until set. Serve warm. Yields 6 dozen.

MARY LAWTON   BUNKER HILL UNIT

"PLAINS SPECIAL" CHEESE RING

1 pound grated sharp cheese
1 cup nuts, finely chopped
1 cup mayonnaise
1 small onion, finely grated

Black pepper
Dash cayenne
Strawberry preserves, optional

Combine all ingredients except preserves; season to taste with pepper. Mix well and place in a 5 or 6 cup lightly greased ring mold. Refrigerate until firm for several hours or overnight. To serve, unmold, and if desired, fill center with strawberry preserves, or serve plain with crackers.

NEVA SKINNER   BIRD UNIT

CHICKEN WING APPETIZERS

12 chicken wings
1 cup white vinegar
1 cup brown sugar
¼ cup corn starch

½ cup soy sauce
Chicken broth
Salt to taste

Remove wing tips, split remainder making two "drumsticks." Place in shallow 9x12 inch pan to brown in oven at 400° for 20 minutes. Drain, saving broth. Combine vinegar, sugar, corn starch, and soy sauce into a smooth paste. Bring to a boil, stirring constantly. If sauce becomes too thick, add reserved chicken broth. Add chicken pieces to sauce, stir and simmer for about 20 minutes. Taste for salt. Serve hot. Makes 4 servings.

MILDRED BADER   HAGAMAN UNIT

OLIVE 'N CHEESE BALL

1 8-ounce package cream
  cheese, softened
8 ounces blue cheese,
  crumbled
¼ cup soft butter or
  margarine

1 tablespoon minced chives
⅔ cup ripe olives, well drained
  and chopped (1 4½-ounce can)
⅓ cup walnuts or pecans,
  chopped

Blend cheeses and butter. Stir in chives and olives. Combine thoroughly. Chill slightly for shaping. Form in ball on serving dish. Just before serving, sprinkle chopped nuts over ball. Trim with parsley. Serve with assorted crackers. Makes 3 cups.

COMMITTEE

MOCK OYSTERS

1 cup whole kernel corn
1 tablespoon butter, melted
2 eggs, separated
½ teaspoon salt

¼ teaspoon thyme (optional)
⅛ teaspoon black pepper
Celery salt
½ cup sifted flour

Combine corn, butter, egg yolks, seasonings and flour. Beat egg whites until they form soft peaks. Fold into corn mixture. Drop from teaspoon into deep fat preheated to 350°. Fry until golden. Drain on paper towel. Serve as appetizer or main course. Makes 5 dozen.

RUTH SHIELDS   MEDORA UNIT

CHILI DIP

1 small green pepper,
  chopped
1 medium onion, chopped
2 tablespoons butter

1 15-ounce can beanless chili
1 can cream of mushroom soup
1 cup (8 ounces) Cheddar
  cheese, grated

Saute green pepper and onion in butter until tender. Add remaining ingredients and heat until cheese melts, stirring occasionally. Serve hot with corn or taco chips. Makes 16 servings.

CATHY MALHAM   MONDAY NITERS UNIT

DILL DIP

½ cup mayonnaise
8 ounces sour cream
½ tablespoon Lowry's salt

1 tablespoon parsley flakes
1 tablespoon onion, minced
2 tablespoons dill weed

Combine all ingredients. Chill. A very good dip for most everything. Makes 1½ cups.

MRS. EDWARD KOERTGE   BRIGHTON EARLY BIRDS UNIT

PARTY HAM DIP

2 8-ounce packages cream
  cheese
1 3-ounce package cream
  cheese
1 carton sour cream with
  chives
1 4-ounce can deviled ham

Salt and pepper to taste
1 heaping tablespoon
  mayonnaise
1 teaspoon Worcestershire sauce
½ teaspoon soy sauce or steak
  sauce
Dash of lemon juice

Blend softened cream cheese with a small amount of milk. Fold in remaining ingredients. Serve with chips or crackers.

LOUISE RIZZIE   GET TOGETHERS UNIT

SOMBRERO DIP

1 pound ground beef
½ cup onions, chopped
½ cup catsup
3 tablespoons chili powder
¼ teaspoon salt
2 8-ounce cans red beans,
  mashed

1 cup Cheddar cheese, shredded
  (for garnish)
1 cup chopped onions (for
  garnish)
2 9-ounce packages corn curls

Brown ground beef and ½ cup onions. Add catsup, chili powder, salt, and mashed red beans. Heat together for 15 minutes in electric skillet. Garnish with cheese and 1 cup chopped onions. Use as dip with corn curls. Makes 10 servings.

ALICE TOSTBERG   HONEY POINT UNIT

CURRY DIP

1 cup mayonnaise
1 teaspoon tarragon vinegar
1 teaspoon onion, grated
1 teaspoon garlic powder

1 teaspoon curry powder
1 teaspoon horseradish
(optional)

Mix ingredients together until well blended. Serve with bite size fresh vegetables.

JANEVA CLARK   CARLINVILLE NIGHT UNIT

CRAB CHEESE FONDUE

1 pound butter
1 pound Velveeta cheese

1 6-ounce package king frozen crab meat (or canned may be used)

Melt butter and cheese over medium heat, stirring continuously until well blended. (This takes forever, but it's essential.) Add crab meat and mix ingredients thoroughly. Place in fondue pot over low flame. Dip bite size squares of French bread into mixture. Peppers, cauliflower, and celery may be used for dipping. Makes 4 to 6 servings.

LAURA WILSON   DANDY DOERS UNIT

HOT CRAB FONDUE

1 5-ounce jar processed
   sharp American cheese
   spread
1 8-ounce package cream
   cheese
1 7½-ounce can Alaska king
   crab, drained and flaked

¼ cup light cream
½ teaspoon Worcestershire
   sauce
¼ teaspoon garlic salt
½ teaspoon cayenne
French bread, Melba rounds, or
   toast points

In top of double boiler, over boiling water, combine cheese spread and cream cheese. Stir constantly until blended and smooth. Add remaining ingredients except for breads and heat until well blended, stirring occasionally. Serve hot in fondue pot or chafing dish with chunks of French Bread, Melba rounds, or toast points. If fondue thickens on standing, stir in a little additional cream. Makes 30 servings.

LINDA SCHIEN   STITCH AND STIR UNIT

PUFFY APPETIZERS

6 ounces cream cheese
1 egg yolk
1 teaspoon onion, grated
(to taste)

Pinch Accent
Crackers

Mix first four ingredients well. Spread on crackers. Broil. The canapes puff up and turn golden brown.

COMMITTEE

FRUITED CHEESE BALLS

1 3-ounce package cream
cheese

¼ cup drained pineapple
¼ cup finely chopped Brazil nuts

Cream cheese until smooth. Add pineapple and blend. Form into ½ inch balls and roll in chopped nuts. Chill. Pierce each ball with a pretzel stick. Serve on tray. Larger balls (1 inch) may be served to garnish a luncheon fruit salad.

THEDA YOUNG   SPANISH NEEDLE UNIT

SAUSAGE BALLS

1 pound Rice's hot sausage
1 pound Cheddar cheese,
grated

3 cups Bisquick

Mix ingredients together well. Drop by teaspoons onto greased cookie sheet. Bake for 30 minutes in 350° oven.

COMMITTEE

DEEP FAT FRIED SOYBEANS

Soybeans
Vegetable oil

Salt

Wash and soak beans overnight; beans will be plump and oversized. Drain and dry on paper towels. Heat oil in electric skillet or deep fryer. Fry beans 7-10 minutes. (Taste test for crunchiness.) Drain well. Put 3 or 4 paper towels in brown paper bag. Add nuts and shake to remove excess grease. Salt to taste. These taste like salted peanuts.

ROBIN MANSHOLT   GILLESPIE NIGHT UNIT

COCKTAIL MEATBALLS
(Microwave)

1 pound ground beef
¼ cup onion, chopped
1 egg, beaten
1 small teaspoon salt

3 tablespoons lemon juice
⅓ cup brown sugar
1 8-ounce can tomato sauce
⅛ teaspoon garlic salt

Combine ground beef, onion, egg, and salt. Mix well. Shape into 18 1-inch balls. Place in 9-inch glass dish; cover. Microwave on Roast for 8 minutes. Drain off fat. Combine remaining ingredients; pour over meatballs. Microwave on Roast for 5 to 6 minutes. Serve with toothpicks.

COMMITTEE

SPICED CIDER
(Microwave)

⅓ cup brown sugar
⅓ cup water
2 teaspoons whole cloves
2 sticks cinnamon

1 teaspoon whole allspice
¼ teaspoon salt
2 quarts cider

Combine sugar, water, and seasonings in 4 cup measure. Microwave at High for 4 to 6 minutes to form a light syrup. Combine with cider in a 3-quart casserole. Microwave 7 to 9 minutes until heated. Strain before serving. Makes about 2 quarts.

COMMITTEE

STANDARD PUNCH

2 envelopes Kool Aid
2 cups sugar
3 quarts water
1 large can pineapple juice

1 12-ounce can frozen orange
juice
1 6-ounce can frozen lemonade
1 16-ounce bottle 7-Up

Combine all ingredients. Makes 40 cups.

COMMITTEE

HOLIDAY PUNCH

½ gallon lime sherbet 1 bottle ginger ale
2 cans Hi-C citrus cooler
  juice

Combine sherbet and citrus cooler, stirring until sherbet is nearly melted. Add ginger ale, stirring to blend. Makes 25 6-ounce servings. Variation: Orange sherbet and orange Hi-C can be used, or any other same color combinations.

NORMA KEAGY   POLK UNIT

HOT CHOCOLATE MIX

1 8-quart box non fat 1 6-ounce jar powdered coffee
  dry milk creamer
1 cup powdered sugar 1 1-pound can instant Quik

Mix all ingredients together. Store in container with tight fitting lid. More powdered sugar may be added to taste. To serve, use ¼ cup chocolate mix to each cup of hot water. Makes 150 servings.

MRS. DONALD COLBURN   BRIGHTON EARLY BIRDS UNIT

SOUPS, STEWS, SANDWICHES

Terry Park was given to Palmyra in 1925 by Mrs. Jenny O'Nell Terry. It has a nine-hole golf course and consists of 80 acres. It is located two miles east of Palmyra. For the past 33 years, this park has been the scene of the annual Terry Park Fair.

Photographed by Jacoby Studios

ITALIAN BEAN VEGETABLE SOUP

2 tablespoons olive oil or
  butter
2 tablespoons parsley,
  minced
1 large clove garlic, minced
½ cup onion, chopped
1 pound pork meat, cut up
1 cup celery, sliced or diced
1 cup carrots, sliced or diced
1 cup zucchini, diced
1 cup fresh or canned green
  beans, cut up

2 cups cabbage, cut up
1 cup or can tomatoes
1 can pork and beans
1 teaspoon salt
¼ teaspoon pepper
1 bay leaf
8 cups boiling water
6 chicken bouillon cubes
1 cup Creamettes or noodles,
  broken

In a heavy Dutch oven, heat olive oil or butter. Add parsley and garlic. Stir. Add onions and pork meat. (Country style spare ribs or pork steak may be used.) Add vegetables in order given. Zucchini may be omitted if not available or substitute one white potato, diced. When all vegetables have been added, stir in seasonings, and the boiling water with the bouillon cubes. Cover and cook for 1 hour, stirring occasionally. Add Creamettes or broken noodles and simmer ½ hour more. Remove bay leaf.

NANCY MAJZEL   GET TOGETHERS UNIT

BEEFY VEGETABLE SOUP

2½ pounds beef shanks
1 tablespoon salt or to taste
6 cups water
2 stalks celery, diced
1 medium onion, diced
2 medium carrots, diced
1 pint tomatoes
¼ cup parsley, chopped

¼ teaspoon basil
¼ teaspoon thyme leaves
¼ teaspoon pepper
1 10-ounce package frozen lima
  beans
1 10-ounce package frozen corn
1 10-ounce package frozen peas

In a large kettle heat beef shanks, salt, and water to boiling. Reduce heat to low and add remaining vegetables and spices except frozen vegetables. Cover and simmer for 2 hours. Stir in frozen vegetables. Continue cooking about 30 minutes until meat and vegetables are tender. This soup freezes well. Refrigerate, covered, until chilled, freeze up to 3 months.

COMMITTEE

CABBAGE SOUP

2½ pounds green cabbage
3 quarts salted water
2 cups water
2 cloves garlic
1 teaspoon caraway seeds
1 teaspoon whole black
pepper
1 teaspoon oregano

2 bay leaves
½ cup flour
1 stick butter
1 quart milk, scalded
4 ounces American cheese slices
Salt to taste
White pepper to taste

Cut up cabbage. Put in soup pot with the salted water. Boil 1 hour, covered. In a smaller pan, bring to boil the 2 cups of water. Add garlic, caraway seeds, black pepper, oregano, and bay leaves. Simmer 10 to 15 minutes. Let stand another 10 minutes. Strain this spice mixture into the cooked cabbage. Blend flour into the butter and mix well. Add this to cabbage and stir while simmering, about 10 minutes. When soup is smooth, turn off heat. Add the milk and cheese. Add salt and pepper to taste. Makes 6 servings.

SYLVIA ZERBOLIO   GET TOGETHERS UNIT

FRENCH ONION SOUP

3 pounds onions, peeled
4 ounces butter or margarine
1½ teaspoons ground pepper
2 tablespoons paprika

1 bay leaf
¾ cup flour
2 teaspoons salt
3 quarts canned beef bouillon

Slice onions ⅛ inch thick. Melt butter in large, heavy soup pot. Saute onions in butter 1½ hours. Add the remaining ingredients except the bouillon. Saute 10 to 15 more minutes. Add bouillon and simmer, covered, for 2 hours. Season to taste and refrigerate over night. Kitchen Bouquet may be added for color. To serve, heat soup. Ladle into soup bowls and top with 3 or 4 slices of French bread and Swiss cheese. Put under broiler at 550° for about 5 minutes.

MARGARET WIRTH   GILLESPIE NIGHT UNIT

MRS. DALE RHODES, GILLESPIE NIGHT UNIT, adds one cup of white wine, and use 1 teaspoon paprika and salt to taste.

24

BEAN SOUP

1 pound white beans
1 ham bone
3 quarts water
½ cup cooked mashed
potatoes

1 medium onion, chopped
1 small bunch celery, chopped
1 clove garlic, chopped
¼ cup parsley

Presoak beans as directed on package. Drain and put beans in a soup kettle with ham bone. Add the water and bring to a boil. Simmer for 2 hours. Stir in the mashed potatoes; add onions, celery, garlic, and parsley. Simmer for 1 additional hour. Remove ham bone, dice meat from it and return meat to soup.

MILDRED P. LEEFERS   SUSTAINING MEMBER

CREAM OF WHEAT DUMPLINGS FOR SOUP

1½ cups water
1½ cups milk
1¼ cups Cream of Wheat
1½ teaspoons salt

½ stick margarine
3 eggs
1½ cups grated Parmesan
cheese (optional)

Bring water and milk to boil in saucepan. Gradually add Cream of Wheat and salt. Stir to prevent lumps. Remove from heat. Beat in margarine and eggs. Add cheese and stir. Drop by teaspoon into simmering broth.

ANNA KALASKIE   GET TOGETHERS UNIT

VEGETABLE SOUP

1 package Lipton onion soup
3 tablespoons sugar
1 small can tomato sauce

3 to 4 pints tomato juice
2 pounds ground beef, browned
3 to 4 cans mixed vegetables

Mix all ingredients together, adding enough tomato juice for right consistency for soup. Bring soup to a boil; simmer at least 2 hours before serving.

DONNA LANDES   SCOTTVILLE UNIT

MARROWBALL SOUP (BEEF SOUP)

1½ to 2 pounds shin bone
  meat
3 medium carrots, thinly
  sliced
1 stalk celery
½ to 1 cup tomatoes
10 slices bread

3 tablespoons marrow from meat
  bone
½ teaspoon salt
½ teaspoon pepper
1 egg
1 teaspoon nutmeg
2 cups cracker meal or more

Scoop out all marrow from shin bone. Place the bone with the meat into a large pot with about 1½ quarts water. Simmer about 3 hours. After meat has simmered, add carrots and celery with leaves and the tomatoes. Soak the bread in water. Squeeze out all the water, mashing together with fingers. Fry out marrow, add 3 tablespoons of the fat to the bread. Add salt, pepper, egg, and nutmeg. Add cracker meal to make a firm consistency. Roll into small balls. Put into soup at least ½ hour before soup is to be served. Remove the meat before adding the balls, and fry until brown. (Meat is served separately from the soup.) The soup is fairly clear with the thin slices of carrot and the celery. The nutmeg makes an interesting and tasty spice in the marrow balls. Makes 10 servings.

MRS. WILLIAM E. (GRACE) WERNER   STITCH AND STIR UNIT

PUMPKIN SOUP

3 10¾-ounce cans chicken
  broth
2 or 3 cups pumpkin, pared
  and cubed
1 cup onion, sliced

1½ teaspoons salt
½ teaspoon dried thyme leaves
5 peppercorns
½ cup whipping cream, warmed
1 teaspoon snipped parsley

Put all ingredients except whipping cream and parsley in Dutch oven. Bring to a boil, then simmer 45 minutes or until pumpkin is tender. Puree mixture and return to Dutch oven. Heat to boiling. Stir in warmed cream and parsley. Serve hot. Canned pumpkin may be substituted.

SYLVIA ZERBOLIO   GET TOGETHERS UNIT

BEEF STEW

2 pounds stew meat, cut up
1 cup carrots, chunked
3 stalks celery, diced
4 to 5 potatoes, chunked
1 small or medium onion, diced

1 teaspoon sugar
1 teaspoon salt
2 tablespoons Minute tapioca
1 cup tomato juice
1 can mushrooms, if desired

Put the first five ingredients into 3 quart casserole in layers as listed. Mix the sugar, salt, tapioca, and tomato juice and pour over top of layered ingredients. Top with 1 can of mushrooms if desired. Cover tightly. Bake at 275° for 3 hours. Makes 6 to 8 servings.

HELEN L. KEELE   POLK UNIT

FIVE HOUR STEW

1½ pounds stew meat
6 medium carrots, cut in large chunks
1 large onion, chopped
3 medium potatoes, quartered

1 teaspoon sugar
2 tablespoons Minute tapioca
1 can tomato soup
¾ can water
Salt and pepper to taste
Garlic salt

Combine all ingredients and bake in a covered roaster at 250°. Do not open for five hours. Makes 6-8 servings.

AUDREY BLOOME   SOUTH OTTER UNIT

FORGOTTEN STEW

½ pounds stew meat
can tomato soup
can cream of mushroom soup
cans water
package dry onion soup

Celery, carrots, potatoes, and onions, whole, or cut in edible pieces
2 tablespoons flour, tapioca, or corn starch

Put all ingredients except onion soup in greased casserole. Sprinkle onion soup over the top. Put foil over top and cover with lid. Bake at 325° for 3 hours. Needs no watching; will be ready when it comes out of oven.

FRANK THOMAS   SUSTAINING MEMBER

MEAT BALL STEW

1½ pounds ground beef
1 cup bread crumbs
¼ cup onion, chopped
1 egg

½ teaspoon salt
½ teaspoon margarine
¼ teaspoon thyme

Mix ingredients and shape into one inch meatballs; brown in skillet.

For stew:
1 can tomato soup
1 10½-ounce can beef broth
4 medium potatoes

4 medium carrots
8 small onions

Combine above ingredients; bring to boil. Add meat balls. Simmer 30 minutes. One bag of frozen stew vegetables may be used.

KATHY GWILLIM   PIASA UNIT

TURKEY CHOWDER

¼ cup onion, finely chopped
5 tablespoons margarine
1½ cups turkey, cooked and
    diced
2 cups broth or water
2 cups raw potatoes, diced
1 cup carrots, diced

½ cup celery, chopped
1 teaspoon salt
¼ teaspoon thyme
¼ teaspoon pepper
1 bay leaf
3 tablespoons flour
2 cups milk

Cook onion in 3 tablespoons margarine until tender but not browned. Add turkey, broth, vegetables, and seasonings. Simmer until vegetables are tender. Melt remaining 2 tablespoons margarine in skillet and blend in flour. Add milk and cook over low heat, stirring constantly until thick. Stir white sauce into turkey and vegetable mixture. Heat thoroughly. Serve immediately in bowls or over hot biscuits. Makes 6 servings.

NORMA SPURGEON   HAGAMAN UNIT

BEEF STEW WITH NOODLES

3 tablespoons cooking oil	1 cup small whole onions
2 pounds beef stew meat in	2 tablespoons parsley, minced
1 inch pieces	1 tablespoon Worcestershire
1 cup flour	sauce
1 teaspoon salt	1 bay leaf
⅛ teaspoon pepper	1 tablespoon flour
1 cup carrots, sliced	1 12-ounce package medium
1 cup celery, sliced	egg noodles

Heat oil in heavy kettle or large sauce pan. Roll beef in flour that has been seasoned with salt and pepper. Brown meat in oil. Cover with boiling water and simmer for 1½ hours. Add the carrots, celery, onions, parsley, Worcestershire sauce, and bay leaf. Simmer for 40 minutes. Thicken broth with 1 tablespoon flour mixed with a small amount of the broth. Add to the meat and vegetable mixture. Bring to a boil. Cook the noodles according to package directions. Spoon hot stew over hot noodles. Makes 6 servings.

FANNIE D. GAUDINO   GET TOGETHERS UNIT

SPANISH STEW WITH DUMPLINGS

1 pound beef stew meat	1 can tomato soup
3 tablespoons cooking oil	1 can water
Salt and pepper to taste	1 can peas and carrots
¼ cup onions, minced	

Brown meat in oil. Add salt and pepper. Cook onions until soft. Add tomato soup and water. Continue cooking until meat is tender. Add the peas and carrots. Cook for 45 minutes over low heat. (This can be left in slow cooker to cook all day.) Before serving, add dumplings. Makes 5 to 6 servings.

Dumplings:

1 egg	Pinch of salt
¾ cup milk	2 cups flour

Beat eggs and milk together. Add salt. Gradually add the flour, stirring until smooth. Drop by large spoonfuls into stew, Cook 12 to 15 minutes. Dumplings will float when done. Makes 6 to 8 dumplings.

MRS. JAMES RONDI   STAUNTON UNIT

FIVE HOUR STEW

1 to 1½ pounds stew meat
1 cup potatoes, diced
1 cup carrots, diced
1 cup celery, diced
1 cup onion, diced
1 tablespoon Worcestershire
   sauce

1 tablespoon tapioca
1 tablespoon sugar
1 teaspoon salt
¼ teaspoon pepper
1 cup V-8 juice

Clean and dice the vegetables then put all the ingredients into a 2½ quart baking dish. Place in 250° oven for 5 hours. Leave the lid on stew the entire time—don't peek. Makes 4 servings.

LINDA GWILLIM   STITCH AND STIR UNIT

HE-MAN STEW

3 pounds stew meat
2 cups seasoned flour
4 tablespoons fat
4 cups water
1 cup onion chunks

2 tablespoons parsley, minced
Salt and pepper to taste
2 cans mixed vegetables with
   juice

Roll meat in flour (after cutting into chunks.) Brown in hot fat. Add water and simmer 1½ hours. Add onion, parsley, salt, pepper, vegetables. Heat 15 minutes, stirring often. (Liquid may be thickened for gravy.) Makes 6 servings.

MRS. ROGER (DOTTIE) GRUEN   JUNIOR HOMEMAKERS UNIT

SANDWICH QUICKIE

GRIND:
1 can luncheon meat
½ pound Cheddar cheese
2 eggs, boiled

2 pieces celery
1 small onion

Moisten with salad dressing. Fill wiener or hamburger buns. Wrap in foil. Bake 10 minutes at 350° or until cheese melts.

MILLIE TURNER   MODELITE UNIT

HORSESHOE SANDWICHES

1 one pound package frozen French fries (baked according to package directions)

2 pounds ground beef, made into patties and fried

Sauce:
¼ cup butter
2 tablespoons flour
1 cup stale beer
2 teaspoons dry mustard
Dash cayenne
¼ teaspoon paprika

2 teaspoons Worcestershire sauce
4 eggs, slightly beaten
½ pound shredded Cheddar cheese

Melt butter in top of double boiler. Stir in flour. Add beer slowly. Cook, stirring constantly till sauce thickens. Add mustard, cayenne, paprika and Worcestershire. Mix well. Add cheese, and continue to cook until cheese melts. Add a little hot mixture to eggs and slowly stir egg mixture into cheese. Pour over toasted English muffins or toast, cooked hamburger patty and baked French fries. Serves 8. Note: Any leftover cheese sauce may be used as a spread for crackers.

DORIS LACY   SUSTAINING MEMBER

HORSESHOE SANDWICHES

¼ cup butter
2 tablespoons flour
2 teaspoons dry mustard
Dash of cayenne
¼ teaspoon paprika
2 teaspoons Worcestershire sauce

8 cups Cheddar cheese, grated or 2 large jars Cheez-Whiz
4 whole eggs, slightly beaten
Split English muffins
Ham as needed

Melt butter in top of double boiler. Stir in flour. Cook, stirring constantly till sauce thickens. Add mustard, cayenne, paprika, and Worcestershire sauce. Mix well; add cheese; cook till cheese melts. Add a little hot cheese mixture to eggs and slowly stir eggs into the cheese. Pour over hot English Muffins topped with ham. Serve with french fries. Makes 8 servings.

MRS. WILLIAM GENETTI   NILWOOD UNIT

SUPPER ON A BREAD SLICE

Long loaf Italian or French
   bread, cut lengthwise
⅔ cup evaporated milk
1½ pounds hamburger
1 cup cracker meal
1 egg

1½ teaspoons salt
⅛ teaspoon pepper
½ cup onion, chopped
1 tablespoon prepared mustard
¾ teaspoon Accent
2 cups grated American cheese

Mix together as for meatloaf. Spread on top of both halves of bread. Place foil on cookie sheet. Don't cover top, but wrap bottom and sides of bread with the foil. Bake at 350° for 25 to 30 minutes. Remove from oven and garnish with grated cheese, if desired. Place back in oven for 5 minutes. Makes 6 to 8 servings.

SUE VIECELI   STITCH AND STIR UNIT

SUPPER ON A SLICE

1½ pounds lean ground beef
1 small can evaporated milk
1 medium onion, grated
1 teaspoon prepared mustard
½ teaspoon salt
½ teaspoon garlic salt
½ teaspoon thyme
1 teaspoon Accent
⅛ teaspoon freshly ground
   pepper

2 teaspoons Worcestershire
   sauce
1 cup Cheddar cheese, grated
1 loaf Italian or French bread
Sliced American cheese—cut in
   strips
Stuffed olives, sliced

Preheat oven to 350°. Combine all ingredients EXCEPT bread, cheese strips and olive slices. Cut loaf of bread in half lengthwise. Place meat mixture on each cut side, spreading evenly to cover completely. Bring heavy duty foil up and around each half to form a boat. Bake for 45 minutes. Arrange cheese strips and sliced olives on top. Bake for 5 minutes more. Makes 12 servings.

LUANNE KOCH   HONEY POINT UNIT

LITTLE REUBENS

Sweet hot mustard
Snack rye bread (sliced)
Canned corned beef

Sauerkraut
Monterey Jack cheese

Spread mustard on rye slices. Layer on corned beef. Drain kraut and put on top of corned beef. Top with cheese. Broil until melted.

COMMITTEE

HOT PIZZA SANDWICH

2 pounds hamburger
8 ounces Mozzarella cheese, shredded
1 15-ounce can tomato sauce
½ bottle chili sauce
¼ cup Parmesan cheese

1 tablespoon oregano
2 teaspoons minced garlic or
⅛ teaspoon garlic salt
Dash of salt
8 rolls or buns

Brown hamburger, drain and cool. Add remaining ingredients. Mix well. Place on hard rolls or buns. Bake at 350° for 20 mintues.

GILDA CALDERWOOD   GET TOGETHERS UNIT

HOT HAM AND CHEESE SANDWICHES

¼ cup chopped onion
½ cup margarine
¼ cup mustard
⅛ teaspoon Accent
1 tablespoon poppy seed
  (optional)

6 hamburger buns
6 slices American cheese
6 slices ham

Combine margarine, onion, mustard, Accent and poppy seed. Spread mixture on both sides of split buns. Place a slice of ham and cheese between each bun sandwich. Place in shallow pan and bake at 350° for 15 minutes. Makes 6 servings.

GILDA CALDERWOOD   GET TOGETHERS UNIT

33

EGG PUFF

10 slices white bread, cubed
6 eggs
3 cups milk
2 tablespoons minced
    parsley

¾ teaspoon dried mustard
2 cups shredded sharp Cheddar
    cheese
2 cups (shrimp, cubed ham,
    bacon, sausage, etc.)

Beat eggs, milk and seasonings. Stir in bread, cheese and meat. Bake uncovered in 11x7 pyrex pan 1 hour at 325°.

JEAN LOVELESS   GILLESPIE NITE UNIT

CHEESE PUFF

2 slices bread
2 slices American cheese
1 egg, slightly beaten
½ cup milk

⅛ teaspoon salt
¼ teaspoon paprika
¼ teaspoon dried minced onion

Make a cheese sandwich with bread and cheese. Spread the outside of sandwich with butter. Place sandwich in small baking dish. Combine remaining ingredients and pour over sandwich. Let stand 15 minutes. Bake at 350° for 30 minutes. Serve hot. Makes 1 serving.

FRANK THOMAS   SUSTAINING MEMBER

SALADS

A typical snow scene in northwestern Macoupin County.

Photographed by Jacoby Studios

APRICOT JELLO

2 small or 1 large package
  apricot Jello
3 cups boiling water
1 small can pineapple tidbits

½ cup nuts
2 bananas, diced
2 cups Dream Whip

Mix Jello and water. Cool. Add remaining ingredients. Refrigerate.

MAXINE MILLER   DO MORE UNIT

APRICOT PINEAPPLE SALAD

1 package orange Jello
1½ cups apricot nectar
1 tablespoon lemon juice
1 cup crushed pineapple,
  undrained

2 bananas, diced
1 cup miniature marshmallows

Dissolve Jello in boiling apricot nectar. Add lemon juice. Cool. When cool, add pineapple, bananas, and marshmallows. Mix thoroughly. Refrigerate until firm.

ANNA K. REGLI   POLK UNIT

APPLE TOPPED CHEESE SALAD (OR DESSERT)

2 3-ounce packages lemon
  flavored gelatin
3 cups boiling water
1 teaspoon lemon rind
1 303-can applesauce
½ cup mayonnaise

1 pound carton cottage cheese,
  drained
Dash salt
½ cup pecans, chopped
1 cup celery, diced

Dissolve gelatin in boiling water; chill until syrupy. Pour half the syrupy gelatin into 2 quart mold. Add lemon rind and applesauce; mix. Chill until set. Beat mayonnaise into remaining half of gelatin. Stir in drained cheese, salt, pecans, and celery. Keep mixture at room temperature until gelatin mold begins to firm. Spoon cottage cheese mixture over top and return mold to refrigerator until firm. Makes 6 to 10 servings.

NELLE J. ALBORN   BARR UNIT

BEET SALAD

1 package lime or lemon
  Jello
1 cup boiling water or juice
1 cup pickled beet juice
1 tablespoon dehydrated
  onion

1 teaspoon Worcestershire sauce
1½ cups pickled beets, finely
  chopped
1 cup celery, finely chopped

Dissolve Jello in hot water. Add chilled beet juice, onion, and Worcestershire sauce. Let cool or even jell. Add beets and celery. Refrigerate.

JENNIE COLE   DO MORE UNIT

BEET SALAD

1 cup beet juice
½ cup vinegar
½ cup sugar
2 teaspoons mustard seed
1 3-ounce package lemon
  Jello

1 No. 303-can beets, drained,
  reserving juice
1 cup celery, chopped fine
1 small onion, grated

Combine beet juice (and water if needed to make 1 cup), vinegar, sugar, and mustard seed. Heat and stir until sugar is dissolved. Add Jello; stir until dissolved. Cool. Cut beets into small pieces. Combine sauce and vegetables. Makes 10 servings.

ANN POLO   BRUSHY MOUND UNIT

BLACK WALNUT SALAD

1 8-ounce package cream
  cheese, softened
½ cup pancake syrup
1 4-ounce package black
  walnuts, chopped

1 large can crushed pineapple,
  drained
1 medium size carton Cool Whip

Mix softened cream cheese and syrup well. Add remaining ingredients and mix. Freeze in 2 quart salad bowl. Remove an hour or so before serving. Makes 20 servings.

ELAINE MILLER   SHAWS POINT UNIT

CAULIFLOWER SALAD

1 head lettuce
1 onion
1 head cauliflower
1 pound bacon

1 cup salad dressing
⅓ cup Parmesan cheese
¼ cup sugar

Cut up lettuce, slice onion, break up cauliflower. Fry bacon crisply and break into small pieces. Put into large bowl. Toss with salad dressing, cheese, and sugar.

MARY DAVIDSON   GET TOGETHERS UNIT

BARB HEYEN, BERTHA ELDRED UNIT and DONNA LITTLE, STITCH AND STIR UNIT, use 2 cups mayonnaise and ½ cup sugar in above recipe.

CHERRY SALAD

1 large can cherry pie filling
¼ cup water
1 cup sugar
2 small packages cherry Jello
1 cup 7-Up or ginger ale

1 small can crushed pineapple, drained
1 small package Cool Whip or whipped cream

Combine first 3 ingredients and bring to boil. Remove from heat and add dry cherry Jello. Stir until dissolved. Cool. Pour in 7-Up or ginger ale. Add crushed pineapple and pour into 9x13 inch pan. Refrigerate until firm. Spread Cool Whip or whipped cream over top. Let set until topping is firm.

MRS. ROBERT FRASER   SOUTH OTTER UNIT

CHEESE BALL SALAD

2 cups American cheese, grated
4 tablespoons stuffed olives, chopped

Mayonnaise
¼ cup nuts, grated
Shredded lettuce

Blend cheese, olives, and enough mayonnaise to hold mixture together; shape into 1 inch balls. Roll balls in grated nuts. Arrange 3 balls to each serving in nest of shredded lettuce. Garnish with spoonful of mayonnaise. Makes 6 servings.

MRS. GEORGE (KAY) TOMPKINS   JUNIOR HOMEMAKERS

CHICKEN SALAD

1 3-pound chicken
1 carrot
1 stalk celery
3 stalks celery
6 candied dill pickle spears

1 tablespoon pickle juice
1 teaspoon celery seed
¼ cup chicken broth
¼ cup mayonnaise

Stew or pressure cook chicken in salt water along with carrot and 1 stalk celery; cook until tender. Cool chicken. Debone and skin chicken. Grind together chicken, 3 stalks celery, and pickle spears. Add to mixture the pickle juice, celery seed, chicken broth, and mayonnaise to make a soft spread. Refrigerate until ready to use on sandwich buns, on cream puff as filling or bread may be used. If spread is too soft, grind enough bread slices to stiffen spread.

DOROTHY KANALLAKAN   HAGAMAN UNIT

CORNED BEEF SALAD

1 6-ounce package lemon
  Jello
1¾ cups boiling water
2 tablespoons vinegar
1 tablespoon onion, chopped
1 cup celery, chopped

1 small green pepper, chopped
3 eggs, hard boiled and chopped
1 cup mayonnaise
½ cup corned beef broken into
  small pieces

Mix Jello, boiling water, and vinegar. Let set until cooled. Add rest of ingredients. Put in refrigerator until jelled. This is pretty if put in Jello mold and turned out on plate to serve. Makes 6 servings.

IRENE PERRINE   BRUSHY MOUND UNIT

COTTAGE CHEESE SALAD

1 large carton small curd
  cottage cheese
1 6-ounce package orange
  Jello
1 or 2 small cans mandarin
  oranges, drained

1 medium size can pineapple
  tidbits, drained
1 9-ounce carton Cool Whip

Stir cottage cheese and dry Jello together. Fold in drained fruits. Fold in Cool Whip. Refrigerate at least over night. Makes 12 servings.

SUSY WOODS   MONDAY NITERS UNIT

STRAWBERRY COTTAGE CHEESE SALAD

½ cup sugar
1 small can crushed
  pineapple, undrained
1 3-ounce box strawberry
  Jello

1 small carton whipped topping
1 cup small curd cottage cheese,
  washed

Add sugar to pineapple; boil until clear. Add Jello; cool. Fold in whipped topping and cottage cheese.

ELAINE SANDERS   JUNIOR HOMEMAKERS UNIT

CRANBERRY SALAD

1 3-ounce package cherry
  Jello
1 cup hot water
1 can cranberry sauce
1 small can crushed
  pineapple

1 cup cream, whipped, or
1 package Dream Whip, prepared
  as package directs
1 3-ounce package cream
  cheese, softened
1 cup marshmallows, quartered

Mix Jello with hot water. Stir sauce into hot Jello mixture. Let set. Mix together pineapple, whipped cream, cream cheese, and marshmallows. Spread on set Jello. Refrigerate.

IRENE SCHRAMM   BARR UNIT

CRANBERRY SALAD

1 pound cranberries
1 orange
2 cups sugar
1 package cherry Jello
1 cup hot water

1 cup nuts
1 cup apples, chopped
1 cup celery, chopped
1 cup crushed pineapple

Grind cranberries and orange. Pour sugar over them and let set until sugar dissolves. Dissolve Jello in hot water. When partially set, add to cranberries. Add remaining ingredients. Mix well and chill in 2½ quart bowl. Makes 12 servings.

LODEMA MEEKS   HAGAMAN UNIT

FROZEN CRANBERRY SALAD

1 package cranberries	2 cups hot water
2 cups sugar	1 cup cream
2 packages lemon Jello	

Grind cranberries and add sugar; mix well. Dissolve Jello in hot water. When it starts to set, add cranberry mixture. Whip cream and fold into cranberries. Pour into mold or dish and freeze about 4 hours.

MARIAN GWILLIM   PIASA UNIT

CRANBERRY SOUR CREAM SALAD

1 package cherry Jello	½ cup celery, chopped fine
1 cup hot water	½ cup nuts, chopped
1 cup whole cranberry sauce	1 cup sour cream (or imitation)

Combine Jello and hot water; stir well. Cool until syrupy consistency. Add cranberry sauce, celery, nuts, and sour cream.Pour into 9x9 inch glass dish or mold. Chill well. Makes 9 servings.

MRS. FRED J. ARMOUR   SHAWS POINT UNIT

CUCUMBERS IN CREAM

2 cucumbers	¼ cup white vinegar
¼ cup sugar	¾ cup sweet light cream

Pare cucumbers and slice as thin as possible. Soak for 1 hour (at room temperature) in salt water. Squeeze them as dry as possible with your hands. Mix together sugar, vinegar, and cream. Pour mixture over cucumbers and soak for 1 hour. Keep at room temperature; do not put in refrigerator.

MARY SCHMIDT   GILLESPIE NIGHT UNIT

GOLDEN GLOW SALAD

1 3-ounce package lemon Jello	1 tablespoon vinegar
1 cup hot water	½ teaspoon salt
1 cup pineapple juice	1 cup crushed pineapple drained
	1 cup carrots, grated

Dissolve Jello in hot water. Add pineapple juice, vinegar, and salt. Chill until slightly thickened. Add pineapple and carrots. Pour into 8 inch dish. Chill until firm. Serve with salad dressing if desired. Makes 6 servings.

MARGARET SMITH   DO MORE UNIT

DUNKARD SALAD

4 green peppers
4 red peppers
2 cups onions
2 cups celery
1 peck ripe tomatoes, diced

2 cups vinegar
2 cups sugar
½ cup mustard seed
½ cup canning salt

Coarsely grind peppers, onions, and celery. Mix rest of ingredients; do not heat. Pour over vegetables. Mix well. Put in large jars and keep in refrigerator. Keeps all winter and tastes like fresh tomatoes. As you use the vegetables, more diced tomatoes may be added to the liquid.
WILMA HAMMOND   DO MORE UNIT

FRUIT COCKTAIL SALAD

1 pound can crushed
    pineapple
1 pound can fruit cocktail
2 tablespoons corn starch
¼ cup sugar
2 egg yolks, beaten

1 cup fruit syrup
1 cup cream, whipped
¼ cup nuts
2 cups miniature marshmallows
2 bananas, sliced

Drain crushed pineapple well; drain the fruit cocktail, saving both juices. Combine corn starch and sugar; add egg yolks and 1 cup of fruit syrup. Cook until thickened; cool. Fold in whipped cream, nuts, and marshmallows. Add fruit cocktail and pineapple. Chill overnight. Add sliced bananas before serving.
PHYLLIS HARMS   NILWOOD UNIT

GERMAN HERRING SALAD

3 herring
5 medium potatoes
3 apples, peeled and cubed
1 onion, chopped
4 sweet pickles, chopped

1 egg, hard boiled
1 tablespoon salad oil
1 teaspoon mustard,
1 raw egg, beaten
½ cup vinegar

Clean herring and cut in small pieces. Boil potatoes, peel and cube. Chop the white of the hard boiled egg (reserve yolk.) Mix together reserved mashed egg yolk, salad oil, mustard, raw egg, and vinegar; add to herring-potato mixture; mix well. Store in refrigerator. Ready to serve in several hours (even better the next day.) Serve with crackers.
JOYCE DUELM   MT. OLIVE UNIT

GERMAN POTATO SALAD

8 cups potatoes, cooked and
cubed
¾ cup bacon, diced
1 cup celery, chopped
1 cup onion, chopped
3 tablespoons flour

⅔ cup vinegar
1⅓ cups water
3 teaspoons salt
⅔ cup sugar
½ teaspoon pepper

Cook bacon in large skillet; drain off fat. Measure fat and return ½ cup to skillet. Add celery and onion; cook about 1 minute. Blend in flour. Stir in vinegar and water; cook, stirring, until thick. Stir in salt, sugar, and pepper. Mix all ingredients with cooked potatoes. Can be made ahead of time.

RUTH SEIFERT   DO MORE UNIT

GERMAN POTATO SALAD

8 or 9 medium potatoes
6 slices bacon
½ to ¾ cup onion
2 tablespoons flour
2 tablespoons sugar

1 teaspoon salt
Dash of pepper
1 teaspoon celery seed
¾ cup water
⅓ cup vinegar

Boil peeled potatoes until tender; cool and slice. Fry bacon until crisp; set aside. Saute the onion in bacon grease. Remove from pan. Add onion and bacon pieces to potatoes. Mix together flour, sugar, salt, pepper, celery seed, water, and vinegar in sauce pan. Cook together a few minutes and pour over potatoes. Keep warm until serving time. Makes 8 servings.

MRS. MARY PEACOCK   GIRARD DAY UNIT

GERMAN POTATO SALAD

½ pound bacon
1 medium onion, diced
2 tablespoons flour
½ cup vinegar
2 tablespoons sugar

½ cup water
6 medium potatoes, boiled, and
sliced
4 eggs, hard cooked

Cut bacon in small pieces and fry until brown. Remove from skillet, pour off drippings. Saute onion in 2 tablespoons bacon drippings. Brown flour in drippings. Mix together the vinegar, sugar, and water; cook until thick. Add to potatoes, onion, and chopped eggs. Serve hot or cold.

DOROTHEA J. McCLUSKEY   CARLINVILLE DAY UNIT

FIVE CUP SALAD

1 cup fruit cocktail,
  undrained
1 cup pineapple tidbits,
  undrained
1 cup Mandarin oranges,
  drained

½ cup coconut (if desired)
½ cup miniature marshmallows
1 small package lemon instant
  pudding
1 banana, diced (if desired)

Mix fruit cocktail, pineapple, oranges, coconut, and marshmallows. Add dry pudding mix and mix well. Fold in bananas. Chill in 2 quart casserole. Better if made night before serving. May be served over cake. Note: One large package lemon instant pudding may be substituted for the small package.

GRACE M. POCKLINGTON   NILWOOD UNIT

HOT FRUIT SALAD

1 large can pineapple chunks
1 large can apricots
1 medium can pears
1 medium can red apple rings

½ cup sugar
2 tablespoons flour
1 cup cooking sherry
¼ cup butter

Drain fruits well. Place fruits in large baking dish. Cook remaining ingredients in double boiler until thickened. Pour hot mixture over fruits. Bake at 350° for 40 minutes. Serves 12 to 15.

BERTIE HAMMANN   GILLESPIE NIGHT UNIT

GREEN AND WHITE MARINADE

1 16-ounce can white corn,
  drained
1 16-ounce can tiny peas,
  drained

1 onion, finely diced
1 green pepper, finely diced
1 cup celery, finely diced

Mix corn, peas, onion, pepper, and celery. Mix Dressing and pour over vegetables. Marinate 2 or 3 hours (or overnight) before serving.

Dressing:
½ cup vinegar
½ cup salad oil

½ cup sugar

Mix ingredients.

MARY ANN ANDERSON   NILWOOD UNIT

45

GOOSEBERRY-MANDARIN SALAD

2 packages lemon Jello
1 can gooseberries, drained
2 cans mandarin oranges,
   drained

Juice 1 fresh orange and grated
   rind
½ cup celery, chopped
⅓ cup nuts

Add enough water to the three juices to make 2 cups liquid. Heat, dissolve Jello in liquid. Chill. When Jello starts to thicken, add fruits, rind, celery, and nuts. Refrigerate.

HELEN M. KELSEY   SHIPMAN UNIT

GRAPE JELLO SALAD

2 packages grape Jello or
   black cherry Jello
2 cups hot water

1 No. 2 can crushed pineapple
1 can blueberry pie filling
¼ cup pecans, chopped

Dissolve Jello in boiling water. Let cool until lukewarm. Add crushed pineapple, blueberry pie filling, and pecans. Pour in 9x12 inch dish or salad mold. Set in refrigerator until firm. Spread Topping on chilled salad. Makes 12 servings.

Topping:
1 package Dream Whip

1 4-ounce package cream cheese

Prepare Dream Whip according to package directions. Blend in cream cheese. Spread on salad. (Cool Whip may be used instead of Dream Whip.)

MARY STEAD   GIRARD NIGHT UNIT

LIME COTTAGE CHEESE SALAD

1 3-ounce package lime
   gelatin
1 cup boiling water
2 cups miniature
   marshmallows
Dash salt

1 9-ounce can crushed pineapple
1 cup small curd cottage cheese,
   drained
1 cup whipped cream
½ cup nuts, chopped

Dissolve gelatin in boiling water; add marshmallows and let melt. Stir in salt and pineapple. Chill until slightly thickened. Fold in cottage cheese, whipped cream, and nuts. Turn into 8x8 inch pan or mold as desired. Makes 6 to 8 servings.

MRS. DARRELL (EVELYN) WALTERS   JUNIOR HOMEMAKERS UNIT

HAM AND TATER LOAF

4 cups (1½ pounds) ham,
  cooked and chopped
¾ cup Hellmann's real
  mayonnaise
½ cup celery, diced

½ cup sweet pickle, diced
3 tablespoons pickle juice
1 teaspoon salt
2½ pounds potatoes, cooked,
  peeled, and cubed

Line 9 inch loaf pan with waxed paper. Mix ham with ½ cup mayonnaise. Press into pan. Mix next 4 ingredients with remaining mayonnaise. Add potatoes and toss. Press lightly over ham layer. Cover and chill 4 hours. Unmold. Serves 6.

NELLE ELDRED POLK UNIT

LIMA BEAN SALAD

2 packages frozen lima beans
1 onion, minced
5 stalks celery, cut in 1 inch
  strips
1 stick butter or margarine
1 can mushroom pieces,
  drained

½ teaspoon salt
½ teaspoon nutmeg
¼ teaspoon pepper
½ pint whipping cream

Cook lima beans as directed on package; drain. Saute onion and celery in butter. Add mushroom pieces, salt, nutmeg, and pepper. Add to cooked lima beans. Stir in whipping cream. Warm and serve in 2 quart casserole. Makes 12 servings.

EVELYN WOODS BIRD UNIT

ORANGE SALAD

1 3-ounce box orange Jello
1 3-ounce box vanilla
  pudding (not instant)
1 3-ounce box tapioca
  pudding (not instant)
3 cups water

2 cans mandarin oranges,
  drained
1 9-ounce carton Cool Whip
1 cup small marshmallows

Put all dry mixes into sauce pan. Add water and bring to a boil. Let cool. Add oranges and Cool Whip. Fold in marshmallows. Chill in refrigerator overnight. Makes 8 to 12 servings.

IMOGENE THEOBALD GILLESPIE NIGHT UNIT

LUNCHEON LAYERED SALAD

1 quart lettuce, thick sliced
½ cup celery, thick sliced
½ cup onion, thick sliced
1 8-ounce can water
   chestnuts, drained and
   thick sliced
½ cup green pepper,
   chopped
1 10-ounce package frozen
   peas, cooked and drained

2 cups chicken or turkey, cooked
   and diced
1½ cups mayonnaise
3 tablespoons sugar
1½ cups mild Colby or Cheddar
   cheese, shredded
8 slices bacon, cooked

In a 13 x 9 x 2 inch pan, layer all ingredients in order listed, crumbling bacon over top. Cover with foil or plastic wrap. Chill at least 8 hours. When ready to serve, cut into 3 inch squares. Makes 12 servings.

MARIANNA RAMEY   CARLINVILLE NIGHT UNIT

ORANGE ICE CREAM SALAD

1 3-ounce box orange Jello
1 cup hot water
1 pint vanilla ice cream

1 small can mandarin oranges,
   well drained

Dissolve orange Jello in hot water. Add ice cream; stir until dissolved. Add oranges to Jello mixture. Stir well. Pour into shallow glass bowl or Pyrex baking dish. Refrigerate until firm. Makes 4 to 6 servings.

FANNIE D. GAUDINO   GET TOGETHERS UNIT

MEXICAN CHEF SALAD

1 pound ground beef
1 16-ounce can kidney beans,
   drained
Salt to taste
1 medium onion, chopped
4 tomatoes, chopped
1 head lettuce, torn in bite
   size pieces

4 ounces cheese, grated
1 medium size package tortilla
   flavored chips
8 ounces Catalina salad dressing
Hot sauce to taste (optional)
2 avocados, sliced

Brown ground beef in small amount of fat; add beans and salt. Simmer for 10 minutes. Toss vegetable pieces with grated cheese. Crush tortilla chips and add to vegetables. Stir in salad dressing and hot sauce. Add meat mixture and sliced avocados. May be served with tortilla chips. Makes 8 servings.

JESSIE KAHL   SHIPMAN UNIT

COPPER PENNIES SALAD

2 pounds fresh carrots
1 medium green pepper
2 medium onions, sliced
1 10¾-ounce can tomato
  soup
⅔ cup sugar

½ cup cooking oil
1 teaspoon mustard
¾ cup vinegar
1 teaspoon Worcestershire sauce
½ teaspoon salt

Peel, slice and cook carrots until crispy tender, about 10 minutes; drain. Add peppers and onions. In sauce pan, heat remaining ingredients, stirring until sugar is dissolved. Pour mixture over vegetables; stir. Makes 10 to 12 servings. Better if made a day or two before serving.

ELSIE MADER   STAUTON UNIT

CUBA LANDGREBE, NILWOOD UNIT, uses 2 cups carrots, 1 cup celery, 1 small onion, ¾ cup sugar, ½ cup vinegar, and omits Worcestershire sauce and salt in above recipe.

DOROTHY McINTYRE, HONEY POINT UNIT, uses ¾ cup sugar, ½ cup vinegar, 1 teaspoon salt, pepper and paprika to taste and omits green pepper and Worcestershire sauce.

ORANGE SHERBET SALAD

2 3-ounce packages orange
  Jello
2 cups boiling water
1 pint orange sherbet
1 can mandarin oranges,
  drained
1 No. 2 can crushed
  pineapple, drained

1 cup juice from fruit
½ cup sugar
1 egg
3 tablespoons flour or corn
  starch
1 teaspoon butter
½ pint whipping cream, whipped
Grated cheese, if desired

Dissolve Jello in water; add sherbet and allow to melt. Add drained fruits to Jello and chill in 9x13 inch Pyrex dish. Combine juice, sugar, egg, and flour in sauce pan. Cook until thick. Add butter and blend well. Let mixture cool. Fold in whipped cream. Spread over well set Jello. Sprinkle with grated cheese, if desired.

MARY DAVIDSON   GET TOGETHERS UNIT

PINEAPPLE-APRICOT DELIGHT

2 3-ounce packages apricot
Jello
3 cups boiling water
1 cup miniature
marshmallows
1 No. 2 can crushed
pineapple, drained and
save juice
2 bananas, crushed with fork
1 egg

½ cup pineapple juice
½ cup sugar
2 heaping tablespoons flour
1 tablespoon margarine or butter
1 8-ounce package Philadelphia
cream cheese at room
temperature
1 envelope Dream Whip or
equivalent of Cool Whip

Mix Jello with boiling water. Beat marshmallows into hot Jello until dissolved; cool. Add pineapple and bananas. Let jell in 3 quart baking dish. (This can be made one night and the rest the next night.) In sauce pan, beat egg and pineapple juice together until frothy. Cook until thick, stirring constantly. Remove from heat and add margarine and cream cheese. Mix well and let cool. Prepare Dream Whip according to package directions. Add Dream Whip to cooled mixture and beat well with mixer. Spread on top of chilled Jello mixture. Let set. Makes 10 to 12 servings.

AVIS E. SMITH   POLK UNIT

ELOISE ECCHER, STAUNTON UNIT uses 2 cups hot water and 2 cups cold water; 2 cups miniature marshmallows, 3 medium bananas, sliced; 1 cup pineapple juice; ¾ cup sugar; adds nuts and coconut, and omits butter.

OVER NIGHT SALAD

1 large head iceberg lettuce,
chopped
2 large carrots, peeled and
grated
1 #303 can green beans,
drained

1 16-ounce jar Libby's sliced
beets
2 tablespoons sugar
½ cup bacon bits
1 pint Hellmann's mayonnaise

Drain beets and blot on paper towel. Layer ingredients in large bowl in order given, except bacon. Cover with mayonnaise; sprinkle sugar over top. Refrigerate over night covered with Saran Wrap. When ready to serve, sprinkle bacon bits over top. Makes 6 servings.

MRS. MILWIDA R. BOYD   SUSTAINING MEMBER

MOTHER'S CABBAGE SALAD

SALADS

1 medium head cabbage	Butter size of egg
½ cup vinegar	1 tablespoon prepared mustard
1 tablespoon sugar	2 eggs
1 teaspoon salt	Celery seed

Put cabbage through food chopper. Mix and heat to boiling the vinegar, sugar, salt and butter. Remove from heat. Beat together the eggs and mustard. Slowly add a little of the hot vinegar mixture to eggs and beat while adding. Add all of the egg mixture to the hot vinegar and heat to boiling, stirring constantly, until slightly thickened. Pour over cabbage while hot. Sprinkle celery seed over cabbage.

NELL WEISS   POLK UNIT

PEANUT SALAD

1 cup Spanish peanuts	½ cup vinegar
1 cup crackers	2 eggs, slightly beaten
2 cups cabbage	½ teaspoon salt
½ cup sweet cream	¼ teaspoon mustard
½ cup sugar	

Grind peanuts, crackers, and cabbage in a food grinder. Set aside. Bring remaining dressing ingredients to a boil; cook until thickened. Pour over peanut mixture and mix well. Makes 6 to 8 servings.

MAXINE OXLEY   SCOTTVILLE UNIT

MRS. RUTH MASKA of MEDORA UNIT submitted the same recipe except she uses ½ teaspoon mustard.

PINK SALAD

1 can cherry pie filling	1 can Eagle Brand milk
1 can crushed pineapple, drained	1 medium size carton Cool Whip
	½ cup pecans, chopped

Toss above ingredients together in a large bowl in order given. Pour into 2 quart glass bowl. Cover and refrigerate overnight. Makes 10 to 12 servings.

MRS. ROBERT BIRK   BRIGHTON EARLY BIRDS UNIT

MRS. ROY WELLER of SOUTH OTTER UNIT uses ⅓ cup lemon juice, ¼ teaspoon almond extract, and one large whipped topping, omitting the nuts.

SALADS

PINEAPPLE APRICOT SALAD

1 No. 303 can crushed pineapple	2 cups boiling water
1 No. 303 can apricots	½ 7-ounce package miniature marshmallows
3 3-ounce packages orange Jello	

Drain crushed pineapple; reserve 1 cup juice. Drain apricots; reserve 1 cup juice. Dissolve gelatin in boiling water; add ½ cup apricot juice and ½ cup pineapple juice. When mixture is cool, add pineapple, apricots, and marshmallows. Pour into 7x11 inch pan. Chill until firm. Spread Topping over set gelatin. Refrigerate until ready to serve. Makes 12 servings.

Topping:

⅓ cup sugar	½ cup apricot juice
1 tablespoon corn starch	½ cup pineapple juice
1 egg	2 slices Cheddar cheese, grated
2 tablespoons butter	1 package Dream Whip

Combine topping ingredients in sauce pan. Cook over low heat, stirring constantly. Cool custard. Fold into prepared Dream Whip. Spread custard mixture over set gelatin. Sprinkle cheese over top.

ADELINE WEIDNER   GILLESPIE NIGHT UNIT

QUICK SALAD

8 ounces cottage cheese	½ cup miniature marshmallows (optional)
1 16-ounce can crushed pineapple, well drained	1 3-ounce package strawberry, orange, or lime Jello
1 teaspoon lemon juice	1 10-ounce carton whipped topping
½ cup pecans, chopped (optional)	

Mix cottage cheese, pineapple, and lemon juice together. Add nuts and/or marshmallows, if desired. Sprinkle Jello on top of fruit mixture and stir well. Fold in whipped topping. Pour into 1½ to 2 quart bowl. Chill or serve immediately. Makes 10 3-ounce servings or 15 to 16 2-ounce servings.

MARY ANN ANDERSON   NILWOOD UNIT

SPRING SALAD

2½ cups rhubarb, diced
1 cup sugar
½ cup water
1 tablespoon lemon juice
1 6-ounce package raspberry
    Jello

½ cup boiling water
2 cups celery, chopped
1 cup walnuts, chopped

Boil rhubarb, sugar, and ½ cup water slowly until rhubarb is tender; add lemon juice. Cool. Dissolve Jello in boiling water. Cool. Add celery, nuts, and rhubarb mixture. Chill. Makes 10 to 12 servings.

GEORGINA V. BLAIR   DO MORE UNIT

ROSY SPRING SALAD

4 cups raw rhubarb, diced
1½ cups water
½ cup sugar
2 3-ounce packages
    strawberry gelatin

1 cup orange juice
1 teaspoon orange rind, grated
1 cup fresh strawberries, sliced

Combine rhubarb, water, and sugar in sauce pan. Cook until tender, about 4 to 5 minutes. Pour over gelatin, stirring until dissolved. Add orange juice and rind. Chill until thick and syrupy. Add strawberries. Pour into lightly oiled 6 cup mold, chill until set. Makes 8 servings.

MRS. PAUL N. ODELL   PIASA UNIT

RED HOT JELLO SALAD

1 2½ to 3-ounce package red
    hots
1 cup boiling water
1 3-ounce package red Jello
1 16-ounce can applesauce

1 8-ounce can crushed
    pineapple, drained
1 3-ounce package cream
    cheese, softened
1 tablespoon milk

Dissolve red hots in boiling water. (This takes some time.) Add Jello; stir until dissolved. Cool until partially set. Stir in applesauce and pineapple. Pour into small to medium mold or bowl; set until firm. Thin softened cream cheese with milk; spread over Jello. Refrigerate. Cool Whip may be substituted for cream cheese topping. Makes 8 to 10 servings.

MARGIE THOMAE   SHIPMAN UNIT

RED HOT JELLO

1¼ cups water
2 to 3 tablespoons red hots
  (candy)

1 3-ounce box red Jello, any
  flavor
1 1-pound can applesauce

Boil 1 cup water and red hots until dissolved; stir in Jello. When dissolved, add ¼ cup water and applesauce. Chill.

MRS. DARRELL (BETTY) MOLEN   JUNIOR HOMEMAKERS UNIT

PEAR AND PINEAPPLE SALAD

1 #2 can sliced pineapple,
  drained and diced
1 #2 can pears, drained and
  diced
¼ cup sugar
¼ cup flour

2 egg yolks plus 1 whole egg
1¾ cups combined juices of
  drained fruits
1 cup cream, whipped
8 ounces American Cheddar
  cheese, shredded

Combine sugar, flour, eggs, and juice. Cook over medium heat until mixture thickens. Cool. Fold in fruit and pour into an 8x8 inch dish. Top with unsweetened whipped cream and top with shredded cheese. Refrigerate several hours before serving.

FRANK THOMAS   SUSTAINING MEMBER

SPICED PICKLE SALAD

2 cups sugar
⅓ cup vinegar
⅔ cup water
3 tablespoons whole cloves
2 tablespoons Knox gelatin

1 pint cold water
1 cup sweet pickles, thinly sliced
2 tablespoons pimientos,
  chopped
½ to ⅔ cup nuts, chopped

Boil sugar, vinegar, ⅔ cup water, and cloves until a thick syrup is formed. Dissolve gelatin in pint of cold water. Add hot syrup to dissolved gelatin; stir well. When mixture begins to thicken, add remaining ingredients. Stir and pour into an 8x8 inch dish. Chill and serve on lettuce.

MRS. RUTH MASKA   MEDORA UNIT

SPINACH SALAD

1 bag spinach
1 can bean sprouts, drained
1 can water chestnuts,
  drained and sliced

2 eggs, hard boiled and sliced
5 slices bacon, cooked crisp and
  crumbled

Wash spinach, drain well. Tear into pieces. Add bean sprouts, water chestnuts, eggs, and bacon. Pour Dressing over and toss in large salad bowl. Makes 8 to 10 servings.

Dressing:
1 cup oil
1 tablespoon A-1 sauce
⅓ cup vinegar

¾ cup brown sugar
1 medium onion, chopped

Put all ingredients in blender container and blend 3 minutes.

BEULAH LAURIE   SHAWS POINT UNIT

SWEET-SOUR CUCUMBERS

9 cucumbers, sliced
2 cups onions, sliced
2 cups green peppers, sliced
  (optional)
3 cups sugar

2 cups white vinegar
1⅓ teaspoons tumeric
1⅓ teaspoons mustard seed
1⅓ teaspoons celery seed
3 tablespoons salt

Mix all ingredients together. Soak overnight in porcelain or glass pan. Pack in sterilized jars; it is not necessary to seal jars. Use jars with tight fitting lids such as peanut butter jars or similar types. Store in refrigerator. (These taste like bread and butter pickles.)

MRS GERALD (NORMA) BOSTON   HONEY POINT UNIT

SAUERKRAUT SALAD

1 can sauerkraut
3 quarts water
1 cup celery, chopped
½ cup onion, chopped

½ cup green pepper, chopped
1 cup sugar
½ cup vinegar
½ cup cooking oil

Boil sauerkraut and water together for 15 minutes; drain. Set aside or run cold water over sauerkraut until cool. Combine celery, onion, and green pepper; mix with cooled sauerkraut. Heat sugar, vinegar, and oil until sugar is dissolved. Pour over the sauerkraut mixture. Chill and serve. Makes 8 servings.

BETTY ROTH   BIRD UNIT

STRAWBERRY SALAD

1 3-ounce package
  strawberry gelatin
1½ cups boiling water
1 10-ounce package frozen
  strawberries
1 3-ounce package lemon
  gelatin

1 cup boiling water
½ cup pineapple juice
1 3-ounce package cream
  cheese, softened
½ cup crushed pineapple,
  drained
1 cup heavy cream, whipped

Dissolve strawberry gelatin in 1½ cups boiling water; add strawberries and stir until berries are completely thawed. Pour into 9x13 inch pan and chill until firm. Dissolve lemon gelatin in 1 cup boiling water; add pineapple juice and cool. Blend in softened cream cheese and crushed pineapple; chill until slightly thickened. Fold whipped cream into lemon mixture. Pour over firm strawberries. Chill until firm. Makes 10 to 12 servings.

BELLE M. JENNINGS   BARR UNIT

STRAWBERRY PRETZEL SALAD

2½ cups pretzels, crushed
¾ cup margarine
3 tablespoons brown sugar
1 large package cream
  cheese
1 large carton Cool Whip

1 scant cup sugar
1 large package strawberry Jello
2 cups boiling water
1 10-ounce package frozen
  strawberries

Mix pretzels, margarine, and brown sugar. Pat lightly into 9x13 inch pan. Bake at 350° for 10 minutes. Let cool. Mix cream cheese with sugar and Cool Whip. Spread over crust. Refrigerate one half hour. Dissolve Jello in water; add frozen berries and stir until thawed. Spread Jello mixture on top and refrigerate until set. Makes 12 servings.

MADELINE SARACCO   GET TOGETHERS UNIT

MARLA ROSENTRETER, MONDAY NITERS UNIT, uses 1 9-ounce package pretzels and 3 tablespoons white sugar.

KAREN BATES, STITCH AND STIR UNIT, uses 1 16-ounce box frozen strawberries, 3 tablespoons white sugar, and ½ cup sugar.

SEA SIDE SALAD

2 envelopes Knox gelatin
1 cup cold water
1 large or 2 small packages
  Philadelphia cream cheese
¾ cup sugar
1 small can crushed
  pineapple

½ pint whipped cream
1 teaspoon vanilla
1 package lemon Jello
1 cup hot water
1 cup cold water

Dissolve gelatin in 1 cup cold water. Heat and stir; cool. Mix cream cheese, sugar, and pineapple together. Add cream cheese mixture to gelatin. Let set until syrupy. Fold in whipped cream and vanilla. Pour into large glass dish. Dissolve lemon Jello in hot water. Add 1 cup cold water and chill until syrupy. Pour over cream cheese mixture. Chill. Makes 10 servings. Note: Any flavor Jello may be used.

PEARL EDWARDS   DO MORE UNIT

SWEET AND SOUR BEANS

4 cups French style green
  beans, drained
1 large onion, sliced paper
  thin
½ cup vinegar

1 cup sugar
¼ cup water
2 tablespoons salad oil
Salt and pepper

Combine beans and onions in a large bowl. Heat vinegar, sugar and water together until mixture boils, stirring to dissolve sugar. Remove from heat. Add salad oil and pour over beans and onions. Season with salt and pepper. Toss gently until well mixed. Cover and chill several hours or overnight. Makes 8 servings.

MRS. ROBERT G. ENGLAND   HONEY POINT UNIT

TIKI FRUIT SALAD

1 can chunk pineapple (in
  own juice)
1 package frozen
  unsweetened strawberries

2 bananas
2 oranges, peeled and chunked
1 can water packed pears, cut up
1 can Shasta tiki punch soda

Drain all fruits except pineapple. Combine fruits and add soda. Chill. Makes 6 to 8 servings. Note: You can use any fruit desired such as apples, fruit cocktail, etc. Also any flavor soda—orange or strawberry. Dieters may use diet soda.

MRS. LEO (BETTY) SCOTT   JUNIOR HOMEMAKERS UNIT

TACO SALAD

1 pound ground beef	1 6-ounce package corn chips,
1 package taco seasoning	broken
mix	¾ cup cheese, shredded
½ cup hot water	2 medium tomatoes, cut up
½ head lettuce in pieces	⅓ cup chili sauce
½ cup onion, chopped	¼ teaspoon hot taco sauce

Brown beef; drain fat. Stir in taco mix and water; simmer 10 minutes on low heat. Place lettuce in large bowl; add beef mixture, onion, corn chips, cheese and tomatoes. Combine chili sauce and taco sauce to make a dressing. Pour dressing over all ingredients and mix. Serve immediately.

MRS. JACK (GLORIA) BARKLEY   JUNIOR HOMEMAKERS UNIT

TACO SALAD

1 pound ground beef	8 ounces Cheddar cheese
1 package taco seasoning	8 ounces Thousand Island
1 head lettuce	dressing
1 small can kidney beans	⅓ cup sugar
1 large onion, chopped	1 tablespoon taco sauce
4 tomatoes, diced	1 package taco chips

Brown ground beef and add taco seasoning, reserving 1 tablespoon seasoning. Layer vegetables, cheese, and meat. Mix dressing, sugar, reserved taco seasoning, and taco sauce. When ready to serve, add dressing and chips to salad.

KATHY GWILLIM   PIASA UNIT

TACO SALAD

1 pound ground beef, cooked	2 cups Mozzarella cheese
1 medium head lettuce	1 medium onion, thinly sliced
4 tomatoes	into rings
1 5½-ounce package taco	1 8-ounce jar Thousand Island
chips	dressing

In large salad bowl, combine ground beef, lettuce torn in pieces, tomatoes cut in wedges, taco chips, shredded cheese, and onion rings. Pour dressing over all and toss lightly. Makes 6 servings.

MRS. EDWARD KOERTGE   BRIGHTON EARLY BIRDS UNIT

VEG-ALL SALAD

2 No. 2 cans mixed
vegetables (Veg-All)
2 No. 2 cans red kidney
beans
2 onions, chopped fine
8 stalks celery, chopped fine

1 green pepper, chopped fine
1½ cups sugar
2 tablespoons prepared mustard
(or horseradish mustard)
2 tablespoons flour
1 cup vinegar

Drain canned vegetables. Set aside in large bowl. In sauce pan, mix together sugar, mustard, flour, and vinegar. Cook until thick. Let cool completely, then pour over vegetables. Set in refrigerator at least one day or night. Makes 20 servings.

MELBA COULTAS   GIRARD NIGHT UNIT

TOMATO ASPIC

1 envelope Knox unflavored
gelatin
1¾ cups tomato juice
(divided)
¼ teaspoon salt

½ teaspoon Worcestershire
sauce
2 teaspoons lemon juice
½ teaspoon sugar
⅛ teaspoon Tabasco

Sprinkle gelatin in ½ cup tomato juice. Place over low heat and stir until gelatin is dissolved. Remove from heat; stir in remaining tomato juice and seasonings. Pour into 2 cup or individual molds. Chill until firm. Serve with salad greens, cucumbers, and black olives. Can use salad dressing or is good served with meat dishes.

JENNIE COLE   DO MORE UNIT

WATERGATE SALAD

1 9-ounce carton Cool Whip
1 3¾-ounce package instant
pistachio pudding, dry
1 1-pound 14-ounce can
crushed pineapple with
juice

¾ cup miniature marshmallows
½ cup pecans, chopped

Mix all ingredients together in a mixing bowl. Pour into a 1½ quart glass bowl; cover. Refrigerate at least 1 hour before serving. Makes 6 to 8 servings.

MRS. DONALD COLBURN   BRIGHTON EARLY BIRDS UNIT

YUM YUM SALAD

1 3-ounce package lemon
  Jello
Water
1 package small
  marshmallows
Juice from pineapple

1 package Dream Whip
1 flat can crushed pineapple,
  drained
1 cup pecans
1 cup American cheese, grated

Dissolve Jello in 2 cups hot liquid using the juice from the drained pineapple and water to make 2 cups. Melt marshmallows in Jello and refrigerate until syrupy. Add Dream Whip which has been prepared according to package directions. Stir in drained pineapple, pecans, and cheese. Pour into shallow glass bowl or baking dish and refrigerate until set.

DENA GIRARDINI   GET TOGETHERS UNIT

ZINGY DINGY LETTUCE SALAD

1 head lettuce, cut up
1 cup celery, chopped
½ cup green pepper,
  chopped
½ cup onion, chopped
1 10-ounce package frozen
  peas (do not thaw or cook)

2 tablespoons sugar
1½ cups mayonnaise
1 cup Cheddar cheese, grated
½ jar Bacos or other brand
  imitation bacon or real bacon

Place in bowl in order given, the lettuce, celery, green pepper, onion, and frozen peas. Sprinkle sugar over all. Spread mayonnaise on top, then sprinkle cheese and Bacos over all. Do not mix. Cover and store in refrigerator. May be made day ahead and stored overnight in refrigerator. Mix slightly before serving.

MARY KRATOCHVIL   MT. OLIVE UNIT

DARLENE WOOLFOLK, SCOTTVILLE UNIT, uses ½ cup chopped celery and ¼ cup onions, and 2 cups mayonnaise in above recipe.

24 HOUR SALAD

2 cups black cherries,
  drained
2 cups pineapple chunks,
  drained

2 oranges, peeled and cut up
24 marshmallows, cut in fourths

Toss fruits and marshmallows together. Blend in Dressing and chill several hours.

Dressing:

2 eggs
2 tablespoons sugar
2 tablespoons lemon juice
2 tablespoons pineapple juice

1 tablespoon butter
Dash salt
1 cup cream, whipped

Cook all dressing ingredients except cream over low heat, stirring constantly, just to boiling. Remove from heat; cool. Fold in whipped cream. Blend into fruit mixture.

MRS. JACK (GLORIA) BARKLEY   JUNIOR HOMEMAKERS UNIT

24-HOUR SALAD

4 eggs
Juice of one lemon

¼ cup cream

Cook in double boiler until thick. Cool.

Add:

½ pint whipped cream
½ pound seeded white
  grapes or white cherries

1 cup shredded almonds
2 cups marshmallows
1 cup pineapple, cut fine

Refrigerate for 24 hours.

MRS. EWELL (JOSEPHINE) HARRIS   SUSTAINING MEMBER

FRENCH DRESSING

1 cup Mazola oil
½ cup vinegar
1 teaspoon salt
¼ teaspoon black pepper

2 teaspoons paprika
2 tablespoons catsup
½ cup sugar
1 small onion, minced

Blend all ingredients in blender for short period. Let stand 24 hours before using. Makes 1 pint.

LUCILLE BALLINGER   SHAWS POINT UNIT

APPLE COUNTRY SALAD DRESSING

1 cup sugar
½ cup white vinegar
1½ teaspoons dry mustard
1 teaspoon salt

1 teaspoon celery seed
4 teaspoons onion flakes
1 cup salad oil

Mix first six ingredients in a bowl. Add salad oil (good quality oil mixes best) slowly and beat until creamy. Refrigerate. Makes about 2 cups.

MRS. JAMES (JANET) HOPPER   PLAINVIEW UNIT

FRENCH DRESSING

1 can tomato soup
1½ cups vegetable oil
Dash of paprika
1 teaspoon red pepper
½ teaspoon salt

½ cup sugar
½ cup vinegar
2 teaspoons dry mustard
2 tablespoons onion, grated
1 clove garlic

Combine all ingredients in jar or bottle; shake well. Refrigerate until needed, shaking well before using. You may choose to remove garlic after it has seasoned the dressing.

MRS. JOHN PARIS   STAUNTON UNIT

RED FRENCH SALAD DRESSING

¾ cup catsup
1 cup sugar
1 cup salad oil
½ cup wine vinegar

2 teaspoons instant minced
   onions
1½ teaspoons garlic powder

Combine all ingredients well using blender or shake well in jar. Makes 2½ cups.

JANEVA CLARK   CARLINVILLE NIGHT UNIT

SALAD DRESSING

⅓ cup sugar
1 teaspoon salt
1 teaspoon dry mustard
1 teaspoon celery seed

3 cloves garlic (optional)
1 onion, minced
1 cup salad oil
½ cup vinegar

Mix all ingredients well, or if you desire a creamy consistency, put dressing in blender. Very good on cole slaw. Can make slaw the day before.

VIOLA HELM   STAUNTON UNIT

SALAD DRESSING

¼ cup (scant) vinegar
2 cloves garlic
¼ cup oil
1 teaspoon Worcestershire
  sauce

2 teaspoons onion
Dash salt
1 whole green pepper
1 egg, hard cooked
1 quart Hellmann's mayonnaise

Put all ingredients except mayonnaise in blender; blend completely. Mix with mayonnaise.

DONNA DILL   SCOTTVILLE UNIT

SALAD DRESSING

¼ cup salad oil
¼ cup vinegar
¼ cup sugar
¼ cup catsup

2 drops Worcestershire sauce
1 clove garlic
Dash of salt

Pour all ingredients into jar and shake well. Will keep indefinitely in refrigerator. Makes 1 cup.

MRS. WM. (HELEN) MANNING   SPANISH NEEDLE UNIT

THOUSAND ISLAND DRESSING

1 small onion, chopped
1 cup mayonnaise
⅓ cup salad oil
¼ cup catsup
2 tablespoons sugar
2 tablespoons vinegar

1 teaspoon prepared mustard
½ teaspoon salt
½ teaspoon paprika
¼ teaspoon celery seed
Dash of pepper

Put all ingredients in blender container; cover and blend until smooth. Chill and serve over your favorite tossed vegetable salad.

ANN REYNOLDS   HAGAMAN UNIT

METHUSELA

Methusela ate what he found on his plate
And never as people do now
Did he note the amount of the calorie count
He ate it because it was chow
He wasn't disturbed as at dinner he sat
Devouring a roast or a pie
To think it was lacking in granular fat
Or a couple of vitamins shy.
He cheerfully chewed each species of food
Unmindful of troubles or fears.
Lest his health might be hurt
By some fancy dessert
And he lived over nine hundred years.

—Author Unknown

SEAFOOD

This monument is located in the Miner's Cemetery in Mt. Olive. It was erected in memory of "Mother Jones," a teacher-educator, who for most of her life, battled industrial slavery.

In 1903, Mother Jones was in Mt. Olive, at the time union miners were mourning the death of eight of their comrades who had been murdered by coal company gunmen at Virden, Illinois. She requested that her last resting place be near those of the brave boys in Mt. Olive.

Her request was granted in 1930. After reaching age 100, she died in Silver Spring, Md.—and her body was returned to Mt. Olive for burial.

It should be noted that this story is of national significance.

Photographed by John Allen

CHEESE AND TUNA CRESCENTS

1 can (6½ ounces) tuna, drained
2 tablespoons instant minced onion, or ½ cup chopped onion
¾ cup (3 ounces) shredded American or Cheddar cheese

1 can (10¾ ounces) condensed cream of mushroom soup
1 can (8 ounces) refrigerated quick crescents or Italian flavor crescent dinner rolls
½ cup milk

Preheat oven to 375°. In small bowl, combine tuna, onion, ½ cup shredded cheese (reserve ¼ cup) and 5 tablespoons soup. Separate crescent dough into 8 triangles. Place 2 tablespoons tuna mixture on the wide end of each triangle. Roll up; start at shortest side of each triangle and roll to opposite point. In small saucepan, heat remaining soup, reserved shredded cheese and milk until bubbly. Pour ½ of soup mixture (¾ cup) into ungreased 8 or 9 inch square pan. Arrange filled crescents over soup. Bake 25 to 30 minutes until golden brown. Serve with remaining sauce. Refrigerate any leftovers. Makes 4 to 6 servings.

DONA HUBERT   DANDY DOERS UNIT

SALMON-RICE CASSEROLE

1 10¾-ounce can condensed cream of chicken soup
1 15½-ounce can pink salmon, drain and reserve liquid
2 teaspoons Dijon mustard

1 teaspoon seasoned pepper
1½ cups Cheddar cheese, grated
1 10-ounce package frozen chopped broccoli, thawed
3 cups cooked rice
Paprika

Combine soup, ½ cup salmon liquid, mustard, pepper, and ¾ cup cheese. Heat to melt cheese. Toss together broccoli and rice. Stir in ½ soup mixture. Spoon into greased shallow 2 quart casserole. Top with flaked salmon. Pour remaining soup mixture over salmon, sprinkle on remaining cheese. Dust with paprika. Bake at 350° for 20 minutes or until hot and bubbly. Makes 6 servings. To freeze, complete casserole except for remaining cheese. Wrap and freeze. To use later, thaw, sprinkle with cheese, dust with paprika, bake as directed.

DOROTHY OLLER   DO MORE UNIT

HERBED FISH BAKE

2 tablespoons butter or
  margarine
2 pounds halibut steak, 1
  inch thick
1½ cups dairy sour cream
2 tablespoons flour
1 4-ounce can sliced
  mushrooms, drained
3 tablespoons mushroom
  liquid

1 teaspoon salt
⅛ teaspoon pepper
½ teaspoon savory
½ teaspoon tarragon
Paprika
Lemon slices
Parsley

In a large casserole, melt butter. Arrange halibut in dish. In a mixing bowl, combine sour cream, flour, mushrooms, liquid, salt, pepper, savory, and tarragon. Mix well. Spoon mixture over halibut in baking dish and sprinkle with paprika. Bake in a 350° oven for 30 minutes. Dip lemon in parsley and arrange on casserole. Serve with additional lemon slices if desired. Makes 8 servings. Note: If fresh fish is used, ¼ cup butter or margarine will be needed.

HESTER CLARK   CARLINVILLE NIGHT UNIT

POTATO CHIP TUNA TETRAZZINI

1 tablespoon butter or
  margarine
¼ cup onion, chopped
1 10½-ounce can cream of
  mushroom soup, undiluted
1 6 oz. can evaporated milk
⅓ cup grated sharp Cheddar
  cheese
1 6½ to 7-ounce can tuna,
  drained

1 3-ounce can sliced
  mushrooms, drained
2 teaspoons lemon juice
¼ cup pimiento, chopped
  (optional)
3 cups potato chips, crushed
Grated Parmesan cheese
Paprika

Melt butter or margarine in pan. Add onions and saute until tender. Add soup, milk, sharp cheese, and heat through, stirring constantly. Add tuna, mushrooms, lemon juice, and pimiento (if using). Pour a thick layer of crushed potato chips into the bottom of a 2 quart casserole. Divide the tuna mixture into thirds. Pour the first third over the bottom layer of chips. Add another layer of chips, another layer of tuna, repeat until finished. Sprinkle top of casserole with grated cheese and paprika. Bake in a 375° oven for 20 to 25 minutes. Serve hot. Makes 8 servings.

MARY KRATOCHVIL   MT. OLIVE UNIT

CRAB MOLD

1 can cream of mushroom
   soup

12 ounces cream cheese

Melt together over low heat.

Combine:
1 package unflavored gelatin   ¼ cup water

Fold in:
¼ cup chopped onion
¼ cup chopped celery

1 can crabmeat
1 cup real mayonnaise

Pour into a mold and refrigerate for 24 hours to enhance the flavor.

JACQUELINE H. THOMAS   EXTENSION HOME ECONOMIST—
                             MACOUPIN COUNTY

PERFECT TUNA RECIPE

1 can cream of mushroom
   soup
¼ cup milk
2 7-ounce cans tuna

2 eggs, hard cooked
1 cup peas, cooked
1 cup potato chips, crushed

In a 1 quart casserole, blend soup and milk. Stir in tuna, eggs, and peas. Bake at 350° for 25 minutes or until bubbly. Stir. Sprinkle chips over top. Bake 5 minutes more. Makes 4 cups.

FANNIE D. GAUDINO   GET TOGETHERS UNIT

QUICK CHOW MEIN TUNA

1 10¾-ounce can cream of
   mushroom soup
½ cup water
1 cup chow mein noodles
1 6½-ounce can tuna

1 cup celery, chopped
¼ cup onion, chopped
Dash of pepper
½ cup chow mein noodles for
   topping

Mix all ingredients in a bowl. Pour into a buttered 1 quart casserole. Top with an extra ½ cup chow mein noodles. Bake at 375° for 15 minutes. This is an exceptionally good quick luncheon dish. Makes 4 servings.

MRS. CLIFFORD BEILSMITH   BRIGHTON EARLY BIRDS UNIT

SALMON LOAF

1 1-pound can salmon	2 tablespoons lemon juice
Milk	1 tablespoon onions, chopped
1½ cups soft bread crumbs	¼ teaspoon salt
1 egg, slightly beaten	¼ teaspoon pepper

Drain liquid from salmon into 1 cup measure; add enough milk to make 1 cup. Flake and bone the salmon. Mix the egg with the bread crumbs. Add lemon juice, onion, salt and pepper. Combine with salmon and liquid. Spoon mixture into a buttered 9x5x2½ inch loaf pan or 1 quart baking dish. Bake at 350° for 1 hour. Remove from oven and spread topping on top.

Topping:

¼ cup sour cream	Dash of dill seed
¼ cup mayonnaise	

Combine ingredients.

SANDY LOVELESS   CARLINVILLE DAY UNIT

SEAFOOD CASSEROLE

½ cup green pepper, chopped	1 small can shrimp
1 cup celery, chopped	1 cup mayonnaise
½ cup onion, chopped	1¾ cups Pepperidge Farm dressing mix
1 large can tuna	

Mix ingredients together. Place in a greased casserole dish. Top with bread crumbs. Bake at 325° for 30 minutes.

SUE VIECELI   STITCH AND STIR UNIT

TUNA ROMANOFF

1 cup cottage cheese	2 teaspoons Worcestershire sauce
1 cup sour cream	⅛ teaspoon Tabasco sauce
2 tablespoons onion, minced	2 cups cooked noodles
2 tablespoons pimiento, chopped	2 6½- to 7-ounce cans tuna
½ cup black olives, slivered	

Combine cottage cheese, sour cream, onion, pimiento, olives, Worcestershire sauce, and Tabasco sauce. Stir in noodles and tuna. Turn into greased 2 quart casserole. Bake at 350° for 40 minutes. Makes 6 servings.

LUANNE KOCH   HONEY POINT UNIT

MEATS AND MEAT SAUCES

Livestock is an important part of the farming industry in Macoupin County. This is a very familiar sight as one drives through the rural area.

Photographed by Frank Thomas

BAR-B-QUE

5 to 6 pounds pork butt,
cooked till tender
1 tablespoon brown sugar
2 onions
2 cloves garlic
1 can tomato paste

2 cups water
½ cup catsup
3 bottles Maulls bar-b-que sauce
1 teaspoon Tabasco sauce
½ bottle Worcestershire sauce
1 tablespoon mustard

Mix all ingredients except meat and simmer for 2 hours. Cut meat very fine. Add to sauce and simmer 1 hour more.

MARY DAVIDSON   GET TOGETHERS UNIT

BARBECUED HAMBURGERS DELUXE

1½ pounds ground beef
1½ teaspoons salt and
pepper
⅔ cup rolled oats

1 cup cream or milk
3 tablespoons onions

Mix all ingredients together; form into small patties. Lightly brown on both sides in small amount of oil. Drain. Add Sauce and simmer 45 minutes or more. Freezes well. Makes 24 small patties or 12 servings.

Sauce:
1 cup tomato catsup
1 tablespoon Worcestershire
sauce
6 tablespoons onions,
chopped

2 tablespoons vinegar
½ cup water
2 tablespoons sugar

Combine all ingredients.
MILDRED LOVE   CARLINVILLE DAY UNIT

BEEF STROGANOFF

1½ pounds stew meat
1 can cream of celery soup
1 can cream of mushroom
soup

½ package Lipton onion soup
mix
⅓ cup water

Mix all ingredients together and pour into covered casserole. Bake at 325° for 3 hours. Makes 4 servings.

ADELAIDE DALY MASTERSON   SUSTAINING MEMBER

BARBECUE SAUCE AND SPARERIBS

1 medium onion, chopped
1 cup celery, chopped
2 tablespoons margarine
1 cup water
1 cup catsup
2 tablespoons Worcestershire
   sauce
1 clove garlic
2 teaspoons prepared
   mustard

3 tablespoons brown sugar
3 tablespoons vinegar
2 tablespoons lemon juice
1 teaspoon salt
⅛ teaspoon red pepper
1 teaspoon chili powder
4 to 5 pounds spareribs
2 tablespoons shortening
1½ cups water

Saute onion and celery in margarine until tender. Add next 11 ingredients and bring to a boil for 4 to 5 minutes. Salt and pepper the spareribs that have been cut into serving size pieces. Brown in shortening in a heavy pan on all sides. Drain off fat. Add water and half the barbecue sauce. Bake in covered medium size baking pan at 350° for about 2 hours until tender. Add rest of sauce, leave uncovered, and bake unitl moisture is cooked away. May need to add more water. Continue spooning sauce over ribs and let brown. Sauce may be used with left over beef and pork roast to make barbecue. Total baking time is 3½ to 4 hours. Makes 7 to 8 servings.

ROSE MARY HEMBROUGH   BIRD UNIT

BARBECUE BURGER MIX

1 pound ground beef
¼ cup green pepper,
   chopped
½ cup onion, chopped
¼ cup celery, chopped
1 8-ounce can tomato sauce
1 tablespoon vinegar

1½ teaspoons Worcestershire
   sauce
⅛ teaspoon pepper
¼ cup catsup
1 tablespoon sugar
1 teaspoon salt

Brown meat; add vegetables. Cook until vegetables are tender. Add remaining ingredients. Mix well; cover. Simmer for 20 minutes.

MAXINE MILLER   DO MORE UNIT

74

BEEF AND BACON ROLL-UPS

2 pounds ground beef
1 cup American cheese,
  shredded
1 egg, beaten
¼ cup onion, chopped
3 tablespoons Worcestershire
  sauce

3 tablespoons catsup
1 teaspoon salt
½ teaspoon pepper
10 slices of bacon

Mix beef, cheese, egg, onion, Worcestershire sauce, catsup, salt and pepper. Place slices of bacon side by side on a board. Place ground beef mixture in center of bacon slices. Wrap bacon around ground beef and seal with toothpicks. Cut into slices the width of the bacon slices. Broil 7 minutes on each side. This recipe is excellent for grilling out of doors. Makes 10 slices.

ILA NELSON   MONDAY NITERS UNIT

BIRD FARM UPSIDE DOWN PIE

1 pound sausage, round
  package
2 medium onions, sliced

1 can tomato soup
1 recipe baking powder biscuits

Cut sausage into patties. Place in cold skillet. Cook over low heat unitl thoroughly cooked. Place patties in casserole. Slowly brown the onions in a small amount of sausage drippings. Place onions in casserole. Pour tomato soup over meat and onions. Make 1 recipe of baking powder biscuits; lightly roll out to fit casserole. Place on top of mixture. Bake at 400° for 15 to 20 minutes. Turn out on platter so meat and onions are on top. Hamburger may be used instead of sausage. Makes 4 to 6 servings.

DOROTHY GREEN   GIRARD NIGHT UNIT

CORN HOT DISH

1 pound ground beef
1 onion, chopped
½ package alphabet
  macaroni
1 16-ounce can cream style
  corn

1 can chicken rice soup
Seasonings to taste
Buttered bread crumbs

Brown meat and onion. Cook macaroni as directed on package. Mix meat, macaroni, corn, and soup. Season to taste. Pour into casserole. Cover with buttered bread crumbs. Bake at 325° for 1½ hours. Makes 4 to 6 servings.

DARLENE ELLIOTT   STITCH AND STIR UNIT

CRUNCHY BEEF CASSEROLE

1 7-ounce package
Creamettes elbow macaroni
1 pound ground beef
1 10¾-ounce can cream of
mushroom soup
1 14½-ounce can whole
tomatoes, cut up

¾ cup shredded Cheddar cheese
¼ cup chopped pepper
¾ teaspoon salt
1 3-ounce can Durkee's French
fried onions

Prepare macaroni as directed on package; drain. Brown ground beef; drain. Combine beef with all ingredients except French fried onions. Pour half the mixture into a 2 quart casserole which has been sprayed with Pam. Add ½ can onions. Pour remaining mixture over onions. Cover and bake at 350° for 30 minutes. Uncover, top with remaining onions and bake 5 minutes longer. Makes 4 to 6 servings.

MARY TAYLOR   BERTHA ELDRED UNIT

GROUND BEEF STEAK SUPREME

1 pound ground beef
1 egg, beaten
⅓ teaspoon pepper
¼ cup celery, finely chopped
¼ cup dry bread crumbs

1 teaspoon salt
3 tablespoons onion, minced
1 cup mushroom soup
½ cup water

Mix above ingredients except soup and water; shape into oval 1 inch thick. Brown in skillet in hot fat on both sides. Pour over meat loaf the soup diluted with water. Cook slowly in covered skillet about 25 minutes. Serve mushroom gravy with boiled or mashed potatoes. Meat can also be shaped into patties and served over toast for a hot sandwich.

DORIS LACY   SUSTAINING MEMBER

HOT METHODIST CASSEROLE

3 pounds raw ground beef
1 cup celery, chopped
1 medium onion, chopped
1 can cream of mushroom
soup

1 can cream of chicken soup
1 cup water
1 cup uncooked regular rice
2 tablespoons soy sauce

Mix all ingredients; add salt and pepper. Put into an ungreased 10x13 inch pan. Bake, uncovered, at 350° for 2 hours or until dry. Makes 8 servings.

SUE VAN NATTAN   STITCH AND STIR UNIT

GRECO

1 yellow onion, chopped
1 green pepper, chopped
3 tablespoons shortening
1 pound ground beef
1 or 2 cans mushrooms,
  drained

2 cups shell macaroni
3 8-ounce cans tomato sauce
1 16-ounce can cream style corn
1 pound sharp Cheddar cheese,
  grated

Fry onion and pepper in oil, butter, or margarine. Fry meat in onion mixture. Add mushrooms and take from heat. Boil macaroni in lightly salted water, drain, and add to meat mixture. Add tomato sauce and corn. Mix well. Pour into greased 3 quart casserole, cover, and refrigerate. When ready to bake, grate the Cheddar cheese on top. Bake in 300° oven for 1 hour. Makes 8 servings.

MRS. LEA B. HEINZ   BERTHA ELDRED UNIT

HAMBURGER CASSEROLE

2 pounds ground beef
1 medium onion, chopped
1 small green pepper,
  chopped
1 can sliced mushrooms,
  drained
Salt

Pepper
Celery salt
About 6 or 8 potatoes, sliced
1 can green beans
1 large can tomato sauce
½ cup milk

Using large skillet, brown ground beef with onion, green pepper, sliced mushrooms, and seasonings. Butter a large casserole dish and place in layers, raw sliced potatoes, beef mixture, green beans and tomato sauce. Repeat layers again, pouring the milk over top. Cover and bake at 350° for 1½ hours. Makes 8 servings.

PAT MILLER   SCOTTVILLE UNIT

PEPPER HASH

1 pound ground beef
1 onion, diced
1 green pepper, diced
2 cups tomatos, canned

½ cup rice, uncooked
½ teaspoon chili powder
2 teaspoons salt
Dash of pepper

Saute onion and green pepper. Add ground beef and brown well. Drain fat. Stir in tomatoes, rice, chili powder, salt, and pepper. Pour into greased 2 quart baking dish. Cover and bake for 1 hour at 350°. Makes 6 servings.

IDA MAE LEACH   BIRD UNIT

HAMBURGER PIE

1 pound ground beef
½ cup onion, chopped
½ teaspoon salt
Black pepper to taste
1 16-ounce can cut green
  beans, drained

1 can condensed tomato soup
5 medium potatoes, cooked
½ cup warm milk
1 egg, beaten
½ cup shredded American
  cheese

In large skillet, cook meat and onion until meat is lightly browned and onion is tender. Add salt and pepper. Add drained beans and soup; pour into greased 1½ quart casserole. Mash potatoes while hot; add milk and egg. Season with salt and pepper. Spoon in mounds over casserole. Sprinkle cheese over potatoes. Bake at 350° for 25 to 30 minutes. Makes 4 to 6 servings. Note: To use packaged instant mashed potatoes, prepare 4 servings according to package directions except reserve the milk. Add egg; season with salt and pepper. Add enough reserved milk so potatoes hold shape.

CHERYL WALKER   GILLESPIE NIGHT UNIT

HAMBURGER PIE

1 cup Bisquick
⅓ cup light cream
1 pound ground beef
1 medium onion, chopped
1 teaspoon salt

¼ teaspoon pepper
½ teaspoon flavor extender
2 eggs
1 cup small curd cottage cheese
Paprika

Heat oven to 350° or 375°. Mix Bisquick and cream together. Knead gently 10 times on surface lightly dusted with Bisquick. Roll dough into circle to fit 9 inch pie pan. Ease dough into pan and fork edges. Saute beef and onions until meat has lost color. Add salt, pepper, and flavor extender. Drain off excess fat. Beat eggs slightly and blend with cottage cheese. Pour over meat. Sprinkle with paprika. Bake 30 minutes or until set and slightly browned. Make 6 servings.

MILDRED LOVE   CARLINVILLE DAY UNIT

ITALIAN BEEF

6 pound rump roast
3 large onions
1 teaspoon salt
¼ teaspoon coarsely ground
   black pepper
¼ teaspoon onion salt

½ teaspoon garlic salt
¼ teaspoon oregano
¼ teaspoon basil
½ teaspoon Italian seasoning
½ teaspoon seasoned salt
1 teaspoon Accent

Fill roaster half full of water. Add roast, onions, salt, and pepper. Cook in oven until tender. Cool. Refrigerate overnight. On second day, remove roast from pan and slice thin. Remove fat from broth and strain. Combine onion salt, garlic salt, oregano, basil, Italian seasoning, seasoned salt, and Accent. Boil with broth from roast. Place beef in layers in roaster and pour broth over it. Bake at 350° for 30 minutes. Remove roast and broth from roaster and let set in refrigerator for a day or two. When ready to serve, warm. Serve on hard rolls. Makes 16 to 20 servings.

ALICE KULENKAMP   GILLESPIE NIGHT UNIT

SAUERBRATEN

4 pounds boneless beef roast
1 cup water
1 cup wine vinegar
2 onions, sliced
1 teaspoon salt
6 peppercorns
2 bay leaves

2 cloves
2 tablespoons vegetable oil
1 medium tomato, chopped
2 tablespoons flour
2 teaspoons sugar
¼ cup water

Place meat in large container. In a sauce pan, bring water, vinegar, onions, salt, peppercorns, bay leaves, and cloves to a boil. Simmer 10 minutes. Cool marinade to room temperature and pour over meat. Refrigerate 2 days turning frequently. Remove meat from marinade and dry. Brown in vegetable oil. Add tomato and marinade liquid. Cover. Bake at 325° for 1½ to 2 hours or in a slow cooker 3 or 4 hours until tender. Remove meat from juices. Remove peppercorns, cloves, and bay leaves. Mix flour and sugar with ¼ cup water. Add to pan juices and cook until thickened. Serve with boiled potatoes and red cabbage. Makes 6 to 8 servings.

ALBERTA WILTON   CARLINVILLE NIGHT UNIT

ITALIAN BEEF

6 pounds rolled rump roast
2 teaspoons basil
1 teaspoon oregano
1 teaspoon red pepper

1 package onion soup mix
3 cups water
Juice from jar of hot peppers

Mix dry ingredients together and sprinkle over meat. Add water and the pepper juice. Bake, covered, at 350° for 2½ hours or until well cooked. Baste often. When cooked, remove from oven and let cool in broth. When cool, remove from broth and slice very thin. When ready to eat, heat meat together with broth on top of stove. Serve on hard rolls with hot peppers. Makes 12 servings.

LUCY OAKLEY   DO MORE UNIT

SWISS CREME STEAK

2 pounds round steak, cut in
   serving size
Salt and pepper
½ teaspoon dried marjoram
Flour
¼ cup butter or margarine

2 medium onions, sliced
½ cup water mixed with
1 beef bouillon cube
½ cup sour cream
2 tablespoons grated Parmesan
   cheese

Sprinkle both sides of meat with salt, pepper, marjoram, and flour. Pound seasonings into meat using meat tenderizing mallet. Heat butter or margarine in a large skillet, with lid; add onion slices and cook until straw colored. Using slotted spoon, lift out onions from skillet and set aside. Add steaks to hot fat and fry on both sides until browned. Add the beef bouillon flavored water with the sour cream and Parmesan cheese. Pour over meat in skillet; add onion slices. Cover tightly and cook over low heat for about 1¼ hours or until meat is tender. Serves 6.

BOBBIE FRUEH   JUNIOR HOMEMAKERS UNIT

OUTDOOR POT ROAST

4 to 5 pound chuck pot roast
1 can undiluted onion soup
1 can undiluted tomato soup
1 cup chili sauce
3 beef bouillon cubes

2 tablespoons Worcestershire
 sauce
1 teaspoon minced garlic
6 potatoes, pared and halved

Place roast on outdoor grill over high heat; sear 10 minutes. Turn and sear 5 minutes. Turn heat to medium low. Transfer roast to heavy duty foil (double layer if there is a bone.) Shape sides to form a pan. Combine remaining ingredients, except potatoes, in bowl. Pour over roast. Close foil securely with butcher fold. Place on grill, close lid, and cook 1 hour. Turn roast in sauce. Add potatoes and close foil again. Continue cooking 1 hour more with lid closed, or until meat and potatoes are tender. Makes 8 to 10 servings.

NANCY SCHIEN   STITCH AND STIR UNIT

POORMAN'S FILET MIGNON

3 to 5 pound chuck roast
1 teaspoon meat tenderizer
1½ cups orange juice
½ cup soy sauce

2 tablespoons brown sugar
1 tablespoon Worcestershire
 sauce

Sprinkle meat with tenderizer. Pierce deeply with fork many times. Allow to stand 1 hour. Cut into filet mignon sizes. Place in stainless steel bowl. Combine remaining ingredients and pour over meat chunks in bowl. Refrigerate at least 24 hours, turning several times. Grill over hot coals to desired doneness.

DOROTHY L. NELSON   BIRD UNIT

STEAK BITES

4 pounds sirloin steak
Seasoned meat tenderizer
1 clove garlic, cut in half
1 cup cooking sherry
½ cup margarine
1 tablespoon dry mustard
½ teaspoon garlic salt

1 tablespoon Worcestershire
 sauce
⅛ teaspoon pepper
⅛ teaspoon hot sauce
1 tablespoon liquid smoke
1 small can mushroom stems
 and liquid

Sprinkle sirloin with tenderizer; rub with garlic on both sides. Marinate in sherry for 30 minutes on each side; reserve marinade. Broil steak until medium well done; cut into bite size pieces. Combine ⅓ cup marinade with remaining ingredients; pour over steak. Heat; serve in chafing dish, if desired. Steak and sauce may be prepared day before serving; heat through just before serving. Makes 5 servings.

GAIL SPUDICH   DANDY DOERS UNIT

MEAT-ZA PIE

1 pound ground beef
½ to 1 teaspoon garlic salt
½ cup fine dry bread crumbs
⅔ cup evaporated milk
⅓ cup tomato catsup or
  tomato paste
1 2-ounce can sliced
  mushrooms, drained

2 or 3 slices processed American
  cheese
¼ teaspoon oregano, finely
  crumbled
2 tablespoons Parmesan cheese
  (or more)

Place beef, garlic salt, and bread crumbs in 9 inch pie plate. Add milk and mix together with a fork. With fork spread mixture evenly over bottom of pan, raising to form a rim about ½ inch around edge. Spread catsup over meat mixture to rim. Arrange mushrooms on catsup. Place cheese, cut into strips, in criss cross pattern over top. Sprinkle with oregano. (Poultry seasoning may be substituted.) Sprinkle generously with grated Parmesan cheese. Bake in preheated 400° oven for 20 minutes or until cheese is melted and lightly browned. Cut into wedges and serve hot. Makes 6 servings.

MRS. LEOLA KAMPER   BRIGHTON EARLY BIRDS UNIT

SICILIAN SUPPER

1 pound ground beef
½ cup onions, chopped
1 6-ounce can tomato paste
¾ cup water
1½ teaspoons salt
½ teaspoon pepper
¾ cup milk

1 8-ounce package cream
  cheese, cubed
½ cup grated Parmesan cheese
½ teaspoon garlic salt
½ cup green pepper, chopped
2 cups egg noodles, cooked

Brown meat, add onion and cook until tender. Add tomato paste, water, salt, pepper, and simmer 5 minutes. Heat milk, cream cheese, and blend well. Stir in ¼ cup Parmesan cheese, garlic salt, and green pepper. In a casserole alternate layers of noodles, meat mixture, and cheese mixture. Bake at 350° for 20 minutes. Sprinkle remaining ¼ cup Parmesan cheese on top. Makes 6 servings.

VICKIE LAUGHLIN   DANDY DOERS UNIT

MEAT LOAF

3 cups dry bread crumbs
1 cup milk
1½ pounds ground beef
¼ cup onion, chopped
2 eggs, beaten

1 teaspoon salt
6 tablespoons brown sugar
½ cup catsup
2 teaspoons dry mustard

Soak bread crumbs in milk. Add ground beef, onion, eggs, and salt. Mix well. Shape into loaf and place in oblong baking pan. Combine brown sugar, catsup, and dry mustard. Pour over loaf and bake at 350° for 45 mintues.

MRS. LUCILLE MATTHEWS   GIRARD DAY UNIT

FAVORITE MEAT LOAF

1½ pounds ground beef
½ cup cracker crumbs
2 eggs, beaten
1 8-ounce can tomato sauce
¼ cup onion, chopped, or
   equivalent in dry onion

2 tablespoons green pepper,
   chopped
1 package Good Seasons Italian
   style dressing mix

Combine all ingredients. Mix well and shape mixture into loaf in 12x7½x2 inch pan. Bake at 350° for 1½ hours. Makes 6 to 8 servings.

ESTHER DOERR   BUNKER HILL UNIT

SWEET AND SOUR MEAT BALLS

2 pounds ground beef
2 eggs
2 tablespoons Cream of
   Wheat

1 small onion, grated
1 teaspoon salt, or more, to taste
⅛ teaspoon pepper

Mix all ingredients and form into medium sized balls. Place meat balls in Dutch oven, pour Sauce over top, and simmer until done (about 1 hour.)

Sauce:
1 medium onion, sliced
½ cup ketchup
½ cup chili sauce
Salt and pepper to taste

Juice of ½ lemon
2 teaspoons sugar
2 teaspoons brown sugar
¼ cup water

Boil all ingredients together.

LORRAINE OBERTINO   GET TOGETHERS UNIT

SICILIAN MEAT LOAF

2 eggs, beaten
¾ cup soft bread crumbs
½ cup tomato juice
½ teaspoon oregano
¼ teaspoon salt
¼ teaspoon pepper

½ teaspoon instant minced garlic
2 pounds ground beef
8 thin slices ham
6 ounces shredded Mozzarella
  cheese
3 slices Mozzarella cheese

Combine eggs, bread crumbs, tomato juice, oregano, salt, pepper, garlic; mix into ground beef. Divide mixture in half and pat ½ into a loaf pan. Arrange ham slices on top and sprinkle the grated cheese on top. Cover grated cheese with the remaining beef mixture. Bake at 350° for 1 hour. Place cheese slices on top and return to oven for 5 more minutes. (Loaf will be pink in center due to ham.) Makes 8 servings.

RUTH LOVELESS   STITCH AND STIR UNIT

PRESS CLUB MEATBALLS AND SAUCE

1 pound ground beef
½ pound sausage
2 eggs
½ cup bread crumbs
1 medium onion, finely
  chopped
¼ teaspoon celery seed

1 teaspoon Parmesan cheese
¼ teaspoon garlic powder
1 teaspoon salt
Dash of oregano
Dash of salad herbs
Dash of pepper
¼ cup catsup

Combine all ingredients and mix well. Roll into bite size balls. Place on baking sheet. Bake at 350° for 30 minutes. Drain well. Makes 6 servings.

Sauce:
1 small onion, chopped
2 tablespoons salad oil
2 tablespoons vinegar
¼ cup prepared mustard
2 or 3 16-ounce cans tomato
  sauce
2 cups water
2 tablespoons brown sugar

1 teaspoon Worcestershire sauce
½ teaspoon oregano
½ teaspoon chili powder
½ teaspoon salt
Dash of garlic powder, sweet
  basil, salad herbs, cinnamon,
  parsley

Saute onion in oil. Drain. Combine with remaining ingredients and simmer for 3 to 4 hours.

LINDA SKAGGS   STITCH AND STIR UNIT

SWEDISH MEAT BALLS

1 cup fine bread crumbs
⅓ cup milk
1 pound ground beef
¼ cup onion, minced
1 egg, slightly beaten

1½ teaspoons salt
⅛ teaspoon pepper
½ teaspoon nutmeg
2 tablespoons butter

In small mixing bowl, mix bread crumbs and milk. In medium mixing bowl, stir together ground beef, onion, egg, salt, pepper, and nutmeg. Add bread crumbs and milk to meat mixture and mix well. Shape into small balls and saute in butter in a heavy iron or non stick skillet. Brown on all sides. Remove meat balls from skillet, reserve drippings for Sauce.

Sauce:
Reserved meat drippings
2 tablespoons flour
1 cup hot water

1 bouillon cube
½ cup milk
½ cup cream

Stir flour into drippings in skillet. Mix in hot water, bouillon cube, milk, and cream. Cook and stir until thickened. Add meat balls to sauce in skillet and simmer 15 minutes. Makes 6 to 8 servings.

VELMA AMBROSE   SCOTTVILLE UNIT

OVEN PORCUPINES

1 pound ground beef
½ cup regular rice, uncooked
½ cup water
⅓ cup onion, chopped
1 teaspoon salt
½ teaspoon celery salt

⅛ teaspoon garlic powder
⅛ teaspoon black pepper
1 15-ounce can tomato sauce
1 cup water
2 teaspoons Worcestershire
   sauce

Heat oven to 350°. Mix meat, rice, ½ cup water, onion, salts, garlic powder, and pepper. Shape mixture by rounded tablespoonfuls into balls. Place meat balls in ungreased 8x8x2 inch baking dish. Stir together remaining ingredients; pour over meatballs. Cover with aluminum foil. Bake 45 minutes. Uncover dish and bake 15 minutes longer. Makes 4 to 6 servings.

ALDA ARTER   HONEY POINT UNIT

JELLY MEAT BALLS

Meat loaf mixture
½ jar pure grape jelly

½ bottle barbecue sauce
Catsup to taste

Prepare your favorite meat loaf mixture and form into balls. Bake at 350° until brown, about 1 hour. Turn once after ½ hour baking time has passed. In a sauce pan, mix grape jelly, barbecue sauce, and catsup. Heat until blended. Pour drippings from meat balls. Pour jelly mixture over meat balls and bake until bubbly, about 30 minutes.

REVAH RIFFEY   DO MORE UNIT

MEAT BALLS

2 pounds ground beef
1 cup cooked rice
¼ cup onion, chopped

Salt and pepper to taste
1 can tomato soup
1 can water

Mix first 4 ingredients and shape into balls. Place in 8x12 inch baking dish. Mix tomato soup with water and pour over meat balls. Bake in 400° oven for 15 minutes. Turn meat balls over, reduce heat to 350° and bake for 30 minutes. Makes 6 servings.

MAGDALENE LANDES   SCOTTVILLE UNIT

PORCUPINE BALLS

1 pound ground beef
⅔ cup long grain rice,
  uncooked
½ cup onion, chopped

1½ teaspoons salt
¼ teaspoon pepper
2 tablespoons fat
2½ cups tomato juice

Mix ground beef, rice, onion, salt, and pepper. Form into meat balls about the size of an egg. Brown in fat about 15 minutes. Simmer in tomato juice 45 minutes.

ELAINE SANDERS   JUNIOR HOMEMAKERS UNIT

MEAT BALLS

1½ pounds bulk pork
sausage
½ cup rice, uncooked
½ medium onion, chopped

1 teaspoon all purpose
seasoning
¼ teaspoon garlic seasoning
1 large can tomato sauce

Mix ingredients except for tomato sauce and form into balls. Place in a large casserole in one layer. Pour tomato sauce over top. Cover. Bake at 300° for 1½ hours or until done. Makes 6 servings.

MRS. ARTHUR WIESE   SOUTH OTTER UNIT

SWEDISH MEAT BALLS

1½ cups bread crumbs
1 cup milk or cream
1 pound ground chuck
¼ pound veal, ground
¼ pound pork, ground
2 eggs
1 medium onion, chopped
1¾ teaspoons salt
¾ teaspoon dill weed

¼ teaspoon allspice
⅛ teaspoon nutmeg
⅛ teaspoon cardamom (optional)
3 tablespoons butter or
margarine
1 10½-ounce can beef broth
⅛ teaspoon pepper
½ cup light cream

Soak bread crumbs in milk or cream for 5 minutes. Add ground meats, eggs, onion, 1½ teaspoons salt, ¼ teaspoon dill weed, allspice, nutmeg, and cardamom. Mix well. Refrigerate, covered, for 1 hour. Shape mixture into 1 inch diameter balls. Brown lightly in hot butter. Place meat balls in heavy Dutch oven as they are browned. Add beef broth, pepper, light cream, remaining ¼ teaspoon salt and ½ teaspoon dill weed to pan drippings. Pour sauce over meat balls. Cover and simmer fcr about 2 hours. Makes 12 servings. Note: Meat balls will have finer texture if meats are ground together twice.

MRS. MERLE LONG   GIRARD DAY UNIT

CHINESE CHOP SUEY

¾ pound pork steak
¾ pound beef steak
3 tablespoons bead molasses
3 tablespoons soy sauce
1 tablespoon vegetable oil or
  shortening
4 cups celery, cut in small
  pieces on angle or
  crosswise

4 large onions, diced or chopped
1 can mushrooms, cut in pieces
1 can bean sprouts
1 or 2 tablespoons corn starch in
  3 tablespoons water
1 cup rice cooked in 2 cups
  water and
1 teaspoon salt

Cut meat in small strips 1½ inches. Brown in vegetable oil or shortening. When browned, add the onions. Cook until onions are tender, about 5 minutes. Boil the celery in separate pan in 2 cups water until tender, about 7 minutes. Add this to the meat and onions using the liquid which should be about 1½ cups. Add the bead molasses and soy sauce and mushrooms. Cook together until the meat is tender, about 30 minutes. Add the bean sprouts and liquid from the beans to make gravy. Cook about 10 minutes more. Thicken with the corn starch and water. Serve over flaked rice. Chow mein noodles may be sprinkled on the top when serving. Makes 8 large servings.

REGINA DRURY   BERTHA ELDRED UNIT

CHINESE HAMBURGER

1 to 1½ pounds ground beef
  (unsalted)
1 cup onions, chopped
1 cup celery, sliced fine
1 can cream of mushroom
  soup
1 can cream of chicken soup

1½ cups warm water (rinse out
  soup cans)
½ cup uncooked rice (regular or
  Minute)
¼ teaspoon pepper
⅛ cup soy sauce
1 small can Chinese noodles

Brown beef, pour off excess fat. Add onion, celery, soups, and water. Heat all together. Add (without reheating) soy sauce, pepper, and rice. Stir and put in large casserole. Bake, covered, 30 minutes at 350°. Remove cover and bake 30 minutes longer. Stir, put noodles on top and heat noodles for about 10 minutes. Serve with soy sauce on the table. Makes 4 to 6 servings.

MRS. GERALD (ALICE) MAYBERRY   POLK UNIT

CHOP SUEY

¼ cup margarine
2 pounds lean beef or pork,
   diced
1¼ cups hot water
2 cups celery, chopped
1½ cups onions, chopped
1 teaspoon salt
¼ teaspoon pepper

⅓ cup cold water
3 tablespoons corn starch
2 teaspoons soy sauce
1 tablespoon brown sauce
1 can bean sprouts, drained
Cooked rice or chow mein
   noodles

Melt margarine in pan. Add meat; stir and sear quickly. Add hot water and cook slowly 30 minutes. Add celery, onions, salt, pepper; cover and cook 30 minutes. Add cold water, corn starch, soy sauce, and brown sauce; cook 5 minutes. Add bean sprouts and bring to a boil. Serve hot over cooked rice or chow mein noodles with soy sauce. Makes 6 servings.

BETTY SULLIVAN   POLK UNIT

VEAL CORDON BLEU

4 boneless veal cutlets
   (about 4 ounces each), or
1 pound veal round steak, ½
   inch thick
4 thin slices boiled or cooked
   ham
4 thin slices Swiss cheese
2 tablespoons flour

½ teaspoon salt
¼ teaspoon pepper
¼ teaspoon allspice
1 egg, slightly beaten
½ cup dry bread crumbs
3 tablespoons shortening
2 tablespoons water

If using veal round steak, cut into 4 serving pieces. Pound meat until ¼ inch thick. Place a slice of ham and cheese on each cutlet. Roll up carefully, beginning at narrow end; secure rolls with wooden picks. Mix flour, salt, pepper, and allspice; coat rolls with flour mixture. Dip rolls into egg, then roll in bread crumbs. In large skillet, brown rolls in shortening about 5 minutes. Reduce heat and add water. Cover; simmer 45 minutes or until tender. Remove cover last 2 to 3 minutes to crisp rolls slightly. Serve on bed of brown or white rice. Makes 4 servings.

JUDY DEWERFF   MT. OLIVE UNIT

PIZZA

1 package dry yeast	1 teaspoon salt
1¼ cups warm water	4 cups flour
2 tablespoons vegetable oil	

To make dough, dissolve yeast in water. Stir in oil. Add salt and flour, mix well. Knead vigorously on floured board until smooth and elastic. Shape into a ball. Rub a little Crisco on your hands and rub off onto ball of dough. Place dough in a bowl. Cover and let rise 1 hour. While dough is rising, make sauce. When dough has risen, shape into 3 balls. Roll each ball out to fit pizza pans, cookie sheets, or jelly roll pans. Slightly oil the pans. Place dough in pans, pulling to fit to edges and up around edge, pressing to pan with fingers. Spread sauce over all 3 doughs. Sprinkle onions over each, then sausage and mushrooms, and top with cheese. Bake at 550° for 15 minutes. Using a pancake turner, lift crusts to be sure bottoms are nicely browned before removing from oven. Makes 3 pizzas.

Sauce:

1 large can tomato sauce	½ teaspoon oregano
1 teaspoon salt	⅛ teaspoon pepper

Mix together tomato sauce with seasonings. Set aside.

Toppings:

1½ pound sausage	Canned, sliced mushrooms, as
1 very large onion	desired
1 pound shredded Mozzarella	
cheese	

Break up sausage and fry until redness is gone. Remove sausage from fat and set aside. Slice onion into fat and saute. Drain and set aside. Drain mushrooms, slice, and set aside.

NANCY MAJZEL   GET TOGETHERS UNIT

DEEP DISH PIZZA

1½ pounds ground beef
½ cup onion, chopped
1 6-ounce can tomato paste
1 2-ounce can mushroom
  slices, undrained
1½ teaspoons oregano
1¼ teaspoons salt

½ teaspoon pepper
Pinch of garlic salt or powder,
  optional
1 cup shredded Mozzarella or
  Cheddar cheese
1 large can refrigerator biscuits

Brown ground beef with chopped onion. Drain off liquid. Stir in tomato paste, undrained mushrooms, and spices. Simmer this together for 5 to 10 minutes. Press biscuits together on pizza pan to make crust. Spread meat mixture on biscuit crust and top with cheese. Bake at 400° for 20 to 25 minutes. Makes 6 to 8 servings.

MRS. JAMES (JANET) HOPPER   PLAINVIEW UNIT

SWEET-SOUR PORK

3 large green peppers
¾ cup oil
1 teaspoon salt
1 small clove garlic
1 egg
2 tablespoons flour
½ teaspoon salt
⅛ teaspoon pepper
1 pound lean pork, cut in ½
  inch cubes

1 cup chicken bouillon
4 slices canned pineapple
2½ tablespoons corn starch
1 tablespoon soy sauce
½ cup vinegar
½ cup sugar
1 can Chinese noodles or cooked
  rice

Cut pepper in chunks and cook in boiling water until tender, about 5 minutes. Drain immediately. Heat oil and 1 teaspoon salt in skillet. Add garlic, finely minced, and cook until brown. In small bowl beat together egg, flour, and ½ teaspoon salt and pepper. Thoroughly coat cubes of pork with this batter. Drop pieces, one at a time, into skillet and brown. Pour off all but 1 tablespoon oil. Add ⅓ of the bouillon, pineapple, and pepper in skillet with browned pork. Cover tightly and simmer 10 minutes. Blend corn starch, soy sauce, vinegar, and sugar with other ⅔ cup of bouillon in small bowl. Add to pork, peppers, and pineapple mixture. Stir constantly until mixture is hot. Serve immediately over Chinese noodles or cooked rice. Makes 4 to 6 servings.

MRS. OPAL BETHARD   BIRD UNIT

COUNTRY STYLE LIVER POT ROAST

3 pounds beef liver
¼ cup flour
½ cup bacon drippings
4 large onions, peeled and
   sliced

1 teaspoon salt
¼ teaspoon paprika
1 cup dairy sour cream
½ cup water

Dredge liver in flour; brown on both sides in hot bacon drippings. Remove meat to a baking dish. Cook sliced onions in drippings until lightly browned. Remove from pan; place on top of meat. Combine seasonings, cream, and water with remaining fat. Pour mixture over meat and onions. Cover and bake at 325° for 1½ hours. Makes 4 to 6 servings.

MRS. ROBERT G. ENGLAND   HONEY POINT UNIT

CHICKEN FRIED LIVER

1½ pounds sliced beef liver
3 tablespoons lemon juice
¼ cup flour
1 teaspoon salt
¼ teaspoon pepper
¼ cup milk

1 egg, beaten
3 tablespoons onions, grated
1 clove garlic, minced
1½ cups fine cracker crumbs
½ cup fat

Cut liver in strips 1 to 1½ inches wide and sprinkle with lemon juice. Combine flour and seasonings; dredge liver in mixture. Combine milk, onion, egg, garlic, and dredge liver again. Roll in cracker crumbs and fry in hot fat 3 or 4 minutes on each side. Makes 6 servings.

ALICE KULENKAMP   GILLESPIE NIGHT UNIT

STEWED LIVER

6 slices bacon
1½ pounds beef liver
Flour
1 large onion, sliced
1 green pepper, sliced

1 envelope onion soup mix
1 1-pound can stewed tomatoes
Salt and pepper
Cooked noodles

Brown bacon. Set aside. Flour liver and brown on both sides. Cook onions and green peppers until clear. Place on liver in a 13x9x2 casserole. Sprinkle onion soup over top and pour on tomatoes. Place bacon on top. Season to taste. Bake, covered, at 350° for 30 minutes. Serve with noodles. Makes 4 servings.

MISS ELLA PAUL   SOUTH OTTER UNIT

ERNESTO'S ENCHILADAS

1½ pounds ground beef
1 package chili seasoning
  mix
1 16-ounce can tomato sauce

1 medium onion, chopped
1 cup Cheddar cheese, shredded
12 corn tortillas
¼ cup water

Brown the ground beef, stir in seasoning mix, tomato sauce, onions, and ¼ cup of the cheese. Simmer 10 minutes. Remove from heat. Spoon 2 tablespoons of filling into each tortilla. Roll, place in a single layer in 10x6 inch baking dish. Top with the rest of the sauce; cover with the water and remaining cheese. Bake, uncovered, at 375° for 15 minutes. Makes 4 to 6 servings.

KAREN HEMBROUGH   STITCH AND STIR UNIT

POLENTA STEZA

Sauce:
1½ tablespoons butter
1 clove garlic, minced
1 or 2 tablespoons parsley,
  minced, optional
½ cup chopped onion
1 pound ground beef
1 teaspoon salt

¼ teaspoon Italian seasoning
⅛ teaspoon pepper
1 small jar mushrooms, not
  drained, optional
2 teaspoons sugar
1 6-ounce can tomato paste
1 15-ounce can tomato sauce

In a heavy sauce pan, melt butter. Saute garlic, parsley and onion over low heat. Add meat; cook until red is gone from meat. Add salt, seasoning, pepper and sugar. Cook slowly 15 minutes. Add mushrooms, tomato paste and tomato sauce. Cover and simmer 1½ to 2 hours, stirring occasionally.

Polenta:
2 cups corn meal
1½ teaspoon salt

8 cups water
2 tablespoons butter

1 pound Brick cheese, sliced   ½ cup grated Parmesan cheese

Put the corn meal and salt into a 3 quart sauce pan. Add the 8 cups of water. Stir until well mixed. Cook over low heat until it begins to boil, stirring constantly. Add butter and stir well. Cover and cook slowly for 30 minutes, stirring occasionally. Pour half of polenta into a 9x13 inch pan. Cover with cheese slices and spread remaining polenta over cheese. Spoon sauce generously over polenta. Sprinkle grated cheese over top. It is ready to eat now, or bake at 350° for 15 minutes or until ready to eat. Serves 6.

NANCY MAJZEL   GET TOGETHERS UNIT

PORK CHOPS DIJONNAISE

4 thickly cut or butterfly pork
  chops
2 tablespoons butter
1 tablespoon oil
6 tablespoons grated
  Parmesan cheese
6 tablespoons heavy cream

6 tablespoons cider
2 teaspoons white wine vinegar
1 cup stock
1½ teaspoons Dijon style
  mustard
Salt and pepper

In skillet or shallow flame proof casserole, heat butter and oil; brown chops lightly on both sides. Mix the cheese to a paste with 1 to 2 tablespoons cream and spread over the top of the chops. Bake in 375° oven for 25 to 40 minutes or until tender, depending on thickness of chops. Transfer chops to a platter and keep warm. Add the cider and vinegar to the pan and boil until reduced to a glaze. Add the stock, remaining cream, mustard, and seasonings to taste. Reheat sauce without boiling and spoon over chops. Makes 4 servings.

MRS. ROBERT G. ENGLAND   HONEY POINT UNIT

RIO GRANDE PORK ROAST

4 to 5 pound boneless rolled
  pork loin roast
½ teaspoon salt
½ teaspoon garlic salt
½ teaspoon chili powder

½ cup apple jelly
½ cup catsup
1 tablespoon vinegar
½ teaspoon chili powder

Place pork, fat side up, on rack in shallow roasting pan. Combine salt, garlic salt, and ½ teaspoon chili powder; rub into roast. Roast in 325° oven for 2 to 2½ hours or until meat thermometer registers 165°. In small sauce pan, combine jelly, catsup, vinegar, and ½ teaspoon chili powder. Bring to boiling; reduce heat and simmer, uncovered, for 2 minutes. Brush roast with glaze. Continue roasting 10 to 15 minutes more or until meat thermometer registers 170°. Remove roast from oven. Let stand 10 minutes. Measure pan drippings and add water to make 1 cup. Heat to boiling and pass with meat.

PATRICIA DUNCAN   POLK UNIT

PORK CHOP—ONE DISH MEAL

Pork chops	Salt
Potatoes, sliced	Pepper
Carrots, sliced	Green beans, optional
Onions, sliced	

The amount of each ingredient depends on the size of the family. Brown pork chops in large heavy skillet. Pour off excess grease. Put potatoes on top of pork chops, then carrots and onions, and green beans, if desired. Add about 1 cup of water. Sprinkle with salt and pepper. Cover and let simmer until pork chops are tender.

BEATRICE BROWN   BERTHA ELDRED UNIT

NEW ENGLAND PORK LOAF

2 slices whole wheat bread	½ cup wheat germ
½ cup milk	2 tablespoons parsley, chopped
2 pounds lean ground pork	1 teaspoon salt
1 egg, slightly beaten	Pinch of basil
½ cup apples, finely diced	Pinch of thyme
½ cup celery, finely diced	

Soak bread and milk in mixing bowl. Add remaining ingredients, mixing until well blended. Shape into loaf in 1 quart loaf pan. Bake at 350° for about 1¼ hours. Makes 8 servings.

MRS. A. D. ANDERSON   SHAWS POINT UNIT

FRENCH HUNTERS DINNER

1 pound ham (or ham butt)	1 No. 2 can mushrooms
1 pound bacon	1 No. 2 can spaghetti
1 large can tomatoes	Salt and pepper to taste
1 No. 2 can corn	Toast
1 No. 2 can lima beans	

Cut ham into small pieces and bacon into ½ slices. Fry until well done. Leave in all the bacon grease. Add a little water. Pour into a large kettle and add the remaining ingredients. Heat thoroughly. Serve over toast. Makes 5 or 6 servings.

MARY CANDLER   SHIPMAN UNIT

HAM LOAF

1½ pounds ham, ground
1 pound fresh pork, ground
2 eggs

½ cup tomato juice
1 cup cracker meal
¾ cup water

Mix together all the ingredients. Form into a loaf. Put into a 9x5x3 inch loaf pan. Bake at 300° for 2 hours, basting with sauce. Makes 10 servings.

Sauce:
1 cup brown sugar
1 teaspoon mustard

½ cup vinegar
½ cup water

Mix all ingredients together.

COMMITTEE

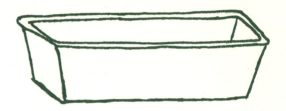

HAM LOAF WITH SAUCE

1 pound smoked ham,
  ground
½ pound lean fresh pork,
  ground
1 egg

½ cup milk
¼ teaspoon dry mustard
Pepper
1 cup corn flakes crumbs

Mix meats well. Add egg, milk, mustard, pepper, and corn flake crumbs. Shape into a roll and wrap in heavy foil and bake 1 hour at 350°. Serve topped with Sauce.

Sauce:
½ cup Cool Whip or whipped
  cream
1 cup salad dressing

1 tablespoon vinegar
2 tablespoons sugar
Horseradish or mustard

Mix all ingredients together.

VERDA BRUNETTO   GET TOGETHERS UNIT

HAM LOAF

2 pounds ground beef
2 pounds ground cooked,
   cured ham
2 pounds ground pork

4 eggs, beaten
4 cups crushed graham crackers
2½ cups milk

Combine all ingredients. Shape into 3 loaves. Put into 9x13 inch pan. Bake at 325° for 1 hour. Remove from oven and poke holes in tops of loaves. Pour Sauce over top. Return to oven and bake about 1 hour longer or until done. Baste occasionally. Makes 24 servings.

Sauce:
1 can tomato soup
⅓ cup vinegar

1 cup brown sugar
1 teaspoon dry mustard

Combine all ingredients.

VELDA ROESLER   MT. OLIVE UNIT

HAM LOAF

4 pounds ham, ground
2 pounds fresh pork, ground
1 medium onion, chopped
4 eggs, beaten
1 cup milk

½ teaspoon paprika
1 tablespoon Worcestershire
   sauce
1 teaspoon dry mustard

Mix all ingredients and shape into 2 loaves. Place in lightly greased 10x14 inch pan. Add about ⅓ cup water. Bake at 350° for 2 hours. After 1 hour, baste with Sauce. Makes 32 servings.

Sauce:
½ cup pineapple juice

⅓ cup brown sugar

Combine ingredients. Note: Grind ham and pork together.

MARY J. FLORI   CARLINVILLE NIGHT UNIT

ITALIAN SAUSAGE CASSEROLE

1 pound ground chuck
1 pound hot bulk pork
  sausage
¾ cup onion, chopped
¾ cup green pepper,
  chopped

1 can Campbell's tomato soup
1 can Cheddar cheese soup
2 teaspoons oregano
1 cup water
¾ package wide egg noodles
Cheddar cheese slices

Saute ground chuck, sausage, onion, and green pepper together until meats are done. Pour off excess fat. Add the soups, oregano, and water. Mix well and refrigerate overnight. When ready to serve, cook the noodles, drain, and put in long baking dish. Cover with meat mixture. Lay slices of Cheddar cheese on top. Place in cold oven. Turn heat to 400°. Bake for 45 minutes or until bubbly.

MRS. VELMA HECK   BERTHA ELDRED UNIT

SAUSAGE AND POTATOES AU GRATIN

1 can cream of mushroom
  soup
½ cup milk
½ cup onion, finely chopped
¼ cup green pepper,
  chopped
1 tablespoon pimiento,
  chopped
½ teaspoon salt

¼ teaspoon pepper
4 cups potatoes, sliced thin
1 8-ounce package precooked
  small sausages, cut into bite
  size pieces
1 tablespoon butter
½ cup Cheddar cheese,
  shredded

Combine soup, milk, onion, green pepper, pimiento, salt and pepper; blend well. Place half the potatoes in a greased 2 quart casserole. Add half the sausage. Cover with half the soup mixture. Repeat layers. Dot with butter. Cover and bake at 350° about 1¼ hours. Remove cover, sprinkle cheese on top, and bake uncovered 15 minutes more or until potatoes are tender. Makes 6 servings.

BETTY REIHER   CARLINVILLE NIGHT UNIT

SAUSAGE AND POTATO SCALLOP

1 pound fresh bulk pork
  sausage
2 tablespoons water
2 tablespoons butter or
  margarine
2 tablespoons flour
¾ teaspoon salt
⅛ teaspoon pepper

1 cup milk
½ cup American cheese, grated
1 teaspoon prepared mustard
2 cups potatoes, cooked, sliced
  and seasoned
1 10-ounce package frozen peas,
  cooked

Shape sausage into 8 patties and place in cold frying pan. Add water. Cover tightly and cook slowly for 5 minutes. Remove cover and pour off drippings. Brown the patties. Melt butter in saucepan. Stir in flour, salt and pepper. Add milk. Cook, stirring constantly, until thickened. Add cheese and mustard. Stir until cheese melts. Combine sauce, potatoes, and peas. Pour into a 1½ quart casserole. Top with pork sausage patties. Bake in a 350° oven for 30 minutes. Makes 4 servings.

FRANCES ANN ROSENTRETER   MONDAY NITERS UNIT

ITALIAN STUFFED ONIONS

8 medium onions
½ teaspoon cinnamon
¾ pound roast pork or veal,
  cooked and ground
1 cup grated Parmesan
  cheese
¼ cup half and half
1 cup bread crumbs

8 pats butter (4 tablespoons)
2 eggs
1 small can mushrooms (pieces,
  stems, and juice)
Salt to taste
Pepper to taste
1 cup raisins, soaked in warm
  water and drained

Boil onions until fork tender. Do not overcook. Carefully remove centers and save the large outer part to be stuffed. Grind the centers of the onions, mix with all the remaining ingredients except bread crumbs and butter. Add only enough crumbs so mixture doesn't get too dry. Stuff onions with meat mixture. Place onions in buttered baking dish large enough to hold onions. Top each onion with a pat of butter. Bake at 350° for 30 to 40 minutes until tops are golden brown.

MRS. JOHN BRUNETTO   GET TOGETHERS UNIT

99

SAUSAGE AND RICE CASSEROLE

1 pound bulk sausage
1 cup onion, cut fine
1 cup celery, cut fine
1 cup water

1 cup raw rice
1 can mushroom soup
1 can chicken soup

Stir sausage in heavy skillet until fat is rendered out. Drain well. Brown onion and celery in small amount of the fat, stirring constantly. Add this and remaining ingredients to the sausage, mixing well. Place into a buttered 9x13 inch baking dish and cover with a lid or foil. Bake at 325° for 1 hour and 45 minutes if glass pan is used. Bake at 350° if using a metal pan. As ovens seem to differ as to baking times, it is advisable to watch closely. Makes 8 to 10 servings.

MRS. FRED J. ARMOUR   SHAWS POINT UNIT

PARTY SPAGHETTI

3 pounds ground chuck
Vegetable oil
¾ pound fresh mushrooms,
  thinly sliced
2 large onions, chopped
¼ cup fresh parsley,
  chopped
2 8-ounce cans tomato sauce
2 5-ounce cans tomato paste
Cooking wine
1½ teaspoons oregano

1½ teaspoons garlic powder
1½ teaspoons cominos
Salt and pepper to taste
8 ounce package cream cheese,
  softened
½ cup sour cream
½ cup chopped chives
2 cups small curd cottage
  cheese
1 pound spaghetti, cooked and
  drained

Brown beef in vegetable oil. Stir in mushrooms, onions, parsley, tomato sauce and tomato paste (rinse cans with cooking wine and add enough wine for ½ cup), oregano, garlic, cominos, salt, and pepper. Cover and simmer 15 minutes. In bowl mix cream cheese, sour cream, chives, and cottage cheese. Cook spaghetti and drain. Into large buttered casserole, pour ½ the drained spaghetti. Cover with all the cheese mixture; add rest of spaghetti. Top with all meat mixture. Bake at 350° for 30 to 40 minutes until bubbly. Makes 12 servings.

SHERRI BUXTON   STITCH AND STIR UNIT

HAMBURGER CASSEROLE

1 pound ground beef,
  browned
1 can tomato soup

1 can Cheddar cheese soup
1 package wide noodles, cooked
1 can mushroom soup

Combine ground beef, noodles, and tomato soup in a medium size casserole. Stir. Top with mushroom soup and cheese soup. Bake in 250° oven for 1 hour or until cheese is thoroughly melted. Makes 4 to 5 servings.

JEAN EDDINGTON   SHIPMAN UNIT

MEDLEY CASSEROLE

1 pound ground beef
1 cup celery, diced
½ cup onion, diced
½ cup green pepper, diced

¾ cup rice, uncooked
1 4-ounce can mushrooms
2 cups tomato juice
Salt and pepper to taste

Combine all ingredients. Put into a 1½ or 2 quart casserole. Cover and bake at 400° for 45 minutes. Uncover and bake another 25 minutes. Makes 4 to 6 servings.

MAGDALENE LANDES   SCOTTVILLE UNIT

SAVORY SAUSAGE RICE

2 pounds bulk sausage
1 cup green pepper, finely
  chopped
¾ cup onion, chopped
2½ cups celery, coarsely
  chopped
2 2⅛-ounce packages of
  chicken noodle soup mix

4½ cups boiling water
1 cup rice, uncooked
½ teaspoon salt
¼ cup melted butter
1 cup almonds, blanched and
  slivered (optional)

Brown sausage in large skillet; pour off excess fat. Add green pepper, onion, and 1 cup celery. Saute. Combine soup mix and boiling water in large saucepan. Stir in rice. Cover and simmer 20 minutes or until tender. Add sausage mixture and salt. Stir well. Pour into greased 12x8x2 inch baking dish. Sprinkle remaining celery over top; drizzle with melted butter. Bake in 375° oven for 20 minutes. Makes 10 servings. If almonds are used, saute all celery with green pepper and onion. Mix most of almonds with other ingredients; save a few to sprinkle on top. Omit melted butter.

NORMA LLOYD   GIRARD NIGHT UNIT

LASAGNA CASSEROLE

1 pound ground chuck
2 teaspoons seasoned salt
Small amount garlic salt
½ teaspoon pepper
1 1 pound 13-ounce can
tomatoes
1 8-ounce can tomato sauce
1 package spaghetti sauce
mix

½ pound lasagna noodles
½ pound Mozzarella cheese,
sliced
½ pound Ricotta cheese (or
cottage cheese)
½ pound grated Parmesan
cheese (optional)

Brown meat in Dutch oven or deep kettle. Add seasoned salt, garlic salt, and pepper. Simmer 10 minutes. Add tomatoes, tomato sauce, and sauce mix. Stir well, cover, and simmer 30 minutes. Meanwhile cook lasagna noodles in boiling salt water until almost tender; drain and rinse. Pour ⅓ of meat sauce into 12x8x2 inch baking dish. Cover sauce with noodles. Arrange slices of Mozzarella cheese and spoonfuls of Ricotta cheese over noodles. Repeat layers, ending with meat sauce and top with Parmesan cheese. Bake at 350° for 20 minutes. Makes 6 to 8 servings.

MRS. JERRE (ALBERTA) STALEY   MODELITE UNIT

LASAGNA

2 pounds ground beef
1 medium onion, chopped
2 6-ounce cans tomato paste
2 6-ounce cans water
1 package spaghetti sauce
mix

1½ teaspoons parsley flakes
9 lasagna noodles
1 large carton small curd cottage
cheese
2 packages shredded Mozzarella
cheese

Brown ground beef and onion. Season with salt and pepper; drain off grease. Add tomato paste and water; simmer for ½ hour. Stir in spaghetti sauce mix and parsley flakes; simmer for 15 minutes. While meat sauce is simmering, cook lasagna noodles in salted boiling water until tender. Grease 9x13 inch pan and starting with noodles, layer meat sauce and then cheeses until you have 6 layers ending with cottage cheese and Mozzarella. Bake at 375° for 40 minutes. Freezes well. May be divided into two 8 inch square pans; one to bake now, one later. Makes 12 servings.

JANET KESSINGER   STITCH AND STIR UNIT

INSIDE OUT RAVIOLI

1 pound ground beef
½ cup chopped onion
1 clove garlic, minced
1 tablespoon salad oil
1 10-ounce package frozen
　chopped spinach
1 1-pound can spaghetti
　sauce with mushrooms
　(add another can of
　mushrooms if desired)

1 8-ounce can tomato sauce, or
　tomato paste
½ teaspoon each salt and pepper
1 7-ounce package shell
　macaroni, cooked
1 cup shredded sharp American
　cheese
½ cup soft bread crumbs
2 eggs, well beaten
¼ cup salad oil

Brown first 3 ingredients with 1 tablespoon salad oil. Cook spinach; drain, reserving liquid. Add water to make 1 cup. Stir spinach liquid into next five ingredients. Add to meat mixture. Simmer 10 minutes. Combine spinach with remaining ingredients. Spread into a 13x7x2 inch pan. Top with meat sauce. Bake at 350° for 20 to 30 minutes. Let stand 10 minutes before serving. Can be frozen. Good made day ahead and kept in refrigerator.

JACQUELINE H. THOMAS　EXTENSION HOME ECONOMIST—
　　　　　　　　　　　　MACOUPIN COUNTY

SPICY MEAT STUFFED TOMATOES

6 large tomatoes
2½ cups garlic and onion
　flavored croutons
¾ cup water
2 tablespoons parsley,
　chopped
1 teaspoon basil, crushed
½ teaspoon oregano, crushed

½ teaspoon thyme
1 pound ground beef
2 tablespoons butter
½ pound fresh mushrooms,
　finely chopped
1½ teaspoons salt
Dash pepper

Slice off tops of tomatoes. Carefully scoop.out pulp to form shell; invert to drain. Crush croutons; reserve ⅓ cup. Combine remaining crumbs, water, and herbs. Saute ground beef until browned, drain off fat. Add meat to crouton mixture. In same skillet, melt 1 tablespoon butter; add mushrooms and saute over medium heat until liquid evaporates and mushrooms brown. Add to meat mixture. Season with salt and pepper to taste. Spoon meat mixture into tomatoes; do not pack tightly but mound slightly. Melt remaining 1 tablespoon butter, stir in reserved crouton crumbs. Sprinkle over tomatoes. Place in shallow 8x11 inch baking dish and bake at 375° for 20 mintues. Makes 6 servings.

MRS. BONNIE SHELTON　PIASA UNIT

STEAK BURGUNDY

4 cups cooked rice
1 pound lean beef (round steak), thinly sliced in 1 inch strips
3 tablespoons vegetable oil
2 cups onions, sliced
1¾ cups beef broth
½ cup Burgundy or other dry red wine

1 4-ounce can sliced mushrooms and liquid
2 cups carrots, sliced
1 tablespoon Worcestershire sauce
2½ teaspoons seasoned salt
2 cups celery, sliced diagonally
2 tablespoons corn starch
¼ cup water

Cook rice according to package directions. Saute steak in oil until brown. Add onions and cook 2 minutes. Stir in broth, wine, mushrooms with liquid, carrots, Worcestershire sauce, and seasoned salt. Bring to a boil. Reduce heat, cover, and simmer 10 minutes. Add celery and continue cooking 10 minutes longer. Mix corn starch in water and stir into meat mixture. Cook, stirring constantly, until thickened. Serve over beds of fluffy rice. Makes 6 servings.

MRS. LEO WELLING   BRIGHTON EARLY BIRDS

SPAGHETTI CASSEROLE

1 pound ground chuck
½ cup onion, chopped
1 clove garlic, minced
1 green pepper, chopped
2 tablespoons shortening
1 can cream of mushroom soup

1 can tomato soup
1 can water
½ pound spaghetti, cooked and drained
½ cup shredded Cheddar cheese

Lightly brown meat, onion, garlic, and green pepper in shortening, stirring occasionally. Add both soups and water, bring to a boil. Add cooked spaghetti and cheese. Mix ingredients together. Turn into a greased 3 quart casserole. Top with additional cheese. Bake at 350° for 45 minutes or more. Excellent for freezing.

FRANCES NORBENT   GET TOGETHERS UNIT

MEXITALIAN SPAGHETTI

2 pounds ground beef
1¼ cups water
1½ cups onion, chopped
½ cup green pepper, chopped
1 teaspoon garlic powder
1 6-ounce can tomato paste
2 8-ounce cans tomato sauce
2 teaspoons Worcestershire sauce

1½ teaspoons salt
½ teaspoon pepper
¼ teaspoon Tabasco sauce
½ teaspoon chili powder
½ teaspoon oregano
1 16-ounce package spaghetti, cooked

Boil meat in water for 5 to 10 minutes. Do not drain. Add remaining ingredients. Cover and simmer 2 hours. Serve sauce over hot spaghetti. Makes 8 to 10 servings.

DONNA BOWMAN   MONDAY NITERS UNIT

RICE AND BEEF CASSEROLE

2 pounds ground chuck
1 can tomatoes
1 cup rice, uncooked (not Minute Rice)
1 cup celery, diced
¾ cup green pepper, chopped
½ cup onion, chopped

2 tablespoons A 1 sauce
2 tablespoons Worcestershire sauce
2 teaspoons salt
¾ teaspoon pepper
1 can onion soup
1 can beef bouillon soup

Mix all ingredients together. Pour into baking dish and bake at 375° for 1 hour and 15 minutes or until done.

FRANCES NORBENT   GET TOGETHERS UNIT

TEXAS HASH

2 large onions, chopped
2 green peppers, chopped
3 tablespoons shortening
1 pound ground beef
2 cups canned tomatoes

½ cup rice, uncooked
1 teaspoon chili powder
1 teaspoon salt
¼ teaspoon pepper

Saute onions and peppers in shortening until onions are yellow. Add ground beef and continue sauteing until mixture falls apart. Add tomatoes, rice, salt, chili powder, and pepper. Pour into a greased 1 to 1½ quart casserole. Cover and bake at 350° for 1 hour and 15 minutes. Makes 3 servings. Note: Baking time can be lessened if rice is soaked in tomatoes for several hours.

MRS. OLA NITZ   BERTHA ELDRED UNIT.

RIBS BY THE YARD

2 to 3 pounds spareribs
½ cup brown sugar
1 tablespoon salt
1 tablespoon celery seed
1 tablespoon chili powder

1 tablespoon paprika
¼ to ½ cup vinegar
1 cup thick tomato pulp or
   tomato puree

Mix dry ingredients and rub half the mixture into the ribs. To remaining mixture, add vinegar and tomato pulp or puree. Marinate ribs 1 hour or longer. Arrange on spit, fasten securely with skewer prongs, and place in position on rotisserie. Start to rotate, basting with sauce frequently. Broil until well done, 40 to 50 minutes, depending on thickness of ribs.

MRS. LILLIAN VANFOSSEN   DO MORE UNIT

OVEN BARBECUED RIBS

3 or 4 pounds ribs
1 large onion, more if desired
Salt and pepper to taste
2 tablespoons vinegar

2 tablespoons Worcestershire
   sauce
1 bottle Maulls barbecue sauce

Cut ribs into serving size pieces. Arrange in small roaster. Cover with sliced onions, salt, and pepper. Mix remaining ingredients and pour over ribs and onions. Bake at 350° for 1½ hours, basting during baking. Makes 3 or 4 servings.

JO MAXEINER   BERTHA ELDRED UNIT

MAZETTI

2 pounds ground beef
2½ cups celery and leaves,
   chopped fine
2 large onions, chopped
2 cloves garlic, chopped fine
1 tablespoon water
8 ounces fine noodles

2 10½-ounce cans tomato soup
1 6-ounce can mushrooms and
   liquid
2 teaspoons salt
½ teaspoon pepper
½ pound grated sharp Cheddar
   cheese

Brown ground beef; add celery, onion, garlic, and water. Cover; cook until tender. Cook noodles, add to beef mixture. Mix in remaining ingredients except cheese. Spread mixture in a 9x13 inch casserole dish. Top with cheese. Bake at 250° for 1 hour. Makes 15 to 20 servings.

MARIANNA RAMEY   CARLINVILLE NIGHT UNIT

HOMEMADE LUNCH MEAT

3 pounds ground beef
2 tablespoons Morton's quick
  curing salt
1¼ teaspoons onion powder

⅛ teaspoon garlic powder
1½ teaspoons liquid smoke
1 cup water

Mix ingredients thoroughly. Shape into 2 rolls and wrap each in foil. Chill 24 hours. Remove foil. Bake on a broiler pan at 300° for 1 hour. Slice and eat warm or cold.

MRS. DAVID SCHAFER   BRIGHTON EARLY BIRDS UNIT

SUMMER SAUSAGE

1 cup water
2 teaspoons liquid smoke
⅛ teaspoon onion salt

¼ teaspoon garlic salt
3 tablespoons tenderquick salt
2 pounds ground beef

Mix water, liquid smoke, and salts. Add ground beef and mix well. Make into two rolls and wrap in foil (shiny side in). Refrigerate 24 hours. When ready to bake, make many holes in bottom of foil with a fork so sausage may drain while baking. Lay on rack over a pan in oven and bake 1½ hours at 325°. Let cool in foil after removing from oven. Rewrap for storage.

LINDA LAMBETH   PIASA UNIT

SUMMER SAUSAGE

2 pounds ground beef
¾ teaspoon mustard seed
¾ teaspoon coarsely ground
  pepper
½ teaspoon minced garlic or
  garlic powder

¼ teaspoon liquid smoke
3 tablespoons Morton's
  tenderquick salt

Mix ingredients as for meat loaf. Put into tightly covered bowl and refrigerate 24 hours. Divide into thirds. Form into sausages and wrap in foil. Boil 1 hour. Put on rack and punch holes in foil. When cooled, remove from foil and rewrap in foil. Refrigerate. Makes 3 sausages.

JOYCE DUELM   MT. OLIVE UNIT

TEXAS HASH

3 medium onions, chopped
1 large green pepper,
  chopped
3 tablespoons shortening
1 pound ground beef
2 cups canned tomatoes
½ cup cooked rice or
2 cups noodles, uncooked

1 teaspoon chili powder
½ teaspoon salt
⅛ teaspoon pepper
Dash of oregano
Dash of A-1 sauce
Dash of Worcestershire sauce

Cook onion and green pepper in butter until onion is yellow. Add ground beef and fry until mixture gets crumbly. Stir into this mixture the remaining ingredients. Pour into a greased 8 inch casserole. Cover and bake at 350° for 1 hour. Remove cover for the last 15 minutes of baking time. Serve hot. If desired, cheese can be sprinkled over top before baking.

PAT CARTY   SHAWS POINT UNIT

REUBEN CASSEROLE

1 large sauerkraut, well
  drained
2 or 3 tomatoes, sliced
2 tablespoons Thousand
  Island dressing
2 tablespoons butter

1 can corned beef, sliced
1 8-ounce package sliced Swiss
  cheese
1 package refrigerator biscuits
¼ cup rye crackers, crushed

Place sauerkraut in 8x12 inch casserole; arrange tomatoes over sauerkraut. Pour dressing over tomatoes; dot with butter. Add corned beef; add cheese. Bake in preheated 425° oven for 15 minutes. Remove from oven, arrange biscuits over top. Sprinkle with crushed crackers. Bake 15 to 20 minutes longer. Makes 5 servings.

HELEN JOHNSON   MT. OLIVE UNIT

ITALIAN MAGNIFIQUE SAUCE

1 pound ground beef
1 onion, chopped
1 8-ounce can tomato sauce
1 8-ounce can tomato puree
1 teaspoon salt
½ teaspoon pepper

½ teaspoon oregano
½ teaspoon sweet basil
2 dashes ground allspice
1 teaspoon sugar
½ teaspoon garlic powder
1 8-ounce can water

Brown ground beef with onion. Mix in remaining ingredients and cook for 20 minutes. Serve over spaghetti.

MRS. STELLA GROVES   SHAWS POINT UNIT

CHERYLL'S ITALIAN SPAGHETTI SAUCE

½ pound ground beef or
   Italian sausage
1 medium onion
1 6-ounce can tomato paste
1 cup water

1 clove garlic, crushed, or
1 tablespoon garlic powder
2 tablespoons Italian seasoning
Salt and pepper to taste

Brown ground beed with onion, season with salt and pepper to taste, and drain on paper towel. Combine other ingredients in a sauce pan, stirring until well mixed. Add ground beef mixture and simmer for 2 hours until done. Makes 4 medium servings.

CHERYLL McNEILLY   MT. OLIVE UNIT

SPAGHETTI SAUCE

2 pounds ground beef
1 large onion, chopped
1 15-ounce chili brick
2 1-pound cans tomatoes
2 8-ounce cans tomato sauce
2 10½-ounce cans tomato
   soup

2 teaspoons oregano
1½ teaspoons whole anise
1 teaspoon sweet basil
2 cloves garlic
Salt and pepper to taste
Water for thinning

Brown the meat and onions together. Add the chili brick which has been broken into pieces. Add remaining ingredients. Simmer for 2 hours.

NANCY SCHIEN   STITCH AND STIR UNIT

BARBECUE SAUCE

12 cups catsup
12 cups water
¾ cup onion, minced
½ cup vinegar
¾ cup Worcestershire sauce

¼ cup salt
2 tablespoons pepper
¼ cup paprika
8 teaspoons chili powder

Mix all ingredients together and simmer for 1 hour. Combine with cooked, shredded beef or pork. Simmer with meat for an additional ½ hour. You may freeze the sauce or the finished barbecue product.

MRS. MELBA K. EICHEN   SHAWS POINT UNIT

BARBECUE SAUCE

2 tablespoons butter
1 medium onion, minced
1 small green pepper, minced
1 tablespoon Worcestershire
   sauce

2 tablespoons prepared mustard
¼ cup catsup
2 tablespoons brown sugar

Melt butter in a small sauce pan. Add onion and pepper and cook slowly for several minutes. Add remaining ingredients. Simmer 10 minutes.

MRS. DAVID SCHAFER   BRIGHTON EARLY BIRDS UNIT

SPAGHETTI SAUCE

½ pound ground beef
½ pound ground pork
2 onions, chopped
1 stalk celery
Olive oil

1 can tomato sauce
1 can tomatoes
1 can mushrooms
Salt, pepper, oregano to taste
2 cloves garlic

In large sauce pan, brown first four ingredients in olive oil. Add the rest of the ingredients and add water as necessary. Simmer for 5 to 7 hours, stirring occasionally. Makes 6 to 8 servings.

PAT GERECKE   MT. OLIVE UNIT

POULTRY, EGGS, & CHEESE

Hudson Hall—Clegg Chapel—is the heart of the Blackburn College Campus. Blackburn College was founded in 1837 by Gideon Blackburn, a Presbyterian minister. Opened in 1857 as a Seminary, in later years it developed into a two-year college, and finally into a four-year private liberal arts college. It is internationally known for its unique student-work program started in 1913 by President William M. Hudson.

Photograph courtesy of Blackburn College

BAKED CHICKEN ON RICE

1 can cream of chicken soup
1 can cream of celery soup
2 cups Minute Rice

½ cup milk
1 fryer chicken, cut into pieces
½ package onion soup

Mix soups and stir in rice and milk. Spread in 9x13 inch pan. Layer chicken on top with skin side up. Sprinkle onion soup over chicken. Cover tightly with foil and bake at 350° for 2 hours without peeking.

ETHEL SPIRES   PLAINVIEW UNIT

CHICKEN BROCCOLI

4 whole chicken breasts
2 packages frozen chopped
   broccoli
2 cans cream of chicken
   soup
1 can cream of mushroom
   soup

1 cup mayonnaise
1 teaspoon lemon juice
½ teaspoon curry powder
1 to 2 cups cheese, shredded
1 cup buttered croutons

Bake seasoned chicken in foil 45 to 60 minutes. Bone and break into bite size pieces. Cook broccoli and drain. Arrange in greased 13x9 inch pan. Layer chicken over broccoli. Combine soups, mayonnaise, lemon juice, and curry powder. Pour over chicken and broccoli. Cover with cheese and top with croutons. Bake at 325° for 25 to 30 minutes. Makes 6 servings. Note: For Chicken Florentine, substitute spinach for broccoli.

IRENE PERRINE   BRUSHY MOUND UNIT

CHICKEN CARUSO

1 2½ to 3-pound fryer, cut up
¼ cup butter, melted
3 cloves garlic
¼ cup onion, minced
1 cup catsup

¼ cup vinegar
2 tablespoons sugar
1 teaspoon salt
¼ cup Worcestershire sauce
½ cup water

Put chicken into baking pan. Combine remaining ingredients and pour over chicken. Cover and bake at 350° for 1½ hours or until tender. Makes 5 to 6 servings.

MRS. JAMES RONDI   STAUNTON UNIT

CHICKEN CASSEROLE

4 whole chicken breasts
2 cans cream of chicken
  soup
½ cup milk or chicken broth
1 cup mayonnaise

1 teaspoon lemon juice
1 cup sharp Cheddar cheese,
  grated
½ package Pepperidge Farm
  dressing mix, dry

Cook chicken breasts (or may use dark meat.) Bone cooked chicken, cut in half, and place in 9x13 inch baking dish. Mix milk or broth with soup and pour over all the chicken. Mix together mayonnaise and lemon juice; pour over chicken. Sprinkle the grated cheese over top. Top with dressing mix. Bake at 350° for 30 to 45 minutes. Makes 8 servings.

MRS. MIKE BRUNETTO   SUSTAINING MEMBER

CHICKEN CASSEROLE

1 3 or 4-pound chicken
1 cup fine cracker crumbs
3 eggs, hard boiled and
  chopped
2 cans cream of chicken
  soup

½ cup onion, chopped
½ cup mayonnaise
Salt and pepper to taste

Stew chicken until tender. Cool; remove skin and bones. Cut chicken into 1 inch size pieces. Grease a 9x13 inch pan. Sprinkle ½ cup cracker crumbs over bottom. Mix chicken pieces, eggs, soup, onions, mayonnaise, salt, and pepper. Pour over cracker crumbs; top with ½ cup cracker crumbs. Bake at 350° for 30 minutes. Makes 6 servings.

KATHY SIEGEL   NILWOOD UNIT

CHICKEN CASSEROLE

3 cups chicken, cooked
1½ cups rice, cooked
2 hard boiled eggs
1 can cream of mushroom
  soup

½ cup onion, chopped and
  sauteed
4 tablespoons butter
½ teaspoon salt and pepper
Paprika

Mix all ingredients together. Pour into greased 8x12 inch pan. Sprinkle with grated cheese or buttered bread crumbs. Bake at 350° for 1 hour. Makes 10 servings.

MARY J. FLORI   CARLINVILLE NIGHT UNIT

CHICKEN CASSEROLE

6 chicken breasts, cooked
   and diced
2 cans mushroom soup
2 cans chicken rice soup
1 cup celery, diced
½ cup onion, chopped

1½ cups Pet milk
1 large can Chinese noodles
1 stick margarine, melted
1 cup Pepperidge Farm dressing,
   dry
Slivered almonds

Mix everything together except butter, nuts, and dry dressing. Place in a 9x13 inch casserole. Sprinkle dressing over top of mixture. Pour melted butter over mixture. Sprinkle with almonds. Bake at 325° for 40 to 50 minutes or until brown. Makes 12 to 15 servings.

MARION E. KLEKAMP   GILLESPIE NIGHT UNIT

CHICKEN CASSEROLE

1 cup cream of chicken soup
¾ cup mayonnaise
2 chicken breasts, boiled
1 cup celery, chopped
2 tablespoons onion, grated

3 eggs, hard cooked and sliced
½ cup slivered almonds
1 medium package potato chips,
   coarsely crushed

Combine soup and mayonnaise. Cut, do not chop, chicken into small pieces. Add chicken, celery, onion, eggs, and almonds to soup mixture. In 8x8 inch or 6x9 inch casserole dish, alternate layers of chicken mixture and potato chips. Bake at 350° for 30 minutes. Makes 4 servings. Note: The ingredients can be prepared ahead of time, then combined just before meal time. To increase serving sizes, use the whole chicken.

ANNA MAY LEACH   BIRD UNIT

CHICKEN AND DRESSING CASSEROLE

8 to 10 slices bread
1 3-pound chicken, boiled
   and deboned
1 can cream of mushroom
   soup—or 1½ cups milk

1 can cream of chicken soup
1 can chicken noodle soup
4 tablespoons margarine, melted
2 eggs

Tear bread into small pieces. Mix all ingredients together. Pour into greased 9x13 inch baking dish. Bake at 375° for 30 to 35 minutes. Thicken chicken broth to make gravy and pour over top when served. Makes 12 servings.

MRS. NORMAN HARMS   MONDAY NITERS UNIT

POULTRY, EGGS AND CHEESE

CHICKEN CHOW MEIN

2 large onions, cut in chunks
3 cups celery, cut in chunks
3 tablespoons cooking oil
1 tablespoon salt
½ teaspoon pepper
2½ tablespoons soy sauce
1 tablespoon molasses
2 cups boiling water
2 chicken bouillon cubes

1 can bean sprouts, rinsed in
  cold water
3 cups chicken, cooked and cut
  in cubes
3 tablespoons corn starch
¼ cup water
Cooked rice or chow mein
  noodles

Combine onions, celery, and cooking oil; place over medium heat. Add salt, pepper, soy sauce, and molasses. Stir, add boiling water and cubes. Boil 10 minutes. Add bean sprouts, stir, and cook 10 minutes. Add chicken. Mix corn starch in ¼ cup water. Add to hot mixture. Stir until thick. Serve with cooked rice or chow mein noodles. Makes 10 to 12 servings.

MARY J. FLORI   CARLINVILLLE NIGHT UNIT

CHICKEN DIVAN

1 package frozen chopped
  broccoli
¾ teaspoon salt
1 chicken, cooked, seasoned
  and deboned
¾ cup salad dressing

1 can cream of chicken soup
½ cup Cheddar cheese, grated
1 cup dry bread, cubed
3 tablespoons margarine, melted
½ cup Parmesan cheese

Cook broccoli with salt until just tender. Place broccoli in bottom of a 10x6½ inch casserole. Put chicken in on top of broccoli. Mix salad dressing and soup and pour over chicken. Spread with grated Cheddar cheese. Top with bread cubes which have been stirred into melted margarine. Sprinkle with Parmesan cheese. Bake 45 minutes at 350°. Makes 4 to 6 servings.

MRS. ALBERT (STEVE) MARKO   BIRD UNIT

CHICKEN DIVAN

1 3 or 4-pound chicken, deboned
2 10-ounce packages broccoli spears of chopped broccoli
2 cans cream of chicken soup
1 cup mayonnaise

1 tablespoon lemon juice
½ teaspoon curry powder
1 cup grated Cheddar cheese
2 slices bread
1 tablespoon melted butter or margarine

Prebake chicken until tender. Boil broccoli to thaw. Butter a 12½x8½ inch casserole. Place chicken in casserole, arrange broccoli on top. Cover with chicken soup mixed with mayonnaise, lemon juice, and curry powder. Cover with grated cheese and bread cut into small cubes and moistened with melted butter. Bake at 350° for 30 minutes. Makes 8 to 10 servings.

LILLIAN TETZLAFF   HONEY POINT UNIT

EASY TURKEY DIVAN

2 10-ounce packages frozen broccoli spears
6 slices turkey or
2 cups turkey pieces
6 slices Swiss cheese
1 14½-ounce can evaporated milk

1 10½-ounce can cream of mushroom soup
1 3½-ounce can french fried onion rings

Heat oven to 350°. Cook broccoli to tender crisp stage. Place in bottom of a greased 1½x7½x1½ inch baking dish with cut spears toward the center. Cover with turkey slices. Top with cheese slices. Cover with a mixture of the milk and mushroom soup. Bake 25 minutes. Cover with onion rings and bake 5 more minutes. Makes 4 to 6 servings. Note: This is a delicious and good way to use leftover turkey. Fresh broccoli may be used in place of the frozen broccoli.

MRS. FLORENCE KOLB   BRIGHTON EARLY BIRDS UNIT

POULTRY, EGGS AND CHEESE

CRUSTY CHICKEN CASSEROLE

1 chicken, cooked
1½ cups flour
1½ teaspoons baking powder
1 teaspoon salt
½ teaspoon poultry
  seasoning or bouillon
  cubes

4 eggs
1½ cups milk
3 tablespoons butter or melted
  chicken fat

Prepare chicken by boning and cutting into bite size pieces and put into 12x8x2 inch pan. Sift flour, baking powder, salt, and seasoning. Beat eggs until light and fluffy. Add milk and mix gradually with dry ingredients. Add butter. Mix until well blended. Pour over chicken in pan. Sprinkle lightly with pepper. Bake at 350° about 50 minutes until golden brown. Serve with Giblet Sauce. Makes 6 servings.

Giblet Sauce:
¼ cup onion, chopped
½ cup butter

⅓ cup flour
3 cups chicken broth

Saute onions in butter. Blend in flour and broth. Simmer constantly until thickened. Season with salt and pepper, if necessary. Cut cooked giblets and add to above sauce.

MARGARET H. FRENCH   MEDORA UNIT

HERB FRIED CHICKEN

1 3-pound fryer, cut up
¼ cup flour
1 teaspoon salt
1 teaspoon pepper
½ teaspoon rosemary leaves

½ teaspoon dried parsley
½ cup butter or margarine
2 tablespoons flour
1½ cups cold water

Combine ¼ cup flour, salt, pepper, rosemary, parsley, and coat chicken. Fry chicken in butter over medium high heat until done. Remove chicken, keep warm. Combine remaining flour and water; add to pan drippings. Stir constantly, cooking until smooth and thick. Pour over chicken. Makes 4 servings.

MRS. WM. (HELEN) MANNING   SPANISH NEEDLE UNIT

ORIENTAL CHICKEN

½ cup cooking oil
3 chicken breasts, boned and cubed
3 cups fresh broccoli flowerets
1 medium sweet pepper
½ pound fresh mushrooms
3 tablespoons scallions, sliced, or instant onions

1 cup chicken broth
3 tablespoons dry cooking sherry
1 tablespoon corn starch
1 tablespoon soy sauce
½ teaspoon hot pepper sauce
1 cup cashew nuts
2 cups prepared rice

Heat oil in wok or skillet. Add chicken for several minutes until meat cooks. Remove meat. Add to oil the broccoli, pepper, mushrooms and onions. Stir constantly for about 4 minutes on high heat. In separate bowl, mix together the chicken broth, sherry, corn starch, soy sauce, and pepper sauce. Add broth mixture to vegetables in wok. Return chicken pieces to wok. Stir for 5 minutes. Add nuts. Serve over rice. Makes 4 servings.

ROSE MARIE VESPER   STAUNTON UNIT

CHICKEN PAPRIKA WITH SPATZLE (DROP NOODLES)

2 to 3 medium onions, chopped
2 or 3 button garlic, chopped

2 to 3 tablespoons paprika
1 3-pound chicken, cut up
Salt to taste

Saute onions and garlic until transparent, add paprika. Stir well and add the chicken and salt. Stir well. Cook chicken slowly over low heat. It will make its own broth. Check chicken and stir to keep from burning. When broth is cooking, add enough water to cover. Cook until chicken is done. Take out of pot to make the spatzle.

Spatzle (Noodles):
1 egg, slightly beaten
1 cup water

1 teaspoon salt
Flour enough to hold batter firm

Mix all ingredients together and beat well. Drop from spoon into boiling broth, cover pot, and cook 10 minutes. Add more water to broth so there will be enough to hold the noodles, adding before batter is put in. When noodles are done, thicken broth with the noodles and pour over the chicken. Makes 6 to 8 servings.

YOLANDA NEWMAN   BERTHA ELDRED UNIT

119

SCALLOPED CHICKEN

5 cups bread, broken into
small pieces
1 teaspoon poultry seasoning
1 teaspoon instant onion

1 stick butter or margarine,
melted
3 cups chicken, cooked
4 cups chicken broth

Mix bread with poultry seasoning, onion, and butter or margarine. Add chicken and mix gently. Add chicken broth and mix thoroughly. Place mixture in a 9x13 inch pan and bake at 350° for 25 to 30 minutes. This may be served with chicken gravy to which more chicken has been added. Makes 8 to 10 servings.

MRS. DONALD COLBURN   BRIGHTON EARLY BIRDS UNIT

ONION BAKED CHICKEN

1 chicken, cut into pieces
1 cup biscuit mix
1 teaspoon salt
½ teaspoon pepper

¼ teaspoon paprika
4 teaspoons margarine
1 package dry onion soup
2 cups hot water

Cut chicken into pieces. Combine biscuit mix, salt, pepper, and paprika. Mix thoroughly. Coat the chicken with the dry mixture and place in a 3 quart casserole. Dot with margarine. Mix together the dry onion soup and hot water. Pour over chicken. Cover and bake at 350° for 1½ hours.

BEULAH BURGER   SOUTH OTTER UNIT

QUICK CHICKEN CASSEROLE

2 cups chicken, cooked
1 10¾-ounce can cream of
celery soup
1 16-ounce can mixed
vegetables, drained

¼ teaspoon garlic salt
1 teaspoon salt
¼ teaspoon pepper
Biscuits

Cook chicken and cut into pieces. Mix together chicken, celery soup, drained mixed vegetables, garlic salt, salt, and pepper. Pour into a 1¾ quart casserole. Bake at 325° until it starts to bubble, about 35 minutes. Add unbaked biscuits to cover top of dish and bake until biscuits are browned. Makes 4 large servings.

MONA R. VAN DOREN   PIASA UNIT

NO PEEK CHICKEN

1 cup rice, uncooked (not
  Minute)
½ cup celery, chopped
1 can cream of chicken soup
1 can cream of mushroom
  soup

1 chicken bouillon cube
2½ cups boiling water
1 chicken, cut up, or 8 pieces of
  chicken you like
½ package Lipton onion soup
  mix

Put uncooked rice in bottom of roasting pan. Add celery on top. Mix soups, bouillon cube, and boiling water; pour over rice and celery. Season chicken. Place in liquid. Sprinkle on onion soup. Seal pan with foil. Bake at 300° for 2 hours. Do not open foil during cooking. Makes 6 servings.

STEPHANIE KOCHINSKI DANDY DOERS UNIT

MEXICAN CHICKEN

1 fryer, cut up
1 medium onion, chopped
1 teaspoon garlic salt
1 teaspoon chili powder

1 can Rotel tomatoes
½ pound Cheddar cheese, grated
1 package soft tortillas
2 cans cream of chicken soup

Cook chicken until tender and debone. Mix with onion, garlic salt, chili powder, tomatoes, and cheese. Soften tortillas in boiled chicken stock and line baking dish. Add chicken mixture. Pour soup over mixture. Bake at 350° for 35 to 40 mintues. Makes 8 servings. Note: Rotel is a brand of tomatoes and green chilies.

EVELYN STAYTON BIRD UNIT

CHICKEN RICE 'N' EASY

1 cup Minute Rice
1 cup milk
1 can cream of mushroom
  soup

1 can cream of celery soup
1 package Lipton onion soup
4 chicken breasts

Mix all ingredients together except chicken. Put mixture into small dutch oven. Lay chicken breasts on top. Cover and bake at 375° for 1½ hours. Makes 4 servings.

KAY LANDERS STAUNTON UNIT

CHICKEN SUPREME

2½ cups chicken, cooked
and cut up
2 cups Creamettes, uncooked
1 cup milk
1 cup chicken broth

1 can cream of mushroom soup
½ pound Velveeta cheese, diced
Small amount grated onion
1 small can mushrooms, if
desired

Mix all ingredients together in buttered 9x12 inch baking dish. Let stand over night in refrigerator. Take out 1 hour before baking. Bake at 350° for 50 minutes. Garnish with hard boiled eggs and pimiento, if desired. Makes 8 to 10 servings.

VERA SCHREITER   CARLINVILLE NIGHT UNIT

CHICKEN TOKAY

6 chicken breasts, split
(about 4 pounds)
1½ teaspoons salt
¼ teaspoon pepper
1 teaspoon rosemary,
crushed
3 tablespoons butter or
margarine
¼ cup onion, chopped, or
1 tablespoon instant minced
onion

2 chicken bouillon cubes,
dissolved in
1 cup boiling water
1 tablespoon lemon juice
4 teaspoons corn starch
1½ cups Tokay grapes, seeded
and halved (about 1 pound)
Parsley, if desired

Rub chicken pieces with a mixture of the salt, pepper, and rosemary. Brown chicken slowly and evenly in hot butter or margarine in large skillet. Remove from skillet. Add fresh chopped onion and cook until lightly browned, stirring occasionally. If instant onion is used, add it to the chicken broth and lemon juice. (Excess fat may be removed from skillet and used to season rice and vegetables served with the chicken.) Add bouillon cube liquid and lemon juice to skillet. Blend corn starch with a small amount of cold water and stir into liquid, blending thoroughly as it is brought to a boil. Cook 3 minutes, stirring constantly. Return chicken to skillet, cover and cook slowly until chicken is tender when pierced with fork (about 20 minutes). Add grapes; heat to serving temperature. Sprinkle with snipped parsley. May also be served without grapes and parsley. Makes 6 servings.

HESTER CLARK   CARLINVILLE NIGHT UNIT

CHICKEN NOODLE CASSEROLE

4 ounce package noodles
1 can cream of chicken soup
½ large can milk

1 can boned chicken
Potato chips, crushed

Cook noodles according to package directions. Drain. Mix noodles with soup, milk, and chicken. Put into a greased 2 quart casserole and top with crushed potato chips. Bake at 350° for 25 to 30 minutes or until bubbly. If desired, mushroom soup may be used instead of chicken soup. Makes 6 servings.

MRS. PEARL SMITH   GIRARD DAY UNIT

CHICKEN OR TURKEY LOAF

2 eggs, beaten
1 cup milk
2 cups soft bread crumbs
1 cup cooked rice
2 cups chicken or turkey,
   cooked and diced

¼ cup celery, chopped
1 tablespoon parsley or celery
   leaves, minced
1 cup rich chicken broth
Salt and pepper to taste
Small amount butter

Mix ingredients in order given. Pour into 7½x12 inch baking dish. Bake at 350° for 45 minutes to 1 hour. Serve with broth gravy into which a small can of mushrooms has been added.

MAGDALENE LANDES   SCOTTVILLE UNIT

TURKEY CASSEROLE

3 tablespoons butter
8 ounces sliced mushrooms
3 tablespoons flour
1½ cups milk
2 cups cooked turkey, diced

2 cups egg noodles, cooked
Parmesan cheese to taste (about
   ¼ cup)
Salt and pepper to taste
3 to 4 slices bread, buttered

Melt butter and saute mushrooms for 5 minutes. Add the flour and stir. Slowly add milk and cook until thick (a chicken bouillon cube may be added if desired.) Add turkey, noodles, Parmesan cheese, salt and pepper. Place in 7x11 inch casserole. Butter 3 or 4 slices of bread and cut into small squares about 1x1 inch. Place on top of casserole. Bake at 350° for 20 minutes .Makes 6 servings.

RACHAEL DEMARTINI   DANDY DOERS UNIT

CHICKEN SUPREME

2 whole chicken breasts
(about 1½ pounds), split
2 tablespoons shortening
1 clove garlic
1 onion, chopped fine
1 small green pepper,
chopped
1 can Campbell's creamy
chicken mushroom soup

⅓ cup milk
¼ teaspoon thyme or rosemary
leaves
1 8-ounce can mixed vegetables,
drained
1 tablespoon chopped parsley

In skillet, brown chicken breasts in shortening with garlic, onion, and green pepper. Pour off fat. Stir in soup, milk, and thyme. Cover and simmer 30 minutes or until done. Stir occasionally. Add remaining ingredients. Heat. Serve with cooked rice. (If mixture is too thick, add more milk or use some of the drained vegetable liquid.) Makes 4 servings.

MRS. LYLE (CLARA) YOUNG   SPANISH NEEDLE UNIT

TURKEY TETRAZZINI

6 ounces spaghetti, broken
¼ cup margarine or butter
½ cup flour
2¾ cups chicken broth
¼ cup dry sherry
1 teaspoon salt
Dash of pepper
½ tablespoon monosodium
glutamate

6 ounce can sliced mushrooms,
drained
¼ cup green pepper, chopped
2 cups turkey or chicken, cooked
and diced
½ cup shredded Parmesan
cheese

Cook spaghetti in boiling salted water until just tender, do not overcook. Drain. Melt butter, blend in flour. Stir broth into flour mixture. Add cream. Cook and stir until mixture thickens and bubbles. Add sherry, salt, pepper, monosodium glutamate, drained spaghetti, mushrooms, green pepper, and cooked turkey or chicken. Turn into a 12x7½x2 inch baking dish. Sprinkle top with Parmesan cheese. Bake in 350° oven about 30 minutes. Makes 6 servings.

MARY SCHMIDT   GILLESPIE NIGHT UNIT

CHICKEN LIVERS CASSEROLE

2 4-ounce cans sliced
  mushrooms
⅓ cup butter or margarine
1 pound chicken livers
1 small clove garlic, crushed
  (optional)
¼ cup flour
1 teaspoon salt
¼ teaspoon pepper

1 cup milk
2 10-ounce packages frozen
  broccoli spears, thawed and
  drained
1 tablespoon fresh lemon juice
1 cup dairy sour cream
1 tablespoon flour
2 tablespoons grated Parmesan
  cheese

Drain mushrooms, reserve ⅓ cup liquid; set aside. Melt butter in large skillet. Add livers and garlic. Saute livers until brown and tender. Stir in ¼ cup flour, mushrooms, and reserved liquid, salt and pepper. Add milk and heat, stirring constantly until mixture thickens. Arrange broccoli in buttered 8x10 inch baking dish. Sprinkle with lemon juice. Top with liver mixture. Combine sour cream and 1 tablespoon flour. Spread over liver mixture. Top with Parmesan cheese. Bake at 350° for 30 to 35 minutes. Makes 4 to 6 servings.

RUTH DEATHERAGE   BARR UNIT

CHICKEN LIVERS WITH PEAS

3 cups carrots, chopped
2 cups peas, fresh or frozen
1½ pounds chicken livers
3 tablespoons margarine
1½ tablespoons flour

1 cup reserved vegetable liquid
  for chicken stock
⅓ cup light cream
Salt and pepper to taste

Cook carrots and peas in salted water until tender. Drain and reserve liquid. Saute chicken livers in margarine until lightly browned. Arrange vegetables in 1½ quart casserole, then put in chicken livers. Add flour to fat remaining from sauteing the chicken livers, adding more fat if needed. Stir in slowly 1 cup reserved vegetable liquid and the cream. Cook until thickened. Pour sauce over ingredients in casserole. Cover and bake in 350° oven for 20 minutes.

MRS. JOSIE JOHNSON   SUSTAINING MEMBER

FRENCH TOAST

12 slices day old bread	1¼ teaspoons baking powder
¾ cup brown sugar	2 egg yolks
Soft butter	1 cup milk
1¾ cups flour	3 tablespoons butter, melted
½ teaspoon salt	2 egg whites, stiffly beaten

Spread bread slices with soft butter. Sprinkle 6 slices with brown sugar, using 2 tablespoons to a slice. Cover these with other 6 slices, butter side down. Cut into quarters. Sift together flour, salt, and baking powder. Drop egg yolks in this and add milk and melted butter. Beat until smooth. Beat egg whites until stiff and fold into above mixture. Dip sandwiches into batter until well covered; put into 1 inch of hot grease in a skillet. Fry over medium heat until both sides are golden brown, turning only once. When done, sprinkle with powdered sugar and serve with tart jelly and platter of crisp bacon. Makes 6 servings.

COMMITTEE

FRENCH TOAST

6 eggs	Juice of ½ orange
½ cup cream	¼ teaspoon nutmeg
⅛ teaspoon salt	¼ cup butter
Grated peel of 1 orange	12 slices day old bread

Beat eggs; gradually add cream. Stir in salt, orange peel, juice, and nutmeg. Melt butter in large skillet or griddle. Cut the crust from bread. Dip the slices in the batter and fry until golden on both sides. Serve with powdered sugar or the following syrup.

Syrup:

1 cup sugar	1 tablespoon honey
3 tablespoons water	½ teaspoon vanilla

Combine sugar and water. Heat until sugar is dissolved. Add honey and vanilla.

COMMITTEE

BRUNCH DISH

12 slices Canadian bacon
12 slices Swiss cheese
1 dozen eggs

½ pint cream
Grated Parmesan cheese

Line 9x13 inch baking dish with Canadian bacon. Layer on the Swiss cheese. Break eggs over all, being careful not to break yolks. Drizzle the cream over the white until yolks peek through. Bake at 450° for 10 minutes. Remove from oven and sprinkle with Parmesan cheese. Return to oven and bake 8 to 10 minutes. Cut into squares and serve immediately. Makes 8 servings.

HELEN JOHNSON   MT. OLIVE UNIT

EGG AND SAUSAGE QUICHE

8 ounces pork sausage
4 eggs, hard cooked and
  chopped
1 cup (4 ounces) natural
  Swiss cheese, shredded
1 cup (4 ounces) natural
  Cheddar cheese, shredded

Pastry for 9 inch pie pan
3 eggs, beaten
1¼ cups light cream
¾ teaspoon salt
⅛ teaspoon pepper

Line 9 inch pie plate with pastry. Bake in 350° oven for 7 minutes. In skillet, cook sausage, drain well. Sprinkle hard cooked eggs in bottom of pie shell. Top with sausage and cheese. Combine beaten eggs, cream, salt, and pepper. Pour over mixture in pie pan. Bake in 350° oven for 30 to 35 minutes or until set. Let stand 10 minutes before serving. Makes 6 servings.

MAXINE RATTERMAN   HONEY POINT UNIT

SAUSAGE CHEESE DELUXE

1 pound sausage
1 pound Velveeta
1 teaspoon garlic salt

1 teaspoon Worcestershire sauce
½ teaspoon soy sauce
2 loaves party rye

Brown sausage. Add cheese and stir until cheese is melted. Add seasonings. Spread on bread. Bake at 350° for 10 to 15 minutes.

KATHY GWILLIM   PIASA UNIT

ASPARAGUS AND SCRAMBLED EGG CASSEROLE

12 to 20 asparagus spears,
  fresh or frozen
¼ to ½ cup water
Salt to taste
2 tablespoons butter
2 tablespoons flour
1 cup milk

Salt to taste
Reserved asparagus liquid
4 to 6 eggs
¼ cup milk or cream
Salt and pepper to taste
1 tablespoon margarine

Clean and cut asparagus into ½ to 1 inch pieces. Cook in as small amount of salted water as possible so asparagus will be steamed not boiled. Drain and reserve liquid. Make a white sauce with 2 tablespoons butter melted, flour, 1 cup milk, and salt to taste. Stir in reserved asparagus liquid and asparagus pieces. Beat eggs together with ¼ cup milk and seasonings. Have 1 tablespoon margarine melted over low to medium heat. Add eggs and stir often until just set. Have asparagus mixture hot and pour over eggs. Serve immediately.

ELINOR WALLACE   GIRARD NIGHT UNIT

DEVILED EGG MOLD

2 envelopes unflavored
  gelatin
1 cup water
½ cup lemon juice
2 teaspoons salt
2 teaspoons Worcestershire
  sauce
⅛ teaspoon cayenne pepper

1½ cups mayonnaise
8 eggs, hard cooked and
  chopped
1 cup celery, finely diced
½ cup green pepper, finely diced
¼ cup pimiento, chopped
¼ cup onion, grated

In small sauce pan, sprinkle gelatin over water. Dissolve over low heat, stirring constantly. Remove from heat; blend in lemon juice, salt, Worcestershire sauce, and pepper. Stir in mayonnaise. Fold in remaining ingredients. Pour into 6 cup mold. Cover and refrigerate until set. Dip mold into warm water for 30 seconds to unmold; invert onto serving platter. Garnish with 2 hard cooked eggs cut in slices, and parsley, if desired. Makes 12 servings.

MRS. LEO (BETTY) SCOTT   JUNIOR HOMEMAKERS UNIT

CHEESE STRADA

20 slices of bread, crust
removed and buttered on
one side
½ pound sharp Cheddar
cheese, grated
1 package frozen broccoli,
thawed

3 to 4 cups diced ham, chicken,
or turkey
7 eggs
Salt and pepper to taste
5 cups milk
⅓ teaspoon dry mustard
1 can mushroom soup

Butter oblong casserole. Put 10 bread slices, buttered side up, in bottom. Sprinkle with cheese, chopped, uncooked broccoli, and meat. Cover with remaining bread slices. Sprinkle with more cheese. Beat the eggs slightly and add milk, dry mustard, salt and pepper. Pour over the bread mixture and refrigerate overnight. Bake at 350° for 1 hour. Remove from oven and let set a few minutes before cutting into squares to serve. Heat mushroom soup for sauce. Makes 10 to 12 servings.

BESSIE BERTOLET   CARLINVILLE NIGHT UNIT

CHEESE SOUFFLE

½ pound Old English Kraft
cheese, grated
8-9 slices white bread
4 eggs, well beaten

2 cups milk
1 teaspoon salt
1 teaspoon pepper
½ cup butter, melted

Cut off bread crusts and cube. Layer bread and cheese in well greased 2 quart casserole. Mix eggs, milk, salt and pepper. Pour over cheese and bread, and add melted butter on top. Refrigerate 12 to 24 hours in covered dish. Bake uncovered at 350° for 65 to 70 minutes. Excellent for breakfast or brunch.

MRS. FLORENCE KOLB   BRIGHTON EARLY BIRDS UNIT

4-STEP CASSEROLE

1½ pound carton small curd
cottage cheese
4 eggs, beaten

¼ cup melted butter
1 cup shredded Cheddar cheese

Mix all ingredients together in a 2-quart casserole and bake uncovered at 325° for 1 hour. Serves 6.

MRS. JAMES (JANET) HOPPER   PLAINVIEW UNIT

PREZNUTZ

½ pound (8 slices) brick
  cheese
½ pound (8 slices) American
  cheese
4 eggs
½ cup flour

½ cup milk
½ stick butter
1 teaspoon baking powder
1 small carton cottage cheese
1 package frozen spinach

Cut cheeses into cubes or strips. Mix all ingredients together. Pour into a greased and floured 1½ quart pan or casserole dish. Bake at 350° for 1 hour. Makes 6 servings.

VICKIE LAUGHLIN   DANDY DOERS UNIT

YAYECHNIK (RUSSIAN EGG CHEESE) AN EASTER TRADITION

12 eggs, well beaten
1 quart milk

1 tablespoon sugar
1 tablespoon salt

Combine above ingredients and cook slowly in double boiler until mixture thickens and coagulates. Drain coagulated mixture into cheese cloth placed in colander. Bring four corners of cheese cloth togehter after shaking, tie, and hang to drain overnight. Remove mixture from cloth after draining, rub with butter, and brown in 400° oven for about 10 minutes.

JULIA ARDEN   BERTHA ELDRED UNIT

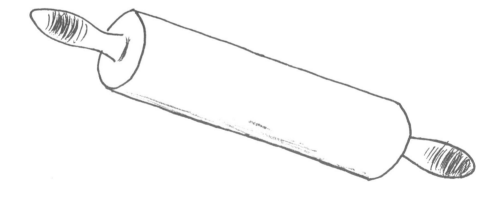

VEGETABLES AND SIDE DISHES

This is a typical farm sceen in Macoupin County where one of the main crops produced is corn.

Old farmers used to say, "Corn should be knee high by the Fourth of July." Now with modernized farming methods, corn is often shoulder high by this date.

Photographed by Jacoby Studios

132

APPLE-PINEAPPLE SCALLOP

1 1-pound 4½-ounce can
  pineapple chunks
¼ cup sugar
1 tablespoon cornstarch
¼ teaspoon salt
¼ cup lemon juice

3 cups sliced tart cooking apples
4 slices dry bread, broken into
  coarse crumbs
¼ pound pasteurized process
  cheese spread, shredded

Drain pineapple, reserve ¾ cup liquid. Combine dry ingredients in heavy saucepan; add pineapple liquid. Cook, stirring constantly, until thickened. Remove from heat, stir in lemon juice, and set aside. Layer fruit, crumbs, and cheese in buttered 2 quart casserole. (Pour on sauce before adding last layer of crumbs and cheese.) Cover. Bake in 350° oven for about 1 hour or until apples slices are tender. Makes 8 servings.

VADA FRANK   PLAINVIEW UNIT

ASPARAGUS CASSEROLE

3 cups asparagus
4 tablespoons fat, melted
2 tablespoons flour
2 cups milk

½ cup American cheese, grated
¼ teaspoon salt
¾ cup dry bread crumbs
2 tablespoons butter

Cook asparagus 5 minutes, place in casserole. Blend fat and flour, add milk gradually and cook slowly until thickened, stirring constantly. Add cheese and salt. Pour sauce over asparagus, sprinkle with crumbs, dot with butter, and bake in slow oven (325°) for 30 minutes. Makes 6-8 servings.

ROSALIE GRICHNIK   SPANISH NEEDLE UNIT

BEETS IN ORANGE SAUCE

1 cup orange juice
½ cup raisins
2 tablespoons corn starch
¼ cup sugar

2 tablespoons beet juice
1 tablespoon vinegar
2 cups cooked beets, drained
  and diced

Combine orange juice and raisins; heat to boiling. Mix together corn starch, sugar, and beet juice. Add to orange juice. Mix and cook until thick. Add vinegar and beets.

MRS. SAM BECHTEL   CARLINVILLE DAY UNIT

HARVARD BEETS

1 can diced beets, drained   ¼ cup vinegar
½ cup sugar   ¼ cup beet juice
½ tablespoon cornstarch

Make a sauce of the sugar, cornstarch, vinegar and beet juice. When thickened add the drained beets. Keep warm to serve. Serves 6.

MRS. FRANCIS SKEEN   GIRARD DAY UNIT

BROCCOLI

4 tablespoons butter   1 10-ounce box frozen chopped
3 tablespoons flour   broccoli
⅛ pound Velveeta cheese,   1 cup cottage cheese
  cubed   2 eggs, beaten

Melt butter. Stir flour into it. Add Velveeta cheese; stir until melted. Add broccoli, cottage cheese, and eggs. Pour into 1½ quart casserole and bake at 350° for 1 hour. Makes 6 servings.

AVIS DADISMAN   DO MORE UNIT

BROCCOLI CASSEROLE

2 10-ounce packages frozen   1 small jar Cheez Whiz
  broccoli   1 can cream of chicken soup
½ cup onion, chopped   1 small can water chestnuts
¼ cup margarine   ½ cup buttered bread crumbs
1 cup Minute Rice, cooked

Cook broccoli according to package directions; drain. Cook rice according to directions. Cook onions in margarine until tender. Combine broccoli, rice, onions, and remaining ingredients except for crumbs. Pour into a buttered 2 quart casserole dish. Top with buttered bread crumbs. Bake at 350° or 375° oven for 20 to 30 minutes or until brown and bubbly. Makes 10 to 12 servings.

LODEMA MEEKS   HAGAMAN UNIT

BROCCOLI BAKE

2 cups Minute Rice
2 cups water
2 packages frozen chopped
  broccoli
½ cup onion, chopped

½ cup celery, chopped
3 or 4 tablespoons margarine
1 can mushrooms
1 small jar Cheez Whiz
1 can cream of mushroom soup

Cook rice and water as directed on package. Cook frozen broccoli as directed. Saute chopped onion and celery in margarine until tender. Add mushrooms and cook down liquid to about half. Add Cheez Whiz and soup. Stir to blend well until heated. Add drained broccoli and rice. Mix well and pour into 14x9x2 inch baking dish. Bake at 375° for 30 to 45 minutes. Makes 12 servings.

MAE STIEHL   MT. OLIVE UNIT

MRS. CLIFFORD BEILSMITH, BRIGHTON EARLY BIRDS UNIT, varies this recipe by sauteing 2 slices of finely chopped bacon with the onion and celery and substituting 1 can of chicken soup diluted with 1 soup can of milk for the mushroom soup and mushrooms.

MRS. ADELINE WEIDNER, GILLESPIE NIGHT UNIT, eliminates mushrooms; substitutes 4 cups cooked long grain rice for the Minute Rice and doubles quantities or broccoli, onion, celery, and soup, for 18 servings.

BROCCOLI AND ONIONS

2 10-ounce packages broccoli
  spears
1 cup Cheddar cheese, grated
2½ teaspoons dry French
  dressing mix

1 3½-ounce can French fried
  onion rings
1 10½-ounce can mushroom
  soup
⅔ cup evaporated milk

Heat oven to 325°. Cook broccoli according to package directions. Drain and place in greased 1½ quart shallow casserole. Sprinkle with grated cheese. Add salad dressing mix and ¾ of the onion rings. Combine soup and evaporated milk. Pour over broccoli mixture. Bake 25 minutes, top with remaining onions, and bake 3-5 minutes longer. Makes 6 servings.

ARDETH JOKISCH   STITCH AND STIR UNIT

BROCCOLI CASSEROLE

1 slice Cheddar cheese,
cut up
1 can cream of mushroom
soup
1 package frozen chopped
broccoli, thawed

3 eggs, hard cooked and
chopped
Chopped olives, optional
Salt and pepper to taste
Buttered bread crumbs

Melt cheese in heated soup. Add broccoli, eggs, chopped olives if desired, and seasoning. Pour into 1 quart casserole. Top with buttered bread crumbs. Bake at 350° until broccoli is tender and mixture is bubbly.

HELEN PITMAN   DO MORE UNIT

CREAMED BRUSSELS SPROUTS

1 pound fresh or 2 packages
frozen Brussels sprouts
3 tablespoons margarine or
butter
1 small onion, chopped

3 tablespoons flour
1 cup chicken broth, seasoned
1/8 teaspoon nutmeg
1/4 cup cream
2 tablespoons parsley

Cook and drain sprouts. Melt the butter or margarine over low heat, add the onion and saute until transparent, about 5 minutes. Stir in the flour. Remove from heat and stir in the chicken broth. Return to the heat and cook, stirring constantly, until the sauce is smooth and thickened. Add salt and pepper to taste. Stir in the nutmeg, cream, and parsley. Gently fold in the sprouts. Makes 6 servings.

JOYCE JOHNSON   HAGAMAN UNIT

HARVEST BEAN CASSEROLE

1 pound ground beef, cooked
and drained
1 onion, chopped
1 green pepper, chopped

1 can tomato soup
1 teaspoon prepared mustard
1 can pork and beans

Saute onion and green pepper. Mix all ingredients together. Bake in casserole at 350° for 30 minutes or longer.

MARVEL F. KILIAN   SUSTAINING MEMBER

136

GREEN BEAN DELUXE

6 slices bacon
¾ cup chopped onion
½ cup green pepper
2 teaspoons flour
2 tablespoons brown sugar
1 teaspoon Worcestershire
  sauce

¼ teaspoon pepper
½ teaspoon salt
¼ teaspoon dry mustard
1 large can tomatoes
2 cans French sliced green
  beans

Fry bacon until crisp; drain grease and save 3 tablespoosn fat to saute onions and green peppers in until tender. Blend flour, brown sugar, Worcestershire sauce, salt, pepper, and dry mustard together in saucepan. Add tomatoes. Cook until mixture is thickened. Pour over drained green beans, sprinkle with bacon pieces and bake in a 1½ quart casserole dish in a 350° oven for 20-30 minutes. Makes 8 servings.

LINDA WATTLES   GILLESPIE NIGHT UNIT

BAKED BEANS—ARMY STYLE

6 strips bacon
1 28-ounce can pork and
  beans
1 large onion, diced
1 medium green pepper,
  diced
1 tablespoon brown sugar

2 tablespoons molasses
1 tablespoon catsup
½ teaspoon salt
¼ teaspoon pepper
¼ teaspoon garlic powder
¼ teaspoon Accent

Grease a 2½ quart baking dish generously. Cut bacon strips in half; put half in bottom of dish. Mix remaining ingredients together: pour into casserole. Cover with remaining bacon. Cover casserole and bake at 400° for 20 minutes. Reduce heat to 250° and bake for 2 hours, uncover during last 10 minutes. Makes 8 servings.

COMMITTEE

LIMA BEANS DELUXE

3 slices bread, cubed
1 stick butter or margarine, melted
3 tablespoons flour
1 cup milk

1 cup cheese, diced
2 cans cooked dry lima beans
4 tablespoons catsup
1 small can pimientos, diced

Cube bread into melted butter; remove cubes and set aside. Stir flour into butter, add milk and liquid drained from beans. Cook until thick. Add cheese and stir until melted. Add the bread cubes, lima beans, catsup, and pimientos. Stir together and pour into casserole. Bake at 350° for 45-60 minutes. Makes 8-10 servings.

MELBA COULTAS   GIRARD NIGHT UNIT

LIMA BEANS MARIE ANN

2 cups shelled baby lima beans, or frozen baby limas
½ pound baby carrots
1 tablespoon butter
2 tablespoons butter
2 tablespoons flour
1½ cups well seasoned chicken stock

Salt and pepper to taste
1 egg yolk
2 to 3 teaspoons heavy cream
1 tablespoon fresh parsley
1 teaspoon savory

Cook beans in boiling water 15 to 20 minutes or until just tender; drain, rinse in cold water, and drain again. If carrots are large, quarter them. Cook in salted water for 15 minutes or until just tender. Melt 1 tablespoon butter in sauce pan or flame proof casserole; add beans and carrots, and keep warm.

To make sauce, melt 2 tablespoons butter. Stir in flour and cook over medium heat until sauce is pale straw color. Take from heat, pour in stock, season to taste, and simmer 2 to 3 minutes until consistency of heavy cream. Mix egg yolk with the cream, stir in a little of the hot sauce, add herbs, and stir into remaining sauce. Heat sauce until it thickens slightly. Do not boil. Pour over beans and carrots; heat until very hot, shaking pan so sauce and vegetables mix. Serve in casserole or transfer to hot serving dish. Good served with veal or lamb. Makes 4 to 6 servings.

BERNA HUHSMAN   STAUNTON UNIT

LIMA BEAN, CHEESE CASSEROLE

4 slices bacon, diced
2 10-ounce packages frozen
  lima beans
½ cup onions, chopped
1 10½-ounce can cheese
  soup

½ cup sour cream
¼ cup soft bread crumbs
1 tablespoon butter

Fry bacon in skillet until crisp, reserve drippings. Drain bacon on absorbent paper. Cook beans as directed on package, drain well. Saute onions in 2 tablespoons drippings until tender. Blend in soup, sour cream, beans and bacon. Pour into a 2 quart casserole. Combine bread crumbs and butter; sprinkle on top of casserole. Bake in a 375° oven for 20-25 minutes. Makes 10 servings.
MILDRED L. REDFERN   CARLINVILLE NIGHT UNIT

ESCALLOPED CABBAGE

1 quart cabbage, finely
  chopped
½ cup water
½ teaspoon salt

4 tablespoons butter
3 tablespoons flour
2 cups milk
1 cup cheese, grated

Boil the cabbage, water and salt together for 8 minutes; drain. Make a cream sauce of the butter, flour and milk. Place half of the cooked cabbage into a 3 quart baking dish. Cover with half of the white sauce. Add ½ cup grated cheese. Add the remainder of the cabbage, white sauce, and grated cheese. Top with fine bread crumbs, if desired. Bake in a 325° oven for 25-30 minutes. Makes 12 servings.

MRS. CHARLES HARP   SHAWS POINT UNIT

FIVE-MINUTE CABBAGE

1½ cups milk
1 quart cabbage, shredded

2 tablespoons butter
Salt and pepper

Scald milk and cook cabbage in it for 2 minutes; add butter and seasonings. Cook rapidly for 3 or 4 minutes, stirring constantly to prevent scorching. The cabbage retains its crispness and is delicate in flavor and color. Makes 6 servings.

MARIE MATHIAS   CARLINVILLE NIGHT UNIT

CABBAGE CASSEROLE

1 medium head cabbage	3 tablespoons butter
1 medium onion	4 tablespoons flour
1 medium green pepper	1 cup milk
1 red pimento (optional)	1 cup cheese, diced
2 or 3 stalks celery	½ cup buttered bread crumbs

Coarsely shred cabbage. Chop onion, pepper, pimento, and celery, Place vegetables in sauce pan, cover with water, salt to taste, and parboil. Pour into colander and drain well. Melt butter in sauce pan over low heat; add flour and blend. Add milk slowly, stirring to blend. Cook, stirring constantly, until sauce boils and thickens. Stir in diced cheese until melted and blended. Pour vegetables and then sauce into greased 1½ quart casserole. Top with buttered bread crumbs and dot with butter. Bake at 325° for 45 minutes or until top is golden brown. Makes 8 servings.

MARY E. SMITH   HAGAMAN UNIT

CABBAGE AND NOODLES

1 small onion	1½ cups noodles
¼ cup margarine	4 cups shredded cabbage

Fry onion in margarine until transparent but not brown. Add 1½ cups noodles (recipe below) cooked in 2 cups water for 10 minutes. Simmer cabbage 5 minutes. Add noodles and water to cabbage and simmer together another 10 minutes. Season to taste. May need to add more water. Makes 6-8 servings.

Noodles:

1 egg, beaten	½ teaspoon salt
2 tablespoons milk	1 cup flour

Combine the egg, milk and salt. Add the flour. Roll in hands to blend well. Roll very thin on floured board. Let stand 20 minutes. Cut and dry for 2 hours. Can be frozen.

LOUISE WOODS   BIRD UNIT

FREDERICK'S CASSEROLE

1 large head cabbage,
shredded
1 medium onion, chopped
Butter

1 pound ground beef
2 cans tomato soup
¾ cup Minute rice, uncooked
½ cup water

Shred cabbage in fairly large pieces. Brown onion in butter. Cook ground beef until brown; drain grease. In a well buttered 13x9x2 inch baking pan, layer ingredients as follows: ground beef, onion, cabbage, tomato soup, season with salt. Repeat all layers. Sprinkle with rice and water. Bake at 350° for 1 hour. (Start baking time with cover on casserole.) Makes 6 servings.

LINDA WATTLES   GILLESPIE NIGHT UNIT

CABBAGE AND HAMBURGER

1 pound ground meat
Garlic
Salt
Onion salt
Pepper

⅓ stick margarine
1 onion, chopped
1 medium head cabbage
⅔ can stewed tomatoes
Grated Parmesan cheese

Brown meat, drain off fat. Season with garlic, salt, onion salt, and pepper to taste. In separate skillet, saute onion in margarine. Add cabbage, which has been shredded. Stir occasionally. When cabbage is translucent, add tomatoes and season to taste. Add meat to cabbage. Heat thoroughly. Top with cheese before serving.

GILDA CALDERWOOD   GET TOGETHERS UNIT

CABBAGE ONE DISH MEAL

3 or 4 tablespoons margarine
¼ cup onion, chopped
1 clove garlic
½ pound ground beef
1 medium head cabbage,
coarsely cut

4 ounces Velveeta cheese
½ cup sour cream (optional)
2 medium size potaotes, cooked
and quartered
Salt and pepper to taste

Melt margarine. Add chopped onion and garlic; saute a few minutes. Add the ground beef; brown lightly. Add cabbage, cook about 15 minutes or until tender. Add cheese. Take off heat after cheese has been melted. Add sour cream, the cooked potatoes, salt and pepper to taste. Makes 3 or 4 servings.

MRS. MARY HEMPHILL   BERTHA ELDRED UNIT

CARROT CASSEROLE

1 pound carrots, sliced
¼ pound Velveeta cheese
½ stick margarine

½ stick margarine
12 soda crackers, crushed

Cook carrots in water until tender. Drain and put into a 1½ quart casserole. Melt cheese with ½ stick margarine. Pour over carrots. Melt the second ½ stick margarine and add the cracker crumbs. Sprinkle over top of carrots. Bake at 350° for 25-30 minutes until bubbly and lightly browned.

ANNA KALASKIE   GET TOGETHERS UNIT

CARROTS WITH ORANGE SAUCE

2 bunches carrots
¼ cup butter
⅔ cup sugar
1 6-ounce can concentrated
   orange juice

1½ tablespoons corn starch
Dash of salt
Maraschino cherries for color

Peel carrots, cut into pieces, and boil in salted water until tender. Drain. Combine rest of ingredients in a saucepan and simmer until thickened. Pour over carrots and marinate at least 5 hours. Heat to serve.

BERTHA O. ELDRED   BRUSHY MOUND UNIT

CURRIED CAULIFLOWER AND PEAS

1 medium cauliflower
2 teaspoons butter
2 teaspoons flour
1½ cups sour cream
1 package frozen peas,
   cooked

1 to 2 teaspoons curry powder
1 teaspoon seasoned onion salt
Toasted curried almonds,
   optional

Trim and wash cauliflower, break into small flowerettes, and cook until tender. In saucepan, melt butter and blend in flour. Add sour cream and cook gently until heated through. Combine all ingredients except almonds and turn into a shallow 2 quart baking dish. Top with almonds, if desired, and bake in 325° oven for 25 minutes until heated through.

DENA GIRARDINI   GET TOGETHERS UNIT

EGGPLANT CASSEROLE

1 to 2 tablespoons vegetable
oil (depending on size of
eggplant)
1 large onion, coarsely
chopped
1 large green pepper, seeded
and cut into 1 inch squares
1 medium eggplant, pared
and cut into 1 inch cubes
½ pound fresh mushrooms,
sliced

1 large tomato, peeled and
chopped
1 teaspoon salt
¾ teaspoon dried leaf thyme
⅛ teaspoon pepper
1 cup packaged herb seasoned
stuffing mix
2 cups (8 ounces) shredded
Swiss cheese, divided

In large skillet, heat oil over medium heat. Add onion and green pepper; saute 3 minutes. Stir. Add eggplant and mushrooms; saute 3 minutes, stirring constantly. Add tomato and seasonings. Cook 2 minutes. Spread stuffing mix over bottom of buttered 2 quart casserole. Layer half the vegetable mixture and 1 cup shredded cheese over the stuffing mix. Top with remaining vegetables. Bake in 350° oven for 35 minutes. Sprinkle with remaining cheese, bake uncovered 10 minutes longer or until cheese melts. NOTE: This tasty casserole makes 6 side dish servings or 4 main dish servings.
MRS. FLORENCE KOLB   BRIGHTON EARLY BIRDS UNIT

EGGPLANT CASSEROLE

1 cup green bell pepper, cut
in ¼ inch strips
½ pound yellow onions,
thinly sliced
2 cloves garlic, minced
4 tablespoons olive oil
½ pound mushrooms, cut in
halves

½ pound eggplant, cut in ½ inch
slices
½ pound zucchini, cut in ½ inch
slices
1 pound red tomatoes, peeled,
seeded and quartered
3 tablespoons parsley
salt and pepper to taste

Saute pepper, onions, and garlic in hot oil until onions are transparent (about 5 minutes). Remove from skillet. Add mushrooms and saute until golden brown; return pepper, onion and garlic to mushrooms. Add half of tomato wedges, zucchini and eggplant. Sprinkle with salt and pepper. Stir gently. Add remaining tomatoes, zucchini and eggplant. Sprinkle with parsley. Cover and simmer over low heat for 10 minutes. Remove cover and cook an additional 5 minutes or until liquid has evaporated. Serves 6 to 8.
MRS. JOSIE JOHNSON   SUSTAINING MEMBER

GOLDEN EGGPLANT CASSEROLE

2½ cups peeled eggplant,
cubed
18 saltine crackers, crumbled
½ cup sharp cheese,
shredded
¼ cup celery, chopped
2 tablespoons chopped
pimiento

1 tablespoon butter or margarine,
melted
½ teaspoon salt
⅛ teaspoon pepper
1 cup cream or evaporated milk

Cook eggplant in boiling, salted water for 10 minutes; drain. Combine with remaining ingredients. Turn into 1 quart casserole. Bake in moderate oven (350°) for 45 minutes. Makes 6 servings.

MRS. M. L. (VIRGINIA) KESSINGER   BIRD UNIT

GUMBO

¼ pound bacon, diced
1 medium onion, diced
1 large green pepper, diced
3 medium tomatoes, diced

1 cup corn (fresh or frozen)
2 cups sliced tender okra pods
Salt and pepper to taste
½ teaspoon oregano (optional)

In medium size skillet, fry diced bacon until crisp. Remove from skillet. In 2 tablespoons drippings, cook onion and pepper until transparent. Do not brown. Add diced and peeled tomatoes, corn, okra pods, and bacon. Seaon to suit taste. Cook over medium heat until okra is tender, approximately ½ hour. Makes 6 to 8 servings.

MRS. A. D. ANDERSON   SHAWS POINT UNIT

NOODLE CASSEROLE

1 pound fresh mushrooms
4 tablespoons butter
½ cup onion, minced
1 8-ounce package wide
noodles

1 cup sour cream
1½ teaspoons salt
¼ teaspoon pepper
1 cup soft bread crumbs

Rinse, pat dry, and slice mushrooms. In large skillet, melt 3 tablespoons butter; add mushrooms and onion. Saute 5 minutes or until mushrooms are golden. Cook noodles; drain. Stir in mushroom mixture, sour cream, salt, and pepper. Spoon mixture into 2 quart casserole. In small sauce pan, melt remaining 1 tablespoon butter; add crumbs and toss lightly. Spoon crumbs around edge of noodles in casserole. Bake at 400° for 5 minutes or until crumbs are golden. Makes 6 servings.

LAURA ELLA ODORIZZI   STAUNTON UNIT

NO-BAKE STUFFED PEPPERS

3 medium green peppers
1 teaspoon sugar
½ teaspoon basil
1 15-ounce can tomato sauce
1 cup rice
2 cups water

2 teaspoons butter or margarine
¾ pound ground beef
1 small onion, chopped
1 teaspoon salt
½ cup Cheddar cheese, grated

Cut peppers in half lengthwise. Remove stem end and seeds. Parboil in boiling, salted water for 10 minutes; drain. Add sugar and basil to tomato sauce; set aside. Cook rice in 2 cups boiling water with ½ teaspoon salt and margarine. Brown beef and onion in large skillet. Stir in ½ cup tomato mixture, ¼ cup rice, and ½ teaspoon salt. Cover and simmer 5 minutes; add cheese. Spoon meat mixture into peppers; place in skillet. Pour remaining sauce around peppers, cover, and simmer 5 minutes. Serve peppers with the rice, top with sauce, and additional cheese. Makes 6 servings.

MRS. GEORGE (KAY) TOMPKINS   JUNIOR HOMEMAKERS UNIT

PINEAPPLE CASSEROLE

2 cups sugar
¾ cup (1½ sticks) margarine
3 eggs, beaten
2 teaspoons milk

1 2-pound can crushed pineapple
1 quart fresh bread crumbs,
  crusts removed

Cream sugar and margarine; add eggs and milk, pineapple and bread crumbs. Mix thoroughly. Pour into casserole. Bake at 350° for 1 hour. Bake immediately after mixing.

FLORENCE ALWARD   SHIPMAN UNIT

PINEAPPLE SCALLOP

1 quart fresh bread crumbs
1 #2½ can pineapple, chunks
  or crushed
1 cup butter

1 cup sugar
3 eggs, beaten
½ cup milk

Mix bread with pineapple (juice and all). Put into a greased 2 quart casserole dish. Cream butter and sugar until fluffy; add beaten eggs and milk to form a batter. Pour batter over pineapple mixture. Bake at 375° for about 40 minutes or until brown. Makes 8-10 servings.

MRS. REBA FERREL   GIRARD DAY UNIT

SCALLOPED CORN WITH OYSTERS

2 cans creamed corn
5 soda crackers, crushed
1 tablespoon butter

Dash of salt and pepper
1 small can oysters, drained
1 cup milk

Place 1 can of corn in a buttered 8x10 inch baking dish. Sprinkle half the crushed crackers over corn. Top with butter, salt and pepper. Place ½ can oysters on top of mixture. Repeat layers of corn, crackers, and the remainder of the oysters. Pour the milk over top. Bake in a 350° oven for 30 minutes, covered. Uncover and bake 15 more minutes to brown lightly. Makes 8-12 servings.

MARGARET WIRTH   GILLESPIE NIGHT UNIT

SCALLOPED CORN AND OYSTERS

2 eggs, well beaten
1 can cream style corn
1 10-ounce can frozen oyster
  stew, thawed
1 cup cracker crumbs
2 tablespoons margarine,
  melted

½ cup or 1 small can evaporated
  milk
¼ cup celery, finely chopped
¼ teaspoon salt
Dash of white pepper
1 tablespoon minced pimiento
Paprika

Combine all ingredients and pour into a buttered 2 quart casserole. Sprinkle a few buttered crumbs on top, if desired. Sprinkle with paprika. Bake at 350° for 1 hour or until just done. Do not overbake. A small carton of fresh or frozen oysters may be added, if desired.

ELDA CREW   CARLINVILLE DAY UNIT

CHEESE POTATOES

4 tablespoons margarine
4 tablespoons flour
1½ cups milk
2 teaspoons salt

¼ teaspoon pepper
1 16-ounce jar Cheez Whiz
6 large potatoes, cooked and
  sliced while hot

Melt together over low heat the margarine and flour. Add milk, salt, pepper, and Cheez Whiz. Stir until thickened. Pour over potato slices in a 1¾ quart casserole. Cover and let stand for 5 minutes before serving. Makes 6-8 servings.

MONA R. VANDOREN   PIASA UNIT

POTATO PANCAKES (KARTAFFELPFANNKUCHEN)

2 large potatoes, grated
  (about 2½ cups)
3 cups water
1 teaspoon lemon juice
1 boiled potato

1 egg, beaten
2 tablespoons milk
½ teaspoon salt
6 to 8 tablespoons vegetable oil

Grate raw potato into water to which lemon juice has been added. Drain well. Beat raw and cooked potatoes with egg, milk, and salt to form a batter. Add slight amount of flour if necessary. Using 3 tablespoons of oil for each batch, drop batter for 3 or 4 pancakes at a time into hot oil in large frying pan. When firm on bottom side, loosen edges and turn. Brown on other side. Remove, drain on paper towels, and serve immediately. If cakes are served with meat, sprinkle with salt. If served with applesauce, etc., sprinkle with sugar. Makes 8-10 pancakes.

ALBERTA WILTON   CARLINVILLE NIGHT UNIT

SCALLOPED POTATOES

2 pounds frozen hash brown
  potatoes
1 can cream of chicken soup
1 pound shredded Cheddar
  cheese

1 small carton (½ pint) sour
  cream
1 stick margarine, melted
1 cup corn flakes
2 tablespoons butter

Place potatoes in buttered 2 quart casserole. Mix soup, cheese, sour cream, and melted margarine together. Pour over potatoes. Crush corn flakes and mix with 2 tablespoons margarine. Sprinkle over casserole. Bake at 350° for 45 minutes. Makes 10 to 12 servings.

ROSE HOPPER   GILLESPIE NIGHT UNIT

MRS. LOIS KABURICK, HONEY POINT UNIT, uses ½ cup finely chopped onion, 1 cup grated Cheddar cheese, and 1 teaspoon salt.

TATER TOT CASSEROLE

1 small package tater tots
1 can cream of mushroom
  soup

1 small package shredded
  Cheddar cheese

Mix all the ingredients together and pour into a 1 quart casserole. Bake in a 350° oven for 40 minutes. Serves 4.

MRS. ROY WELLER   SOUTH OTTER UNIT

PARTY MASHED POTATOES

5 pounds, or 9 large,
  potatoes
1 8-ounce package cream
  cheese
1 cup dairy sour cream

2 teaspoons onion salt
¼ teaspoon pepper
2 tablespoons butter
Paprika
Chopped parsley

Peel potatoes, cut in pieces, and boil in salted water until done; drain. Mash until smooth. Add remaining ingredients and beat until light and fluffy. Cool. Spread into a buttered 13x9 inch baking dish. Cover and refrigerate (can be fixed the day before baking). To bake, dot with butter and bake at 350° for about 45 to 60 minutes or until potatoes are heated through. Garnish with paprika and chopped parsley. Makes 8 to 10 servings.

SYLVIA MAE FRITZ   PIASA UNIT

TATER TOT PIE

2 cups chicken, cooked and
  chopped
1 medium onion, chopped
1 can cream of chicken soup

½ cup milk
1 can French style green beans,
  drained
Frozen Tater Tots

Put chopped chicken into 1½ quart baking dish. Add onion. Mix soup with milk and pour half of this mixture over the chicken and onions. Add the green beans over soup in dish and season lightly with salt and pepper. Pour remaining soup mixture over all. Place a layer of Tater Tots on top. Bake at 350° for 45 minutes to 1 hour. Makes 6 servings.

MRS. WILSON BRIEGEL   CARLINVILLE NIGHT UNIT

SWEET POTATO SURPRISE

6 sweet potatoes, cooked
1¼ cups brown sugar
1½ tablespoons cornstarch
1 teaspoon orange rind,
  grated

1 teaspoon cinnamon
1 cup apricot juice
1 cup apricots, drained
2 tablespoons butter
½ cup chopped pecans

Cut cooked sweet potatoes in halves and arrange in buttered 7½x12 inch baking dish. Combine sugar, cornstarch, orange rind, cinnamon, and apricot juice in saucepan and cook until thick, stirring constantly. Stir in apricots, butter, and pecans. Pour over sweet potatoes. Bake in moderate oven (375°) for 25 minutes. Makes 6 to 8 servings.

MRS. VERNA SCHAEFER   PIASA UNIT

BAKED SWEET POTATOES

3 cups sweet potatoes,
  mashed
⅓ cup margarine
2 eggs
½ cup milk
½ teaspoon salt

1 teaspoon vanilla
1 cup sugar
1 cup brown sugar
⅓ cup flour
½ cup margarine
½ cup ground nuts

Mix together the sweet potatoes, margarine, eggs, milk, salt, vanilla, and sugar. Pour into a greased 9x9 inch baking dish. Melt together the brown sugar, flour, and margarine. Add the nuts. Pour over the sweet potato mixture. Bake at 350° for 30 minutes. Makes 6-8 servings. Best when served warm.

LENA CONRADY   BARR UNIT

SWEET POTATO CASSEROLE

3 cups cooked sweet
  potatoes, mashed
1 cup sugar
½ stick margarine, softened
¼ teaspoon salt
½ cup evaporated milk

Topping:
¾ cup brown sugar
¼ cup flour
½ stick margarine, softened
1 cup pecan halves

Stir together the mashed sweet potatoes, sugar, butter, salt and evaporated milk. Stir until creamy. Turn mixture into a buttered 9x9 inch casserole dish. For topping, mix together the brown sugar, flour, margarine, and pecans. Crumble mixture by hand and spread over top of casserole. Bake in 350° oven for 45 minutes. Makes 6-8 servings. NOTE: You can used canned sweet potatoes (drained) and mash them, but it is best when made with fresh sweet potatoes that have been cooked and mashed. Chopped pecans may be used.

MRS. JOHN DAVIS   BERTHA ELDRED UNIT

RICE PROVENCAL

1 pound rice
2 cans beef consomme
1 can French onion soup
2 cans water

1 can water chestnuts, sliced
Pinches of rosemary, basil, and
  thyme

Mix all together. Bake, covered, at 350° for 45 minutes. Uncover and bake 45 minutes longer in 9x13 inch greased pan. Makes 12 servings.

JEAN GORE   CARLINVILLE NIGHT UNIT

WILD RICE AND HAMBURGER

1 package Uncle Ben's long
  grain wild rice
2 pounds round steak,
  ground
1 medium onion, diced
½ cup celery, diced

2 tablespoons soy sauce
1 can water chestnuts, sliced
1 can chicken and rice soup
1 can cream of mushroom soup
1 small can sliced mushrooms
¼ cup slivered almonds

Cook rice as directed on package. Brown beef, onions, and celery. Add remaining ingredients except slivered almonds. Cover and bake in greased casserole at 325° for 25 minutes. Uncover, add slivered almonds, and bake 15 more minutes.

GLORIA BEASLEY   CARLINVILLE NIGHT UNIT

MUSHROOM RICE

3 cups hot cooked rice,
  cooked in chicken broth
1 4-ounce can mushrooms,
  drained and sliced
1 cup green peas, cooked

2 tablespoons butter, melted
¼ teaspoon onion powder
Salt and pepper to taste
2 tablespoons pimiento, diced

Combine rice, mushrooms, peas, butter, seasonings and pimiento. Heat until vegetables are hot. Toss lightly. Serves 6.

HATTIE HICKS   BERTHA ELDRED UNIT

RICE CASSEROLE

1¼ to 1½ cups rice
1 can onion soup
1 can chicken soup or beef
  broth

1 can mushrooms, undrained
1 stick margarine

Combine first four ingredients in a greased 1½ quart casserole. Cut up the stick of margarine on top. Bake at 350° for 1 hour. Makes 6 servings.

VIOLA HELM   STAUNTON UNIT

RATATOUILLE WITH SAUCE

3 cloves garlic, finely minced
2 onions, thinly sliced
⅓ cup olive oil
1 green pepper, cut in thin
round slices
2 medium eggplants,
unpeeled and diced
2 medium zucchini, cut into
¼ inch slices
1 20-ounce can whole
tomatoes, undrained

1½ teaspoons basil
1½ teaspoons parsley
1½ teaspoons salt
Fresh ground pepper to taste
½ pound whole mushrooms
1½ pounds Italian sausage,
sliced
1 cup Swiss cheese, grated

Saute garlic and onion in oil until soft. Add green pepper, eggplant, and zucchini; cook 5 minutes over medium heat, tossing well. Add undrained tomatoes and seasonings. Simmer 15 minutes; cover and simmer 15 more minutes. Add mushrooms to vegetables during last 10 minutes of cooking time. Meanwhile, cook Italian sausage in skillet until done and drain well. Add sausage to vegetables; sprinkle with grated cheese. Cover and simmer until cheese melts. Makes 8 servings.

MRS. WM. (HELEN) MANNING   SPANISH NEEDLE UNIT

SAUERKRAUT RICE CASSEROLE

1½ pounds ground beef
½ pound ground pork
1 cup rice, precooked 10
minutes
1 teaspoon salt
¼ teaspoon pepper

2 cups sauerkraut, drained
1 large can tomato sauce
¼ to ½ cup grated Parmesan
cheese
1 cup onion, chopped

Cook beef, pork, and onion together until all redness is gone and meat is browned. Add rice, salt, pepper, sauerkraut, and tomato sauce to meat. Place in 2½ to 3 quart casserole. Cover and bake at 375° for 35 to 40 minutes. Sprinkle Parmesan cheese on top during last 10 minutes of baking.

VERDA BRUNETTO   GET TOGETHERS UNIT

GREEN RICE

2 eggs, beaten
2 cups milk
1 medium onion, minced
1 cup grated sharp Cheddar
   cheese

1 package frozen (chopped
   spinach or chopped broccoli)
1 cup Minute Rice

Mix all ingredients together and bake in a casserole at 375° for 45 minutes.

JEAN LOVELESS   GILLESPIE NIGHT UNIT

SAUERKRAUT CASSEROLE

1½ pounds ground beef
1 15-ounce can tomato sauce
2 cans water
1 #303 can sauerkraut

1 cup rice
1 teaspoon salt
1 teaspoon pepper

Brown meat. Mix meat with all other ingredients in a 3 quart casserole. Bake at 375° for 1 hour.

JOSEPHINE BAIMA   GET TOGETHERS UNIT

SPINACH SOUFFLE

2 pounds small curd cottage
   cheese
¼ pound brick cheese
   (4 slices)
¼ pound American cheese
   (4 slices)

1 stick butter
2 10-ounce packages frozen
   spinach, chopped and drained
6 eggs, beaten
6 to 8 tablespoons flour

Cube cheeses and butter. Add all the ingredients, beaten eggs last. Stir. Grease 9x13 inch pan with butter, pour in mixture. Bake at 350° for 1 hour until bubbly brown. After baking, it is best to let stand 1 hour or leave in warm oven. Can be baked and frozen, or frozen and baked. Makes 10-15 servings.

CONNIE SCHRIER   SHIPMAN UNIT

CHEESY SPINACH CASSEROLE

4 10-ounce packages
  chopped spinach, cooked
2 envelopes dry onion soup
  mix
2 cups sour cream

¼ teaspoon garlic powder
⅛ teaspoon pepper
1 cup grated sharp Cheddar
  cheese

Drain the cooked spinach well. Combine spinach, onion soup mix, sour cream, and seasonings in large bowl. Pour into a 9x12 inch baking dish; top with cheese. Bake in 350° preheated oven for 35 minutes or until hot and bubbly. This may be refrigerated for several days before baking, if desired. Makes 8-10 servings.

HELEN JOHNSON   MT. OLIVE UNIT

BAKED SQUASH

3 pounds yellow summer
  squash
½ cup onion, chopped
½ cup cracker crumbs
2 eggs

1 stick butter or margarine
1 tablespoon sugar
1 teaspoon salt
½ teaspoon pepper

Wash and cut up squash. Boil until tender, drain thoroughly, then mash. Add all ingredients to squash, except use only ½ the butter. Melt the remaining half of the butter. Pour the squash mixture into a 9x13 inch baking dish, top with melted butter. Sprinkle with more cracker crumbs or bread crumbs. Bake at 375° for 1 hour until lightly browned.

JOSEPHINE BAIMA   GET TOGETHERS UNIT

BAKED SQUASH WITH SAUSAGE AND APPLES

2 acorn squash
Salt
1½ cups apples, finely diced

¾ cup sausage, cooked and
  crumbled

Halve acorn squash crosswise; remove seeds; salt. Turn upside down in shallow pan. Add water to depth of ½ inch. Bake at 375° for 45 minutes or until tender. Combine apples and sausage. Fill squash halves, return to oven, and bake an additional 35 minutes. Serve with rolls, jam, and coffee. Makes 4 servings.

MRS. LILLIAN VANFOSSEN   DO MORE UNIT

SQUASH CASSEROLE

1½ pounds yellow squash, sliced
1 medium carrot, sliced
1 medium onion, sliced
3 cups Pepperidge Farm stuffing

3 tablespoons margarine
8 ounces sour cream
1 can cream of chicken soup
1 small jar pimiento

Cook squash, carrot, and onion until just tender; drain. Do not overcook. Saute stuffing with margarine. Place half of this mixture in greased 2½ quart casserole. Put vegetables over crumbs. Combine sour cream, soup, and pimento. Pour over vegetables. Put remaining half of crumb mixture over top. Bake at 350° for 30 to 45 minutes until bubbly. Makes 8 servings.

SYLVIA MAE FRITZ   PIASA UNIT

SPINACH CASSEROLE

1 stick margarine
¼ cup flour
4 eggs, beaten
1 large carton cottage cheese

¼ cup shredded Cheddar cheese (some for top)
2 boxes frozen chopped spinach, cooked and drained

Melt margarine. Blend in flour. Add beaten eggs, cottage cheese, and Cheddar cheese. Mix in spinach. Pour into 2 quart casserole. Sprinkle a small amount of shredded Cheddar cheese on top. Bake at 325° for 45 minutes. Makes 8 servings.

HELEN (NELLIE) FISHER   BERTHA ELDRED UNIT

SPAGHETTI WITH SPINACH SAUCE

1 clove garlic, minced
¼ cup butter
½ cup oil
1 package frozen chopped spinach

1 onion, chopped
1 package spaghetti
¼ to ½ cup grated Parmesan cheese

Saute garlic and onion in butter and oil until tender. Cook spinach according to package directions and add onion mixture. Cook slowly, covered, for 15 minutes. Boil spaghetti according to directions. Drain and add spaghetti to spinach sauce with the grated cheese.

MADELINE SARACCO   GET TOGETHERS UNIT

SPINACH SOUFFLE

1 package spinach, chopped
3 eggs, beat until light
3 tablespoons flour

¼ pound Velveeta cheese, diced
½ stick margarine, softened

Heat spinach in water until thawed; drain. Combine eggs, flour, cheese, butter, and spinach; pour into casserole. Bake at 350° for 30 to 40 minutes or until brown.

CLARA FUESS   BERTHA ELDRED UNIT

VEGETABLE CASSEROLE

1 can peas, drained
1 can asparagus, drained
1 can water chestnuts,
   drained and sliced

1 can cream of mushroom soup
1 cup shredded Cheddar cheese
2 cups croutons
1 stick margarine, melted

Layer vegetables in greased 2 quart casserole. Spread soup over top, sprinkle on cheese. Stir the croutons into the melted butter. Sprinkle over top of casserole. Bake at 350° for 30 minutes.

MRS. LOUIS GRANDONE   GET TOGETHERS UNIT

VEGETABLES A LA DELICIOUS

1 can green beans, drained
1 can wax beans, drained
2 cups tomatoes and juice
½ cup purple onion, sliced
1½ cups carrot strips
   2 inches long
2 cups celery strips
   2 inches long

¾ cup green pepper strips
4 tablespoons butter
1½ tablespoons sugar
3 tablespoons Minute tapioca
⅛ teaspoon pepper
2½ teaspoons salt

Mix all the ingredients together well and pour into greased 3 quart casserole. Bake, covered, at 350° for 2 hours . Makes 8 servings.

NANCY COLE   STITCH AND STIR UNIT

VEGETABLE CASSEROLE

1 can mushroom soup
½ stick butter
1 1-pound can tiny peas
1 3½-ounce can sliced
  mushrooms

1 can cut asparagus
1 5-ounce can sliced water
  chestnuts
Grated cheese or bread crumbs

Heat soup with butter. Drain vegetables. Toss lightly in a 1½ quart casserole dish. Pour soup over the vegetables. Top with cheese and/or crumbs. Bake at 350° for 15 minutes until cheese melts and browns slightly. Makes 8-10 servings.

MAXINE RATTERMAN   HONEY POINT UNIT

ZUCCHINI CASSEROLE

¼ cup margarine, melted
3 cups bread cubes
4 cups zucchini, sliced thin
1 medium onion, sliced
3 tomatoes, sliced

1 ½-pound package American
  cheese
½ teaspoon salt
½ teaspoon pepper

Pour melted margarine over bread cubes, mix thoroughly. Grease 1½ quart casserole and alternate layers of zucchini, onion, tomatoes, cheese, and bread cubes. Season. Repeat process ending with bread cubes. Cover, bake 1 hour and 15 minutes at 350°.

MRS. KATHY (LOREN) FILE   JUNIOR HOMEMAKERS UNIT

STUFFED ZUCCHINI

4 zucchini, ½ pound each
1 small onion, minced
1 pound ground beef
4 thin slices bread, crumbed

Several sprigs parsley, minced
¾ teaspoon salt
⅛ teaspoon pepper
½ cup grated Cheddar cheese

Cover zucchini, boil 8 minutes. Cut in half lengthwise. Scoop out flesh, leaving shells ¼ inch thick. Turn shells flesh side down to drain. Drain pulp and cut up fine. Brown onion and beef. Drain well. Stir in pulp, half of the bread crumbs, parsley, salt, and pepper. Pile into shells. In small dish mix remaining crumbs and cheese. Sprinkle over meat. Bake in shallow pan at 350° for 25 minutes or until brown. Makes 4 servings.

CATHERN BEST   PLAINVIEW UNIT

BREADS

An old flouring mill built in 1854 provided flour, meal and livestock feed for Scottville community until 1908. A familiar landmark for more than a century, it survived time and the elements until the summer of 1978 when at last it succumbed to the wrecking bar and bulldozer.

"THE OLD MILL" is now only a fond memory.

Photographed by Frank Thomas

ANGEL BISCUITS

6 cups flour
¾ cup oil
1 teaspoon baking soda
1 teaspoon baking powder
1 teaspoon salt

3 tablespoons sugar
1 package yeast
½ cup warm water
2 cups buttermilk

Dissolve yeast in the warm water. Mix all ingredients together and put in a large greased bowl, covered, in the refrigerator. Let set overnight. Keeps a week or longer. These biscuits do not need to rise. Take a small amount, roll, and cut like biscuits. Bake at 350° for 10-12 minutes on cookies sheet. Makes 35-40 biscuits.

MRS. CHARLES THURSBY   BARR UNIT

MAGIC BISCUITS

2 packages dry yeast
¼ cup warm water
5 cups flour
1 teaspoon baking soda
1 teaspoon salt

4 teaspoons baking powder
4 tablespoons sugar
1 cup shortening
2 cups buttermilk

Dissolve yeast in warm water. Sift flour, soda, salt, baking powder, and sugar together. Cut in shortening with pastry blender. Add yeast mixture and buttermilk to dry mixture. Mix to stiff dough. Knead on floured board or table. Pinch off biscuits or roll and cut out. Allow to rise 10 minutes. Bake at 425° for 15 minutes. Makes 25-30 biscuits. The dough can be stored several days in the refrigerator and made into biscuits as desired, allowed to rise 15-20 minutes before baking. For even greater convenience, the dough can be rolled, cut, placed on baking sheets, and frozen. The frozen biscuits can be stored several weeks in a tight, waterproof container. If the frozen biscuits are placed in the oven as soon as it is turned on, they will thaw and rise as the oven heats.

LINDA LAMBETH   PIASA UNIT

NASHVILLE HOUSE FRIED BISCUITS

2⅔ packages or 1/6 cup dry
  yeast
2 cups warm water
1 quart milk

¼ cup sugar
½ cup lard or shortening
6 teaspoons salt
7-9 cups flour

Add yeast to ⅔ cup warm water. Add other ingredients and let dough rise. Work into biscuits and drop into hot fat. The fat should be slightly hotter than 350°. If fat should be too hot, the biscuits will be soggy in the centers. They may be frozen individually and stored in plastic bags. When you work them up, don't let the biscuits rise too high.

DORMA L. CLOSE   SCOTTVILLE UNIT

OATMEAL DROP DOUGHNUTS

1 cup sugar
1 cup quick oatmeal
2¼ cups flour
1 teaspoon cinnamon
½ teaspoon salt
¼ teaspoon nutmeg

2 teaspoons baking powder
2 eggs, beaten
1 cup sweet milk
1 teaspoon vanilla
1 teaspoon lemon extract

Mix first 7 ingredients. Add remaining ingredients. Mix well. This makes a stiff batter. Drop by teaspoon into hot oil heated to 375°. Fry for 3 to 4 minutes. Makes 5 dozen.

MRS. CHARLES HOHM, SR.   BARR UNIT

QUICK YEAST DOUGHNUTS

½ cup boiling water
2 tablespoons shortening
⅓ cup sugar
¾ teaspoon salt
½ cup rich milk or Half and
  Half

1 teaspoon vanilla
1 yeast cake or 1 package dry
  yeast
¼ cup lukewarm water
1 egg, beaten
3¼ cups flour

Pour boiling water over shortening, sugar and salt. Add milk, vanilla, and a little nutmeg. Cool until lukewarm. Soften yeast in lukewarm water and add to the above. Stir in beaten egg and 2 cups flour. Beat hard then add remaining flour. Place in greased bowl and cover and put in refrigerator overnight or several hours. Roll out ½-inch thick and fry in hot grease. Do not let rise.

MRS. WAYNE (NEFFA) OVERBEY   MODELITE UNIT

BAKED DOUGHNUTS

5 tablespoons margarine
½ cup sugar
1 egg
1½ cups flour
2¼ teaspoons baking powder
¼ teaspoon nutmeg

1 teaspoon salt
½ cup milk
1 teaspoon vanilla
1 tablespoon sugar
1 teaspoon cinnamon

Cream margarine and ½ cup sugar; add egg and mix well. Sift flour, baking powder, nutmeg, and salt. Add to creamed mixture alternately with milk and vanilla. Generously grease muffin tins; fill ½ full. Top with mixture of 1 tablespoon sugar and cinnamon. Bake at 350° for 20 to 25 minutes. Makes 12.

WILMA WARGO   GET TOGETHERS UNIT

BEER BREAD

3 cups self-rising flour
4 tablespoons sugar
1 teaspoon salt

1 can beer
½ stick margarine

Sift dry ingredients together into bowl. Stir in beer and mix well. Pour into greased 9¼ x 5¼ x 2¾-inch loaf pan. Melt margarine and pour over dough before baking. Bake at 350° for 45 minutes. Remove from pan and cool on rack. Makes 10 ¾-inch slices.

MRS. ZELMA L. TUCKER   BRIGHTON EARLY BIRDS UNIT

BRAN MUFFINS

2 cups boiling water
4 cups Nabisco 100% Bran
1 cup shortening (margarine
  or Crisco)
4 cups sugar (less, if desired)
4 eggs, beaten

2 cups Kellogg's All Bran
1 quart buttermilk
5 cups flour, sifted
5 teaspoons baking soda, level
½ teaspoon salt—more, if
  desired

Pour boiling water over Nabisco bran. Cream shortening and sugar. Add beaten eggs. Add Kellogg's All Bran and buttermilk. Don't stir too much. Add flour, soda, salt. Last, add the water and Bran mixture. Will keep in the refrigerator a long time. Don't stir, just dip out into muffin pan. Use as needed. Bake at 400° for 15 minutes. Makes 78 small muffins. They freeze well.

MRS. WILBUR KAHL   SHIPMAN UNIT

6 WEEKS BRAN MUFFINS

1 15-ounce box raisin bran
3 cups sugar
5 cups flour
5 teaspoons baking soda

2 teaspoons salt
1 cup melted shortening or oil
1 quart buttermilk
4 eggs, beaten

Mix together the raisin bran, sugar, flour, baking soda and salt in a large bowl or dishpan. Add the melted shortening or oil, buttermilk, and eggs and mix well. Store in covered container in the refrigerator and use as desired. Fill greased muffin tins ⅔ full and bake at 400° (lower heat for dark pans to prevent burning) for 15-20 minutes. Makes 5 dozen.

Mix keeps six weeks. Baked muffins can be frozen and reheated.

MRS. ALLEN COLE   BARR UNIT

REFRIGERATOR MUFFINS

1 cup boiling water
1 cup Bran Buds
1 cup sugar
½ cup shortening or
   margarine
2 eggs, beaten

2 cups buttermilk
2½ cups flour
2½ teaspoons baking soda
2½ teaspoons salt
2 cups All Bran

Mix the boiling water and Bran Buds together; let cool. Cream sugar and shortening. Add the eggs and buttermilk. Sift together the flour, baking soda and salt. Add to the above mixture. Add the Bran Bud mixture and the All Bran. Bake in muffin tins in a 400° oven for 15 to 20 minutes. Store in airtight container in refrigerator before baking. Will keep for 4 to 6 weeks. Raisins and/or nuts, dates, wheat germ, blueberries, etc. may be added if desired.

GEORGINA V. BLAIR   DO MORE UNIT

LOG CABIN OATMEAL PANCAKES

1 tablespoon melted butter
   or margarine
1 tablespoon brown sugar
1 egg, beaten

½ cup milk
¼ teaspoon salt
½ cup flour
1 cup rolled oats

Combine melted butter, sugar, egg, and milk. Add salt and flour. Add oats and any of the variation extras you like, or any others you can think of. Pour or spoon thick batter onto hot griddle. Fry until golden brown on both sides. Serve with butter and maple syrup.

Variations: chopped fresh apple, raisins, nuts, cinnamon, banana

MARY ANN HARP   SHAWS POINT UNIT

BANANA BREAD

½ cup oil
1 cup sugar
2 eggs, beaten
3 bananas, mashed
2 cups flour
1 teaspoon baking soda

½ teaspoon baking powder
½ teaspoon salt
½ teaspoon vanilla
3 tablespoons milk
½ cup nuts, chopped

Beat oil and sugar together. Add eggs and bananas; mix well. Add remaining ingredients except nuts and beat well. Add nuts. Line bottom of a 9 x 5 x 3-inch loaf pan with waxed paper or foil. Pour in mixture. Bake in 350° oven for about 1 hour. Cool well. Wrap in foil or airtight container.

LINDA GWILLIM   STITCH AND STIR UNIT

BANANA BREAD

1⅓ cups sugar
2 cups cake flour
¼ teaspoon salt
1 teaspoon baking powder
½ teaspoon baking soda
½ cup buttermilk

½ cup shortening
2 eggs, beaten
3 bananas, mashed
½ teaspoon vanilla
½ cup pecans, broken (optional)

Combine sugar, flour, salt and baking powder. Dissolve baking soda in buttermilk. Add milk to dry ingredients. Add shortening, eggs, bananas, and vanilla. Mix well. Stir in nuts. Pour into greased 9 x 5-inch loaf pan. Bake at 350° for 40 minutes. Makes 1 loaf.

SANDY ENGLAND   STITCH AND STIR UNIT

BANANA BREAD

2 cups sugar
1 cup shortening
6 ripe bananas, mashed
4 eggs, well beaten

2½ cups cake flour
1 teaspoon salt
2 teaspoons baking soda

Cream the sugar and shortening. Add bananas and eggs. Sift the flour, salt and baking soda together three times. Blend the wet and dry ingredients; it is important not to overmix. Pour batter into 2 loaf pans. Bake at 350° for 45-50 minutes. Makes 2 1-pound loaves.

GWEN BOEHME   MT. OLIVE UNIT

BANANA NUT BREAD

½ cup butter	1 cup bananas, mashed
1 cup sugar	1 teaspoon baking soda
2 eggs	1 tablespoon warm water
2 cups flour	½ cup nuts, chopped
3 tablespoons sour milk	

Cream butter and sugar. Add eggs and beat well. Add flour alternately with sour milk. Add mashed bananas. Dissolve soda in warm water, add to batter. Fold in the chopped nuts. Pour into a greased and floured 9 x 5 x 2½-inch loaf pan and bake at 350° for 1 hour. Cool on rack 10 minutes before removing from pan. Makes 16 ½-inch slices.

MRS. ZELMA L. TUCKER   BRIGHTON EARLY BIRDS UNIT

BUTTERMILK NUT BREAD

2 eggs	4 cups sifted flour
⅞ cup sugar	½ teaspoon salt
⅞ cup light brown sugar	1 teaspoon baking powder
2 tablespoons shortening	2 teaspoons baking soda
2 cups buttermilk	1 cup pecans, broken

Beat eggs, add sugars and shortening and beat well. Add buttermilk and stir well. Sift flour, salt, baking powder and baking soda. Add to the first mixture. Add nuts and stir just enough to dampen ingredients. Pour into two 9x5-inch loaf pans that are well greased and floured and lined on the bottom with waxed paper. Bake about 47 minutes at 350° for metal pans and at 325° for glass.

ROSE MARY HEMBROUGH   BIRD UNIT

COCONUT BREAD

2 cups flour	1½ cups coconut
3 teaspoons baking powder	1 egg, beaten
1 teaspoon salt	1½ cups milk
1 cup sugar	1 teaspoon vanilla

Stir all ingredients well. Do not beat. Pour into greased 9 x 5 x 3-inch loaf pan. Bake at 350° for 1 hour.

ELEANOR ROSS   BARR UNIT

BLUEBERRY BUCKLE (QUICK COFFEE CAKE)

¾ cup sugar
¼ cup shortening
1 egg
½ cup milk
2 cups sifted flour

2 teaspoons baking powder
½ teaspoon salt
2 cups canned blueberries,
   drained

Mix together thoroughly sugar, shortening and egg. Stir in milk. Sift together flour, baking powder, and salt; add to creamed mixture. Carefully stir in blueberries. Spread in greased and floured 9 x 9-inch pan. Sprinkle on topping Bake at 375° for 40 to 45 minutes or until toothpick comes out clean.

Topping:
½ cup sugar
⅓ cup sifted flour

½ teaspoon cinnamon
¼ cup butter

Mix ingredients together until crumbly.

COMMITTEE

COFFEE CAKE

4 cups sifted flour
¼ cup sugar
½ teaspoon salt
1 cup shortening

2 cakes yeast
1 cup milk
2 eggs, slightly beaten

Combine flour, sugar, salt and shortening as for pie crust. Dissolve yeast in milk, add eggs. Add yeast mixture to the flour mixture and stir until all flour is moistened. Cover and chill overnight. Divide dough into fourths. Roll out as for pie crust, brush with melted butter, and spread on Filling mixture. Fold sides to middle and ends. Put on greased cookie sheets. Cut almost through the dough. Let rise about 1 hour or until light. Bake at 350° for 20 to 25 minutes. Frost while warm with powdered sugar glaze.

Filling:
1 can Solo filling (prune,
   apricot, or date)

½ cup brown sugar
1 teaspoon cinnamon

Combine ingredients.

MARY E. HERIFORD   SCOTTVILLE UNIT

COFFEE CAKE OR ROLLS

1 yeast cake
½ cup lukewarm water
1 cup scalded milk
⅔ cup Crisco
½ cup sugar

1 teaspoon salt
1 cup mashed potatoes
2 eggs, well beaten
4½ cups flour

Dissolve yeast in lukewarm water. To the scalded milk add shortening, sugar, salt and potatoes. When cool add the yeast water, then the eggs. Add flour 1 cup or so at a time and beat hard. Knead well, put in 9 inch pie tins and grease the top. Makes 4-5 coffee cakes. Bake at 350° for 20-25 minutes. Each coffee cake serves 6 or 7. If you do not want to use at one time, the remainder will keep in the refrigerator one week or longer. Rolls are just as good.

ESTHER LAWRENCE   SPANISH NEEDLE UNIT

QUICK COFFEE CAKE

2 cups flour
2 teaspoons baking powder
¾ teaspoon salt
½ cup sugar

6 tablespoons butter
½ cup milk
1 egg

Sift together flour, baking powder, salt and sugar. Cut in butter until fine crumbs. Combine milk and egg and add to flour mixture. Stir well. Pour batter into 9 x 9-inch pan. Mix topping ingredients together and sprinkle over top of batter. Bake at 350° for about 30 minutes or until it tests done. Serves 12.

Topping:
1½ tablespoons melted
   butter
4 tablespoons sugar

1 tablespoon flour
1 teaspoon cinnamon

MRS. FRANCIS SKEEN   GIRARD DAY UNIT

COFFEE CAKE

½ cup shortening
¾ cup sugar
1 teaspoon vanilla
3 eggs

2 cups flour
1 teaspoon baking powder
1 teaspoon baking soda
½ pint sour cream

Cream shortening, sugar, vanilla and eggs. Add the dry ingredients alternately with the sour cream. Put half of the batter in a lightly greased 9x13 inch pan. Add half the topping, the remaining batter, and the rest of the topping. Bake in a 350° oven for 30 minutes or until it springs back when touched. Serve warm. Makes 12 servings.

Topping:
6 teaspoons butter, melted
1 cup brown sugar

2 teaspoons cinnamon
1 cup chopped nuts

EVELYN GATES   MODELITE UNIT

COFFEE CAKE

1 cup sugar
1 stick butter
2 eggs
1 cup sour cream
1 teaspoon vanilla

2 cups flour
1 teaspoon baking soda
1 teaspoon baking powder
Pinch of salt

Cream sugar and butter, add eggs, sour cream, vanilla, flour, soda, baking powder, and salt. Mix together; batter is very stiff.

Topping:
1 cup sugar
1 teaspoon cinnamon

½ cup nuts

Combine sugar, cinnamon and nuts. Pour half of the cake batter into a greased angel food cake pan, sprinkle with half of the topping mixture. Repeat with remaining batter and topping. Bake at 350° for 45 to 55 minutes. Makes 16 servings.

AGNES RAAB   CARLINVILLE NIGHT UNIT

COFFEE CAKE

4 cups sifted flour	2 cakes yeast
¼ cup sugar	1 cup milk
½ teaspoon salt	2 eggs, slightly beaten
1 cup shortening	

Combine flour, sugar, salt and shortening as for pie crust. Dissolve yeast in milk, add eggs. Add yeast mixture to the flour mixture and stir until all flour is moistened. Cover and chill overnight. Divide dough into fourths. Roll out as for pie crust, brush with melted butter, and spread on Filling mixture. Fold sides to middle and ends. Transfer to greased cookie sheets. With sharp knife, slit dough, being careful not to cut bottom. Let rise about 1 hour or until light. Bake at 350° for 20 to 25 minutes. Frost while warm with powdered sugar glaze.

Filling:

1 can Solo filling (prune, apricot, or date)	½ cup brown sugar
	1 teaspoon cinnamon

Combine ingredients.

MARY E. HERIFORD   SCOTTVILLE UNIT

SOUR CREAM COFFEE CAKE

2 cups sifted flour	1¼ cups sugar
1 teaspoon baking powder	2 eggs
½ teaspoon baking soda	1 cup sour cream
1 cup butter	1 teaspoon vanilla

Sift flour once, measure and add baking powder, baking soda, then sift again. Cream butter and sugar until fluffy. Add eggs, beat well. Add dry ingredients alternately with sour cream and vanilla. Mix well. Put half of batter in well greased and floured 13 x 9-inch pan.

Topping:

½ cup brown sugar	2 tablespoons cinnamon
1 cup nuts	

Mix topping ingredients together. Sprinkle half of the topping on batter in pan. Add remaining batter and sprinkle remaining topping on mixture. Pat lightly to hold topping in place. Bake at 350° for 40 minutes.

MARGARET LEBETER   MT. OLIVE UNIT

JEWISH COFFEE CAKE

1 box white cake mix
1 package instant vanilla
  pudding
½ cup salad oil

4 eggs
1 12-ounce carton sour cream
  (1½ cups)
2 teaspoons vanilla

Combine cake mix, vanilla pudding, oil, eggs, sour cream and vanilla. Beat at medium speed for 4 minutes.

Filling Ingredients:
¾ cup brown sugar
2 teaspoons sugar

¾ cup chopped nuts
2 teaspoons cinnamon

Mix filling ingredients together. Grease sides and bottom of angel food cake pan. Add in the following order: ⅓ batter, ⅓ filling, swirl slightly with table knife. Repeat two more times. Bake at 350° for 50-60 minutes. Cool in pan for at least one hour before removing. Freezes well and really is better the second day.

MRS. ELDON O. ARMOUR   SHAWS POINT UNIT

CINNAMON ROLLS

2 yeast cakes
1 pint warm water
6 eggs, beaten
1 cup butter or margarine,
  melted

1⅔ cups sugar
6 teaspoons salt
Flour

Dissolve yeast in warm water. Add remaining ingredients, adding enough flour to make a rather stiff dough. Work until smooth and elastic. Put in greased bowl and let rise until double in bulk. Work down, let rise again. Roll out dough, spread with butter and sprinkle with sugar-cinnamon mixture. Roll up jelly roll style. Cut in slices. Place slices in 2 9x13 inch pans. Let rise until double. Bake at 375° for about 20 minutes. Ice, if desired. Makes about 5 dozen.

MRS. LOIS KABURICK   HONEY POINT UNIT

CINNAMON LEAF RING

2 cups milk, scalded
2 packages active dry yeast
¾ cup shortening
¼ cup butter or margarine
½ cup sugar
2 teaspoons salt

4 egg yolks OR 2 eggs, beaten
6 cups flour, sifted before
   measuring
1 cup raisins, optional
1 cup nuts, optional

Cool milk to lukewarm (110°). Sprinkle yeast over top. Let stand to soften. Cream shortening and ¼ cup butter. Add ½ cup sugar and salt. Cream together until light and fluffy. Add egg yolks or 2 eggs, yeast mixture, raisins and nuts, and enough flour to make a soft dough. Knead until smooth and elastic on lightly floured board. Place in greased bowl. Cover, let rise until double (about 1 hour). Divide dough in half. Roll out dough to ¼-inch thickness. Cut into rounds with 2-inch biscuit cutter. Dip biscuits in melted butter or margarine (below).

1 cup melted butter or
   margarine

2 tablespoons cinnamon
2 cups sugar

Combine the cinnamon and sugar. Roll butter dipped biscuits in sugar mixture. Place on end into bundt pan which has been buttered. Let rise until double, about 30 minutes. This will also make 2 coffee cakes. Bake at 350° for 30 minutes.

CORA MATLACK   SHIPMAN UNIT

CINNAMON BREAD

¼ cup oil
1 cup sugar
1 egg
1 cup buttermilk

1 teaspoon baking soda
2 cups flour
¼ teaspoon salt

Mix well all ingredients. Place ½ of batter into greased 9 x 5 x 3-inch bread pan. Combine ½ cup sugar and 1 tablespoon cinnamon. Sprinkle half of this over batter in pan. Cover with remaining batter. Sprinkle remainder of sugar and cinnamon on top of batter. Swirl with knife. Bake at 375° for 45 minutes. Makes 16-18 servings.

MARGIE THOMAE   SHIPMAN UNIT

CORN BREAD

1 cup self-rising corn bread
  mix
½ cup oil
2 eggs

½ cup sour cream
½ cup milk
1 8-ounce can cream style corn

Beat eggs. Add the other ingredients. Mix well. Bake at 350° for 30 minutes or unit done in an 8 x 8 x 2-inch pan. Makes 9 servings.

NAOMI M. NEWBY   SHIPMAN UNIT

GOOEY BUTTER CAKE

1 Duncan Hines butter
  cake mix
2 eggs, slightly beaten
1 stick margarine, melted

2 eggs
1 box powdered sugar
1 8-ounce package cream
  cheese, softened

In a 9 x 13-inch pan, mix dry cake mix, the slightly beaten eggs, and margarine. In mixer bowl combine the second 2 eggs, powdered sugar, and cream cheese. Spoon this mixture into pan over cake mixture. Bake at 350° for 35 minutes. Serves 8-10.

IMOGENE THEOBALD   GILLESPIE NITE UNIT

GRAPE NUTS BREAD

1 cup Grape Nuts cereal
2 cups sour milk or
  buttermilk
1 egg, unbeaten
¾ cup sugar
3 tablespoons melted
  shortening

3¼ cups flour
4 teaspoons baking powder
1 teaspoon baking soda
1½ teaspoons salt

Combine Grape Nuts cereal and sour milk and let stand 15 minutes. Beat egg and sugar together thoroughly, then add to Grape Nuts mixture. Add shortening and mix well. Sift together the flour, baking powder, baking soda, and salt. Add to Grape Nuts mixture and beat until batter is smooth. (This will be a very stiff batter.) (This is a good place to use your mixer "dough hooks.") Turn into two well greased loaf pans 8 x 4 x 3-inches. Let stand 45 minutes. Bake at 350° for 1 hour or until done. Makes 2 loaves.

AURELA WEIDNER   BERTHA ELDRED UNIT

CHOCOLATE CHERRY BREAD

2 packages active dry yeast	2 eggs
¼ cup warm water	Melted butter or margarine
½ cup sugar	1½ cups (4-ounce bar) sweet
¼ cup shortening or oil	cooking chocolate, finely
2 teaspoons salt	shaved
1 cup milk, scalded	¾ cup maraschino cherries,
5 cups flour, sifted	drained and finely chopped

Soften yeast in water. Measure sugar, shortening, and salt into large bowl. Add hot milk, stirring until sugar is dissolved and shortening is melted. Cool to lukewarm. Stir in about 1½ cups flour and beat well. Beat in yeast and eggs. Stir in enough more flour to make a soft dough. Turn out onto lightly floured surface and knead until smooth and satiny, 5 to 8 minutes. Shape into ball and put in lightly greased bowl, turning greased side up. Cover and let rise in warm place until doubled, about 1½ hours. Punch down. Divide dough in half and shape into smooth balls. Cover and let rest 10 minutes. Roll out one ball of dough to 16 x 8-inch rectangle. Brush with butter. Sprinkle ¾ cup chocolate evenly over dough. Then sprinkle with 6 table-spoons cherries. Starting at narrow end, roll up tightly jelly roll fashion just to center of rectangle. Roll up other end similarly to center, pushing 2 rolls together slightly to form a scroll. Place in greased 9 x 5 x 3-inch loaf pan, flat side down. Repeat with other ball of dough. Brush tops with butter and let rise in warm place until doubled, about 45 minutes. Bake at 350° for about 35 minutes or until golden. Remove loaves from pans. Brush with butter. Cool. Makes 2 loaves.

MRS WILLIAM GENETTI   NILWOOD UNIT

PICCA (Potato Bread)

1 package dry yeast	1 pint potatoes, grated
2½ tablespoons sugar	2 eggs
2 tablespoons salt	1 tablespoon salt
3 pints lukewarm water	

Combine first four ingredients; thicken with flour and let rise to double. Add potatoes, eggs and salt. Thicken with flour until not sticky. Put in 11 x 17 x 2-inch pan and let rise to double. Bake at 350° for 35 to 40 minutes. Cool and slice. May be used fried the next day. Recipe may be divided in half using 9 x 14-inch pans.

EVELYN L. NIEHAUS   MT. OLIVE UNIT

LEMON BREAD

⅓ cup butter, melted
1 cup sugar
2 eggs
¼ teaspoon almond extract
1½ cups flour
1 teaspoon baking powder

1 teaspoon salt
½ cup milk
1 tablespoon lemon peel, grated
½ cup nuts, chopped
3 tablespoons fresh lemon juice
¼ cup sugar

Blend butter and sugar well. Beat in eggs one at a time. Add extract. Sift flour, baking powder, and salt together. Add dry ingredients to egg mixture alternately with milk. IMPORTANT: Blend just to mix. Fold in peel and nuts. Pour into greased loaf pan. Bake at 325° for 60 to 70 minutes. Remove from oven. Mix lemon juice and sugar. Spoon over hot loaf in pan. Cool 10 minutes. Remove from pan and cool on rack. Wrap. Do not serve for 24 hours. Freezes well.
ELOISE ECCHER   STAUNTON UNIT

ORANGE SLICE BREAD

1 cup hot coffee
2 cups orange slices (candy),
   diced
1 cup dates, diced
1 stick margarine
1 cup sugar

2 eggs
4 cups flour
1 cup buttermilk
1 teaspoon baking soda
1 teaspoon salt
1 teaspoon vanilla

Pour hot coffee over orange slices and dates. Let cool. Cream together margarine, sugar and eggs. Add flour, buttermilk, soda, salt, and vanilla to creamed mixture. Add the orange slices and dates mixture. Pour into greased and floured pans and bake at 325° for 50 minutes. Makes 7 small pans.

LUCILLE MAHAN   BARR UNIT

MRS. WILLIAM KESSINGER, BIRD UNIT uses 2 cups sugar, 2 sticks margarine, and 1 cups nuts in her recipe.

PITA BREAD (GREEK)

1¼ cups warm water
1 package yeast
¼ teaspoon sugar

3 cups flour
1 teaspoon salt
2 tablespoons olive oil

Place ¼ cup water in small bowl, add yeast and sugar, stir to blend. Let stand until dissolved. Place the flour, salt, and oil in medium size bowl. Add yeast mixture and remaining 1 cup water. Beat well. Turn out onto floured surface and knead 5 to 10 minutes. Place in clean bowl, oil top, cover with towel, and let rise about 1½ hours. Turn out and knead lightly. Roll into a log 8 inches long and cut into 8 pieces. With rolling pin, roll each piece into a round 6½ inches in diameter. Place each round on 6½-inch round of aluminum foil. Let stand, uncovered, for 1 hour. Place oven rack at lowest position. Place four rounds at a time, still on foil, directly on oven rack. Bake until puffed and just starting to brown at 500° for 5 to 7 minutes. Remove and cool on racks. Makes 8 servings. Breads may be served flat and buttered or wrapped around meat mixture taco fashion.

PAT GERECKE   MT. OLIVE UNIT

PUMPKIN BREAD

⅔ cup shortening
2⅓ cups sugar
4 eggs
1 16-ounce can pumpkin
⅔ cup water
3⅓ cups flour
2 teaspoons baking soda

1½ teaspoons salt
½ teaspoon baking powder
1 teaspoon ground cinnamon
1 teaspoon ground cloves
⅔ cup nuts, coarsely chopped
⅔ cup raisins

Heat oven to 350°. Grease bottoms only of 2 9 x 5 x 3-inch loaf pans. Mix shortening and sugar in large bowl. Add eggs, pumpkin, and water. Blend in flour, baking soda, salt, baking powder, cinnamon and cloves. Stir in nuts and raisins. Pour into pans. Bake until wooden pick inserted in center comes out clean, about 70 minutes. Cool slightly. Loosen sides of loaves from pans, remove from pans. Cool completely before slicing. To store, wrap and refrigerate no longer than 10 days.

MRS. LYLE (CLARA) YOUNG   SPANISH NEEDLE UNIT

ZUCCHINI BREAD

3 eggs
1¾ cups sugar
1 cup oil
1 tablespoon vanilla
2 cups raw, unpeeled ground
  zucchini
1 tablespoon orange peel,
  grated

3 cups flour
1 teaspoon salt
1 teaspoon baking soda
¼ teaspoon baking powder
2 teaspoons cinnamon
½ cup nuts, chopped

Beat eggs until light and fluffy, add sugar, and beat well. Stir in oil, vanilla, raw unpeeled ground zucchini squash, and grated orange peel. Sift flour, salt, soda, baking powder, and cinnamon together. Add to zucchini mixture. Add the chopped nuts. Grease or oil 2 8½ x 4½-inch pans and line with waxed paper or grease and flour Teflon pans. Bake at 325° for 50 to 60 minutes. This freezes well.

MRS. LEO LOTT   SUSTAINING MEMBER

ALICE KULENKAMP, GILLESPIE NIGHT UNIT uses 2 cups sugar, 3 teaspoons cinnamon, and ¼ cup nuts. She omits the orange peel.

POVATICA (NUT ROLL)

1 cup sour cream
3 tablespoons butter
5 tablespoons sugar
⅛ teaspoon baking soda

1½ teaspoons salt
2 eggs
1 cake yeast
3 cups flour

Bring sour cream to a boil in a large saucepan. Remove from heat. Stir in butter, sugar, baking soda, and salt until blended. Cool to lukewarm. Add eggs, yeast which has been crumbled, and stir until yeast is dissolved. Mix the flour in with wooden spoon. Turn out on lightly floured board or cloth and knead lightly a few minutes to form a soft ball. Cover and let stand 5 minutes. Divide dough into 3 equal parts. Roll each out ¼-inch thick and spread with Filling. Roll up like a jelly roll and lay in greased pan. Cover with cloth and let rise 1½ hours. Bake at 350° about 35 minutes or until done. Makes 3 rolls.

Filling:
1 pound walnuts, ground
1 cup milk

1 cup sugar
1 stick butter

Stir together all ingredients. Cook until thick. Cool before spreading on dough.

HELEN TIBURZI   GET TOGETHERS UNIT

PARKER HOUSE ROLLS

1 package yeast, dry or fresh　　3 tablespoons sugar
¼ cup lukewarm water　　　　　1 teaspoon salt
1 cup milk　　　　　　　　　　1 egg, beaten
3 tablespoons margarine　　　　3½ cups flour, sifted

Start three hours before time to serve. Dissolve yeast in water. Heat milk with margarine, sugar, and salt. Do not boil. Cool to lukewarm. Add egg, mix well. Add yeast mixture to flour and mix well. Let rise until double in bulk. Knead on floured board and roll out about ½-inch thick. Cut with a 2 or 3-inch cutter. Put just a bit of margarine in center of roll and fold over. Place on cookie sheet. Let rise again. Bake at 400° for 10-15 minutes.
MILDRED L. REDFERN　CARLINVILLE NIGHT UNIT

PARKER HOUSE ROLLS

6 to 6½ cups flour　　　　　　1 cup margarine, softened
⅓ cup sugar　　　　　　　　　2 cups hot tap water
2 to 3 teaspoons salt　　　　　1 egg
2 packages dry yeast

Combine in large bowl 2¼ cups flour, sugar, salt and yeast. Add ½ cup margarine. Mix at low speed. Gradually pour 2 cups hot tap water into dry ingredients. Add egg. Beat at moderate speed 2 minutes. Beat in ¾ cup flour or enough to make a thick batter. Continue beating for 2 minutes. Add additional flour, approximately 2¼ cups. Turn dough onto floured board and knead until smooth and elastic. Let rise until double in size. Punch down again. Roll out dough ½-inch thick. Cut into 2 ¾-inch circles. Spread with remaining melted butter. Fold over in half and seal edges. Bake at 425° for 18 to 20 minutes. Makes 4 dozen.
LAVERNA M. CAVENY　MEDORA UNIT

SWEET ROLLS

1 package frozen Parker　　　　1 stick margarine, melted
　House rolls　　　　　　　　　1 teaspoon cinnamon
1 box vanilla pudding (not　　　½ cup nuts, chopped
　instant)　　　　　　　　　　1 cup brown sugar

Grease large angel food pan, with solid bottom, generously. Cover with frozen rolls, which have been thawing. Sprinkle dry pudding over dough; pour on melted butter. Mix cinnamon, nuts, and brown sugar. Sprinkle over dough. Cover; let stand overnight at room temperature. In the morning, bake at 350° for 45 minutes until brown; do not under bake. Let set about 10 minutes then turn out onto plate. Makes about 16 servings.
PEARL STAREK　BERTHA ELDRED UNIT

CRESCENT ROLLS

1 cake or package yeast	1 cup hot water
3 tablespoons warm water	2 eggs, beaten
½ cup shortening	1 cup sugar
1 teaspoon salt	4 cups flour

Dissolve 1 cake or package of yeast in 3 tablespoons warm water. Set aside. Add ½ cup shortening and 1 teaspoon salt to 1 cup hot water. Let cool until lukewarm. Beat 2 eggs, add ½ cup sugar. Add to water mixture. Add yeast and stir in 2 cups flour. Beat well. Add 2 more cups flour gradually, cover and place in refrigerator overnight. Three hours before serving, roll cold dough out and cut in triangle shapes. Spread with soft butter. Roll up wedges starting at larger end. Let rise 3 hours to desired size. Bake at 425° for 10-12 minutes. Makes 2 dozen.

MRS. CHARLES HOHM, SR.   BARR UNIT

HONEY ROLLS

¼ cup butter	2 packages yeast, dissolved in
½ cup sugar	¼ cup warm water
½ teaspoon salt	2 eggs, beaten
1 cup milk, scalded	4 to 5 cups flour

Combine butter, sugar, salt, and milk in mixing bowl and mix well. Cool to lukewarm. Add yeast that has been dissolved in the warm water and the eggs. Mix well again. Gradually add flour and be sure the mixture is well blended. Turn onto lightly floured board Knead until smooth and elastic, about 8 minutes. Place dough in greased bowl, turning upside down to grease the top. Cover, let rise in warm place until double. Punch down, place on board and roll out thin. Spread with melted butter. Roll and slice crosswise (½ to ¾-inch thick). Put in greased pan, let rise until double in size.

Topping:

⅓ cup butter	1 egg white, beaten stiff
2 teaspoons warm honey	Chopped nuts, if desired

Mix topping ingredients together and sprinkle over rolls in pan. Bake at 375° for 15 to 20 minutes. Turn oven up to 400° for the last five minutes or so for browning. Makes about 24 rolls.

CLEE W. MOORE   CARLINVILLE DAY UNIT

ICE BOX ROLLS

1 package dry yeast
½ cup potato water,
  lukewarm
1 cup milk, scalded
1½ cups sugar
⅔ cup shortening or
  margarine

1 teaspoon salt
2 eggs, well beaten
1 cup mashed potatoes
5½ to 6 cups flour

Dissolve yeast in the lukewarm potato water. Scald the milk. Stir in sugar, shortening, and salt. Cool. Add eggs. Add mashed potatoes and yeast mixture. Stir in one cup of flour and beat with electric mixer or with a spoon until batter is smooth. Gradually add enough remaining flour to make a fairly stiff dough. Turn onto lightly floured surface and knead 8 to 10 minutes. Place in a greased bowl. Turn over to grease top. Cover and place in refrigerator overnight. Shape dough into balls and place one inch apart in a greased pan. Brush tops with melted butter or margarine. Let rise until double, about one hour. Bake at 350° for 40 to 50 minutes for bread; 375° for 20 minutes for rolls. Remove from pans; cool on racks. This dough will rise some in the refrigerator and will keep for several days. Makes 40 rolls or 2 loaves of bread.

MRS. LEOLA KAMPER   BRIGHTON EARLY BIRDS UNIT

EASY STRUDEL

1 cup flour
1 teaspoon salt
¼ cup butter or margarine

1 egg yolk
¼ cup cold water
Powdered sugar

Prepare flour, salt, and butter as for pastry; add yolk mixed with the water. Mix well. Flour a cloth and roll dough until paper thin. Mix filling and spread on ⅔ of the dough. Having cookie sheet right next to the dough, start rolling the dough so the strudel rolls right onto the greased cookie sheet. Brush strudel with butter and bake at 425° for 20 minutes, then at 375° for 45 minutes. Sprinkle with powdered sugar when cool.

Filling:
8 apples, sliced thin
¼ cup nuts, chopped
½ cup raisins
1 cup sugar

Cinnamon
⅔ cup bread crumbs
2 tablespoons butter

Mix the apples, nuts, raisins, and sugar, adding more sugar if apples are very tart. Add cinnamon to taste. Brown bread crumbs in butter. Add to apples and mix filling ingredients thoroughly. Spread on rolled dough.
VLASTA KING   MOUNT OLIVE UNIT

YUGOSLAV (POTECA) POVITICA NUT ROLL

5 cups flour, sifted
1 cup milk
1 cup sugar
¼ pound soft butter
3 tablespoons oil
3 egg yolks, beaten

3 yeast cakes
1 teaspoon salt
¼ cup warm water
2 teaspoons vanilla

Crush yeast into the lukewarm water and put aside to rise. Bring milk to boil and add sugar, butter, oil, salt, and vanilla. Add beaten egg yolks. In large bowl sift flour. Add yeast to milk mixture and gradually add to flour, stirring well. Work slightly in bowl and then place on floured board and continue working until completely smooth. Put back into mixing bowl, cover, and place in warm spot to rise until double in bulk. Divide dough in half. Roll dough out until ¼-inch in thickness. Spread with ½ of the filling and roll as for jelly roll, using a cloth to aid in rolling. Bake in well greased shallow pan at 300° for 1 hour. Makes 2 loaves.

Filling:
1 cup milk
2 cups walnuts, ground
½ cup sugar

Juice and rind of one lemon
Pinch of salt
½ cup honey

Bring milk to a boil. Add the rest of the ingredients. Simmer 5 minutes. Cool completely.

OLGA TRAGOVICH   GET TOGETHERS UNIT

EASY REFRIGERATOR ROLLS

2 packages active dry yeast
  (not compressed)
2 cups water or potato water
  110° to 115°
½ cup sugar

2 teaspoons salt
6½ to 7 cups flour
1 egg
¼ cup shortening, softened

Dissolve yeast in water in mixing bowl. Add sugar, salt, and about ½ the flour. Beat thoroughly 2 minutes. Add egg, shortening, and beat in gradually the remaining flour until smooth. Knead 6 minutes. Cover with damp cloth; place in refrigerator. Punch down occasionally. Two hours before baking, cut off amount needed. Return remaining dough to refrigerator. Shape into rolls, place on greased baking sheet or 8 x 8-inch pan, brush with melted butter, and let rise until light (about 2 hours). Bake at 400° for about 20 minutes. Makes 32 medium-size rolls.

CLARA FUESS   BERTHA ELDRED UNIT

ORANGE ROLLS

1 envelope dry yeast
¼ cup warm water
¼ teaspoon sugar
¼ cup sugar
1 teaspoon salt
2 eggs

½ cup dairy sour cream
1 cup butter, melted, divided half
3½ cups flour
¾ cup sugar
2 tablespoons grated orange rind

Dissolve yeast in warm water in large mixing bowl with ¼ teaspoon sugar. Let mixture stand for 2 to 3 minutes, then stir to dissolve yeast completely. Set bowl aside for about 5 minutes or until mixture almost doubles in volume. Beat in ¼ cup sugar, salt, eggs, sour cream, and 6 tablespoons melted butter. Gradually add flour, 2 cups at a time, beating well after each addition. Knead remaining flour into dough. Cover and let rise in warm place until double in bulk, about 2 hours. Punch down dough, knead on floured board about 15 times. Divide dough in half; roll into 12 inch circles. Combine ¾ cup sugar and grated orange rind. Brush dough with 1 tablespoon melted butter and sprinkle with half the orange rind-sugar mixture. Cut into 12 wedges and roll up into crescent shape. Repeat with second half of dough. Place rolls, point side down, in buttered 12 x 9-in pan. Cover and let rise until doubled, about 1 hour. Bake at 350° for 20 minutes or until golden brown. As soon as rolls are removed from oven, pour warm Glaze over top.

Glaze:

¾ cup sugar
½ cup dairy sour cream

2 tablespoons frozen orange
    juice concentrate, thawed
¼ cup butter

Combine ingredients, bring to a boil, and boil 3 minutes, stirring constantly.
ELINOR WALLACE   GIRARD NIGHT UNIT

SURE SHOT ROLLS

¼ cup shortening
1 cup hot water
6 tablespoons sugar
½ teaspoon salt

1 package yeast
2 tablespoons warm water
1 egg, well beaten
3 to 3½ cups flour

Mix shortening, hot water, sugar and salt. Cool. Dissolve yeast in warm water. Add egg, yeast and flour to shortening mixture and mix well. Let rise 2½ hours. Roll to ¼ inch thickness and spread with melted butter. Cut into 3 or 4-inch squares and fold in half, sealing in melted butter. Let rise about 20 min. Bake at 375° for 20 minutes. Makes 18-24 rolls. This dough may be used for cinnamon rolls, crescents, or other shape rolls.

MRS. DARRELL (BETTY) MOLEN   JUNIOR HOMEMAKERS UNIT

NO KNEAD REFRIGERATOR ROLLS

1 cup boiling water
¾ cup sugar
¾ cup margarine
1¼ teaspoons salt
½ cup warm water

2 packages yeast
½ cup cold water
2 eggs, beaten
6 cups flour

In a large bowl using the electric mixer, combine the boiling water, sugar, margarine, and salt. Set aside until cool. Mix the warm water and yeast together in a small bowl. Add the cold water, eggs, and flour and yeast mixture to the mixture in the large bowl using mixer up to about 4 cups of flour. Mix in remaining flour with a large spoon. Cover with Saran Wrap and refrigerate at least 2 hours (but can stay up to a week). Make into desired number of rolls. Refrigerate remaining dough. Let rise 1 hour before baking. Bake at 350° about 20 minutes or until done. Makes 24-36 rolls.

BARBARA GREAVES   STITCH AND STIR UNIT

STICKY BUNS

¾ cup milk, scalded
2 tablespoons sugar
1 teaspoon salt
¼ cup corn oil
1 package yeast
¼ cup warm water
1 egg, well beaten
3½ cups flour, approximately

3 tablespoons margarine
¼ cup brown sugar, packed
½ cup pecan halves
3 tablespoons margarine
¼ cup brown sugar, packed
2 teaspoons cinnamon
½ cup dark corn syrup

Mix the milk, sugar, salt, and oil. Dissolve the yeast in the warm water. Add the egg. Stir in flour to make a stiff dough. Turn dough onto lightly floured board, knead until smooth and elastic. Place in greased bowl, turning greased top up. Cover; let rise until double. Punch down. Meanwhile spread 3 tablespoons margarine, ¼ cup brown sugar, and pecans in a 9 x 13-inch pan. Place dough on lightly floured surface. Roll into 12 x 11-inch rectangle, ¼-inch thick. Spread dough with 3 tablespoons margarine, ¼ cup brown sugar and cinnamon. Roll up beginning with long side. Cut roll into 1-inch slices and place in pan. Pour corn syrup over rolls. Cover and let rise again until doubled. Bake at 400° for 20 to 25 minutes. Turn out onto large plate immediately.

COMMITTEE

APPLE STRUDEL

2 cups flour
½ teaspoon salt
1 egg, beaten
3 tablespoons butter or
  margarine, melted
½ cup lukewarm water
¼ cup butter, melted
4 to 5 cups apples

½ cup fine bread crumbs
  browned in butter or margarine
1 cup golden raisins
¾ cup sugar
Dash of cinnamon
1 egg yolk, beaten
1 teaspoon milk

Place flour and salt into a bowl; make well in the center and put in egg and 3 tablespoons shortening. Stir, gradually adding water to make a soft dough. Work dough with fingers until it comes away from sides of bowl. Turn out onto bread board and knead about 10 minutes until dough is silky smooth. Form into ball, place in ungreased bowl, and cover tightly with aluminum foil to prevent a crust from forming. Let rest in a warm place for 2 hours or more. In the meantime, spread a clean tablecloth over kitchen table, dusting cloth with flour. Wash, peel, core, and thinly slice the apples. Set aside. When the dough is ready, place in center of floured cloth and pull apart about 18 inches in diameter. Spread dough with ¼ cup melted butter. Flour both hands. Reaching under dough with back of hands, start stretching dough carefully from the center toward the outside, walking around the table as necessary. Work gently or you'll puncture the dough. Stretch dough paper thin (about 30 x 48 inches.) Combine prepared apples with browned bread crumbs, raisins, sugar and cinnamon. Spread length of dough with filling up to about 12 inches from opposite end. Lift corners of cloth from end covered with filling and start to roll the dough, jelly roll fashion, by pulling the cloth upwards. Shape the strudel into a U-shape; then slide onto a well buttered baking sheet. Bake in 350° oven for 50 minutes. Brush strudel with glaze made of the egg yolk and milk. Bake 20 more minutes. Sprinkle with powdered sugar. Serve hot or cold.

MRS. LARRY SCHWANDNER   STAUNTON UNIT

COOL-RISE MAPLE PECAN RING

5½ to 6½ cups flour
½ cup sugar
1 teaspoon salt
2 packages dry active yeast

½ cup margarine, softened
1½ cups very hot tap water
2 eggs

In large mixing bowl, mix 2 cups flour, sugar, salt, and yeast. Add margarine. Gradually add hot water and beat 2 minutes at medium speed, scraping bowl occasionally. Add eggs and ½ cup flour or enough to make stiff batter. Beat at high speed 2 minutes. Stir in enough additional flour to make soft dough. Knead 8 to 10 minutes on lightly floured board. Cover with plastic wrap, then a towel. Let rest 20 minutes.

Filling:
¾ cup pecans, chopped
⅓ cup brown sugar, packed

1 teaspoon maple flavoring

Combine pecans, sugar, and flavoring. Set aside. Punch down dough. Divide in half. Roll dough into 16 x 8-inch rectangle. Brush with melted margarine and sprinkle with half the filling mixture. Starting with long edge, roll up dough; pinch to seal edge. Place sealed edge down in a circle on greased cookie sheet. Seal ends together firmly. Cut ⅔ way into ring with scissors at 1 inch intervals; turn each section on its side. Repeat with remaining dough and filling mixture. Brush rings with oil and cover loosely with plastic wrap. Refrigerate 2 to 24 hours. When ready to bake, remove from refrigerator, uncover, and let stand at room temperature for 10 minutes. Bake at 375° for 20 to 25 minutes or until done. Cool on wire racks. When cool, frost with favorite icing an sprinkle with additional pecans.

CATHY MALHAM   MONDAY NITERS UNIT

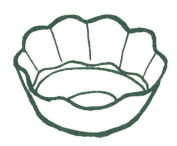

CROATIAN APPLE STRUDEL

4¼ cups sifted flour
1½ cups warm water
3 tablespoons oil

3 tablespoons soft butter
¾ teaspoon salt

Mix ingredients and knead on floured board until dough no longer sticks to hands. Do not use excess flour. Sprinkle flour over large tablecloth; divide dough into equal parts. Place one ball in middle of cloth; grease with a little oil. Put oil in other ball and set aside. Wait half hour before rolling out dough. Roll as for a pie, not too large. Wait another 20 minutes (a must). Now the dough will stretch easily. While dough is resting, peel, slice thinly or shred apples to make six cups. If dough dries out standing too long it will crack when rolled. Sprinkle melted butter and sugar over entire dough. Place apples over dough and roll as for a jelly roll. Place on greased cookie sheet. Using fork, poke holes in dough for steam to escape (prevents sogginess). Brush top with melted butter. Bake at 350°, 50 minutes or until golden brown.

HELEN TIBURZI   GET TOGETHERS UNIT

EASY WHOLE WHEAT BREAD

3 cups whole wheat flour
¼ cup sugar
1 tablespoon salt
2 packages yeast

2¼ cups milk
¼ cup oil
1 egg
3 to 4 cups white flour

Combine whole wheat flour, sugar, salt, and yeast in large mixing bowl. In saucepan, warm milk and oil to 120° to 130°. Add warm liquid and egg to flour mixture. Beat ½ minute at low speed, three minutes at medium speed. Then, by hand, gradually stir in 3 to 4 cups white flour. Knead on floured surface about one minute until smooth and elastic. Place dough in large greased bowl. Turn to grease all sides. Cover and let rise in warm place until double in size, about one hour. Punch down. Shape into two loaves. Place in 2 greased standard sized loaf pans. Cover and let rise in warm place until double, about one hour. Bake at 350° for 40-45 minutes or until loaf sounds hollow when lightly tapped. Turn out onto racks immediately. You may replace half the whole wheat flour with rye flour and add 1 tablespoon caraway seeds and ½ teaspoon fennel seed.

PAT GERECKE   MT. OLIVE UNIT

AN OLD RECIPE FOR LIGHT BREAD

2 packages yeast
3⅓ cups warm water
3½ tablespoons sugar
3½ teaspoons salt

3½ tablespoons shortening
1 cup (or more) of bran
8½ cups flour, more or less

Dissolve yeast in warm water. Stir in remaining ingredients working in flour last. Knead on pastry cloth until springy and not sticky. Round dough up and set into large greased bowl, turning greased side up. Let rise in a warm place until double in size. Punch down and knead again. Divide into loaves, place in greased pans. Use 3 3¾ x 7½ x 2¼-inch pans or 2 4½ x 8½ x 3-inch pans. Using pastry brush, grease loaf tops with shortening or margarine. Let rise again until double and dough is above tops of pans. Bake at 375° (350° for glass pans) for 10 minutes, then at 350° (325° for glass pans) until brown all over. Total time is about 50 minutes. Cool on racks. Using pastry brush, spread margarine on crust. Dough may also be shaped into rolls.

MARGARET SCHOFF   CARLINVILLE NIGHT UNIT

TENDER WHOLE WHEAT BREAD

2 cups milk
1 tablespoon salt
3 tablespoons sugar
4 tablespoons shortening

1½ packages Red Star yeast
⅓ cup warm water
2 cups whole wheat flour
3½ to 4 cups white flour

Heat milk, salt, sugar, and shortening until shortening melts. Cool to luke-warm. Add yeast to warm water, stir to dissolve. Sift whole wheat flour into milk mixture together with 1 cup of the white flour. Stir and add the yeast mixture. Beat two minutes by hand. Stir in the remainder of the flour until dough is easy to handle. Knead on lightly floured board for 10 minutes or until satiny. Let rise in a greased bowl until double (about one hour) in a warm place (80°). Turn onto a lightly floured board. Let rest a bit while greasing 2 9 x 5 x 3-inch loaf pans. Shape into two loaves. Return to warm place. Let rise until double again (about 1 hour). Bake at 350° for 40 minutes. If the tops start getting too brown, cover with aluminum foil for the last 20 minutes. Cool on a rack.

ROSEMARY GABRIEL   BUNKER HILL UNIT

SUGAR AND SPICE PUFFS

1 cup milk
¼ cup water
¼ cup dairy sour cream
3 tablespoons shortening or
  oil
3 to 3½ cups flour
1 cup rolled oats
¼ cup sugar

1¼ teaspoons salt
1 teaspoon orange or lemon
  peel, grated
1 package active dry yeast
1 egg
½ cup butter, melted
¾ cup sugar
2 teaspoons cinnamon

In saucepan, heat milk, water, sour cream, and oil until very warm, about 120 degrees. In large bowl, combine warm liquid, 1 cup of flour, oats, ¼ cup sugar, salt, orange peel, yeast and egg. Beat 2 minutes at medium speed. By hand, stir in remaining flour. On well floured surface, knead about 5 minutes. Dough will be soft and slightly sticky. Place in greased bowl. Cover; let rise in warm place until light and double in size, 45 to 60 minutes. Grease muffin cups. Punch dough down and divide into 24 pieces. Shape into balls and place in muffin cups. Cover and let rise until light and double in size, about 35 to 45 minutes. Bake in 375° oven for 15 to 20 minutes or until golden brown. Cool 5 minutes, then remove from pan. Roll warm rolls in butter, then in sugar-cinnamon mixture. Makes 24.

COMMITTEE

REFRIGERATOR ROLLS

2 packages dry yeast
2 cups warm water
½ cup sugar
2 teaspoons salt

6½ to 7 cups sifted flour
1 egg
¼ cup shortening, softened

Dissolve yeast in water in large mixing bowl. Add sugar, salt and about half of the flour, beat well about two minutes. Add egg and shortening, mix well. Mix in gradually the remaining flour, mix well. Cover with a damp cloth and place in refrigerator, punch down occasionally. About two hours before baking, cut off amount needed, return remaining dough to refrigerator. Shape into rolls, medium size, and place in greased 9 x 13 x 2-inch baking dish or pan. Let rise until light (1½ to 2 hours). Heat oven to 400°. Bake 12 to 15 minutes or until done. Makes 3 dozen.

BEATRICE BROWN   BERTHA ELDRED UNIT

YEAST NUT TORTE

1 package dry yeast
¼ cup lukewarm water
1 cup milk, scalded and
 cooled
1 cup butter, melted

3 egg yolks, slightly beaten
1 teaspoon salt
⅓ cup sugar
4 cups flour

Dissolve yeast in water. Mix milk, butter, egg yolks, salt, and sugar in large bowl. Add yeast mixture, then flour and beat thoroughly with spoon. Cover tightly with waxed paper and place in refrigerator overnight. Next day, roll out on floured pastry cloth into rectangle about 12 x 18 inches. Spread Filling on dough; roll up, starting with narrow edge, as you would a jelly roll. Place in a greased 10-inch tube pan. Pinch edges together to form the circle. Let rise in warm place about 45 minutes. Bake at 350° for 1 hour.

Filling:
1 cup sugar
3 egg whites

1 cup pecans, finely ground

Beat sugar gradually into egg white which have been beaten to a soft peak. Fold in nuts. Spread on dough. Note: Alternate method—Make Nut Bread by cutting dough in half after rolling into 12 x 18-inch rectangle. Spread half the filling on each half of dough and roll along length of dough. Place in prepared 9 x 5-inch pan, seam side down. Let rise 1 hour. Bake 45 minutes.

DORIS LACY   SUSTAINING MEMBER

HOT ROLL BUTTERCAKE

1 package Pillsbury Hot Roll Mix

Prepare hot roll mix according to package directions. Spread in 9 x 13-inch pan. Let rise, covered, about 30 to 35 minutes. Preheat oven 20 minutes. While dough is rising, prepare topping.

Topping:
3 sticks butter or margarine
2¼ cups sugar
2 large eggs

2 tablespoons white corn syrup
2 teaspoons vanilla

Cream butter and sugar. Add rest of ingredients and mix well. Spread on risen dough. Bake at 350° for 35 minutes. Makes 16 servings.

SUSY WOODS   MONDAY NITERS UNIT

JUST ENOUGH

I've dreamed many dreams that never came true
I watched them vanish with dawn
But I've had enough of my dreams come true
To make me want to dream on.

I've prayed many prayers when no answer came
Though I waited patient and long
But I've had answers to enough of my prayers
To make me want to pray on.

I've trusted some friends who have proven untrue
And left me to grieve alone
But I have enough of my friends true blue
To make me want to trust on.

I've sowed many seeds that fell by the way
For the birds to feed upon
But I've gathered enough golden sheaves in my arms
To make me want to sow on.

I've drained the cup of disappointment and grief.
And I've gone many days without song
But I've sipped enough nectar from the roses of life
To make me want to live on.

Author Unknown
Contributed by Mrs. A. D. Anderson

DESSERTS

Residents of Macoupin County are proud of their State Park. This photo shows the entrance to Beaver Dam State Park located seven miles southwest of Carlinville. The park was named after the lake which was originally built by beavers many years ago.

In 1947, the State of Illinois purchased 425 acres and converted it into the State Park.

Photographed by Jim Frank

APPLE CRISP

5 to 6 cups apples, pared and
   sliced
1 cup flour, sifted
1½ cups sugar
1 teaspoon baking powder

¾ teaspoon salt
1 egg
⅓ cup margarine, melted and
   cooled
½ teaspoon cinnamon

Place apples in an 8 x 12-inch baking dish. Mix next 5 ingredients with a fork until crumbly. Sprinkle over apples. Pour melted margarine over mixture. Sprinkle with cinnamon. Bake in 350° oven for 30 to 40 minutes. Makes 12 servings.

MARTHA SAUERWEIN   BUNKER HILL UNIT

MARIE W. PAYNTER, PIASA UNIT, uses 6 apples peeled and sliced, and adds ½ cup water and ½ cup sugar to the apples. She also uses 2 eggs, ¼ cup butter and ¼ teaspoon salt in the batter and bakes it at 375° for 40 minutes. Makes 6 servings.

APPLE CRISP DESSERT

½ cup butter, melted
½ cup flour
¾ cup oatmeal

¾ cup brown sugar
2 cups apples, thinly sliced

Mix first four ingredients. Peel and slice apples into bottom of 8 x 8 x 2-inch baking pan. Sprinkle crumb mixture over apples. Bake at 375° for 40 minutes or until apples are done. May be served plain or with whipped cream, cream, milk, or ice cream. Good, fast and easy. Makes 6 to 8 servings.

RUTH SHIELDS   MEDORA UNIT

CINNAMON APPLES

1½ cups sugar
¾ cup water
1 tablespoon red cinnamon
   candies

6 to 8 tart apples, peeled and in
   sections or whole

Boil sugar, water and cinnamon candies. Drop prepared apples into the syrup. Cook slowly until done, basting with the syrup.

Note: More or less cinnamon candies may be used for desired color.

ELIZABETH REDINGTON   HAGAMAN UNIT

APPLE PIZZA

2½ cups sifted flour
1 teaspoon salt
1 cup lard
1 egg yolk
⅔ cup milk
1 cup crushed corn flakes

8 to 10 apples, pared and sliced
  thin
1 cup sugar
1 teaspoon cinnamon
1 egg white, beaten

Measure flour and salt into bowl; add lard. Cut into flour as for pie dough. Beat egg yolk into milk and add to flour; mix. Be sure egg and milk are stirred in well. Divide dough in half. Roll one half out to fit into a 13-inch pizza pan, allowing dough to fit up edge of pan as for pie crust. Sprinkle crushed corn flakes over bottom. Add sliced apples until they are ½-inch thick; sprinkle cinnamon and sugar over apples.

Roll out other half of dough as a top crust. Crimp edges together and cut slits in top. Beat egg white until stiff (do not add sugar), and spread on top crust. Bake at 400° for 15 minutes; reduce heat to 350° and bake until apples are cooked. Ice with thin powdered sugar frosting.

DOLORES KLAUS   HONEY POINT UNIT

APPLE CAKE PUDDING

1 cup margarine
2 cups sugar
2 eggs
6 apples, diced
2 cups flour

2 teaspoons baking soda
¼ teaspoon salt
¾ teaspoon nutmeg
2 teaspoons cinnamon
1 cup nuts

Mix margarine, sugar and eggs together. Add apples. Sift together the flour, baking soda, salt, nutmeg, and cinnamon. Add flour mixture and nuts to apple mixture and mix well. Pour into greased and floured 9 x 13-inch pan. Bake at 375° for 40 minutes. Pour sauce over cake. Makes 12 servings.

Sauce:
½ cup brown sugar
½ cup sugar
½ cup coffee cream

1 teaspoon vanilla
1 teaspoon butter

Mix all ingredients together and bring to a boil, except the vanilla and butter. Remove from heat and stir in the vanilla and butter.

DENA GIRARDINI   GET TOGETHERS UNIT

APPLE PUDDING

2 cups apples, diced	1 teaspoon cinnamon
1 cup sugar	1 cup flour
1 egg	¼ teaspoon salt
¼ cup butter or margarine	½ cup nuts
1 teaspoon baking soda	

Mix first 3 ingredients in mixer bowl on low speed for 1 or 2 minutes. Add shortening and mix another minute. Add rest of ingredients which have been sifted together (except the nuts). Mix a little of the flour with the nuts to keep them from settling to the bottom of the pan. Mix well. Pour into a greased and floured 9 x 13-inch pan. Bake at 350° for 45 minutes. Serve warm with vanilla sauce or use as a moist cake. Makes 12 large servings.

JOSIE STAMPE   SHIPMAN UNIT

APPLE PUDDING

1 cup sugar	1 teaspoon cinnamon
¼ cup butter	1 teaspoon baking soda
1 egg, beaten	¼ teaspoon salt
1 cup flour	2 cups apples, peeled and diced
¼ teaspoon nutmeg	½ cup nuts, chopped

Cream together the sugar, butter, and beaten egg. Sift dry ingredients and add to creamed mixture along with the diced apples and chopped nuts. Pour batter into 8 x 8 x 2-inch pan. Bake at 350° for 45 minutes. Serve with whipped cream or other topping.

MRS. C. H. POCKLINGTON   NILWOOD UNIT

HOT APPLE DESSERT

6 baking apples	¼ cup raisins
½ cup sugar	20 marshmallows

Peel and slice apples. Place in 1½-quart casserole to cover bottom. Sprinkle on sugar and raisins. Cover and bake in 350° oven for 30 to 35 minutes. Remove cover. Place marshmallows on top of hot apples. Bake 10 more minutes to brown lightly. The marshmallows will puff up, then collapse and melt into apples after removed from the oven. Makes 6 servings.

CHRISTINE SELVO   CARLINVILLE NIGHT UNIT

APPLE GOODIES

3 cups apples, peeled and
  sliced
1 cup sugar
1 tablespoon flour
Pinch of salt
1 teaspoon cinnamon

¾ cup oatmeal
¾ cup flour
¼ teaspoon baking soda
¼ teaspoon baking powder
⅓ cup butter, melted
¾ cup brown sugar

Mix together the apples, sugar, 1 tablespoon flour, salt, and cinnamon. Spread into 9 x 13-inch pan. Combine the remaining ingredients and pour over the apples. Bake at 350° for 40 minutes. May be served hot with whipped cream or ice cream. Makes 12 to 15 servings.
MRS. JAMES RONDI   STAUNTON UNIT

APPLE NOODLE KUGEL

8 ounces wide noodles
3 eggs, slightly beaten
3 cups apples, thinly sliced
½ cup cottage cheese
½ cup sour cream

½ cup raisins
¼ cup sugar
½ teaspoon salt
3 tablespoons butter

Cook noodles according to package directions. Combine eggs, apples, cottage cheese, sour cream, raisins, sugar, and salt. Mix with cooked and drained noodles. Pour into greased 8 x 12-inch baking dish or a 2-quart baking dish. Dot with butter. Bake at 350° for 1 hour until lightly browned. Serve warm with sour cream. Makes 6 to 8 servings.
JOSEPHINE BAIMA   GET TOGETHERS UNIT

CREAMY APPLE SQUARES

1 package yellow cake mix
½ cup butter or margarine,
  softened
2 apples, thinly sliced
1 cup sour cream

1 egg
¼ cup brown sugar, firmly
  packed
½ teaspoon cinnamon

Heat oven to 350°. Combine cake mix and softened butter. Mix until crumbly. Reserving ⅔ cup for topping, press remaining mixture into bottom of ungreased 13 x 9-inch pan. Arrange apple slices over base. Blend sour cream and egg, spread evenly over apples. Add brown sugar and cinnamon to the reserved topping mixture. Sprinkle over sour cream mixture in pan. Bake for 25 to 30 minutes until topping is golden brown and bubbly. Serve warm. Refrigerate leftovers. Makes 12 to 15 servings.
MRS. HENRY GRYSIEWICZ   STAUNTON UNIT

APPLESAUCE PINWHEELS

2 cups flour
½ teaspoon salt
3 teaspoons baking powder
1 tablespoon sugar
4 tablespoons shortening

¾ cup milk
½ to ¾ cup applesauce
Cinnamon or other spice
1 tablespoon butter

Sift first 4 ingredients together in bowl; cut in shortening and add milk. Roll into a rectangle on lightly floured board. Spread on applesauce and sugar; dot with butter. Roll up like jelly roll. Cut into one-inch slices; place them in greased muffin tins. Bake at 425° for 20 minutes until golden brown. Makes 6 to 8 servings.

Note: Don't spread the applesauce too thick or you will have trouble. I have used apple butter in place of applesauce. Grease muffin tins well.

MRS. GEORGE E. ADAM   STAUNTON UNIT

BREAD PUDDING

⅓ cup white raisins
2 cups soft bread crumbs
½ cup sugar
¼ cup butter, melted

4 egg yolks, beaten slightly
1 cup milk
4 egg whites

Soak raisins in hot water for 5 minutes. Drain and put into mixing bowl with bread crumbs and sugar. Add butter and toss lightly. Combine egg yolks with milk. Pour over bread mixture and stir. Beat egg whites until stiff; fold into pudding. Pour into 1½-quart casserole. Bake at 350° for 30 to 40 minutes. Serve warm with vanilla ice cream or Vanilla Sauce.

Vanilla Sauce:
2 tablespoons butter
2 cups milk
1½ tablespoons cornstarch
¼ teaspoon salt

3 tablespoons sugar
1 teaspoon vanilla
1 egg yolk, beaten

Melt butter in a saucepan. Add milk, bring to a boil. Mix cornstarch, salt, sugar, and stir gradually into the milk. Cook 3 to 5 minutes. Remove from heat and add vanilla and egg yolk.

SYLVIA ZERBOLIO   GET TOGETHERS UNIT

BAVARIAN CHEESECAKE

2 cups finely crushed vanilla
  wafers
2 tablespoons sugar
1 teaspoon cinnamon
¼ teaspoon nutmeg
⅓ cup margarine
1¼ pounds (3 8-ounce)
  cream cheese, softened

1 cup sugar
3 eggs
1 tablespoon lemon juice
1 teaspoon grated lemon rind
½ teaspoon vanilla
2 cups sour cream
3 tablespoons sugar
1 teaspoon vanilla

Combine ingredients for crumb crust and press firmly and evenly against bottom and sides of lightly greased 8-inch spring form pan. Refrigerate 30 minutes. Cream cheese and 1 cup sugar together until light and fluffy. Add eggs, one at a time, beating well after each addition. Thoroughly blend in lemon juice, lemon rind and ½ teaspoon vanilla. Pour into chilled crust. Bake in moderate oven (375°) for 45 minutes. Remove from oven and let cool for 30 minutes. Meanwhile, blend together sour cream, 3 tablespoons sugar and 1 teaspoon vanilla. Carefully spread sour cream mixture over baked cheese filling. Bake in very hot oven (400°) for 10 minutes. Cool. Refrigerate overnight before serving. Makes 12 servings.

JACQUELINE H. THOMAS   EXTENSION HOME ECONOMIST—
                       MACOUPIN COUNTY

COTTAGE PUDDING

2½ cups flour
3 teaspoons baking powder
Pinch salt
2 eggs, beaten

1 cup sugar
½ cup butter
1 cup milk
1 teaspoon vanilla

Sift flour, baking powder, and salt. Cream sugar and butter; add beaten eggs. Mix flour mixture into creamed mixture; add milk and vanilla. Bake in a #8 iron skillet at 350° for 35 to 40 minutes. Serve with Sauce.

Sauce:
½ cup brown sugar
½ cup sugar
2 tablespoons flour
Pinch of salt

Cream
⅔ cup milk
Lump of butter

Moisten brown sugar, sugar, flour and salt with cream; mix until smooth. Add milk and butter. Cook until thickened.

MAXINE OXLEY   SCOTTVILLE UNIT

CHEESE CAKE

2 pounds Philadelphia cream
  cheese
1½ pints sour cream
1 tablespoon cornstarch

6 eggs
1¼ cups sugar
1 teaspoon vanilla

Soften cream cheese. Add sour cream and cornstarch. Set aside. Beat eggs, sugar, and vanilla together. Add to cheese mixture and beat lightly. Pour mixture into a spring pan. Bake 1 hour at 300°. Turn off oven, leave cake in the oven for 1 hour after it has finished baking. If the top is not brown enough, place under broiler for a few minutes. Let stand in spring pan until ready to serve. Keep in refrigerator. There is no crust to this cake. Makes 10 to 12 servings.

BERNA HUHSMAN   STAUNTON UNIT

BUTTERSCOTCH TORTE

1¼ cups flour
1 cup nuts, chopped
½ cup margarine
1 8-ounce package cream
  cheese
1 cup powdered sugar
1 large carton Cool Whip

3 cups milk
1 3-ounce package butterscotch
  pudding mix
1 3-ounce package coconut
  pudding mix
1 small carton Cool Whip

Combine flour, nuts, and margarine to make crust. Spread in 9 x 13-inch pan and bake at 350° for 15 minutes. Cool. Mix cream cheese, powdered sugar, and large carton of Cool Whip; spread on cooled crust. Gradually add milk to combined pudding mixes, stirring constantly while cooking over medium heat. Cool. Spread on above mixture. Top with small carton of Cool Whip. Sprinkle on nuts, if desired. Refrigerate. Makes 10 to 16 servings.

COMMITTEE

CHOCOLATE PUDDING CAKE

1 cup brown sugar
½ cup cocoa
2 cups water
12 large marshmallows, cut
  into quarters

1 package devil's food cake mix
1 cup nuts, broken

Mix brown sugar, cocoa, and water until well blended. Pour into greased 13 x 9 x 2-inch pan. Scatter marshmallows over mixture. Prepare cake mix as directed on box. Spoon over the mixture in pan. Sprinkle nuts on top. Bake at 350° for 45 to 50 minutes. Pudding will be on the bottom when done. Top with whipped cream. Makes 10 to 12 servings.

MARVEL F. KILIAN   SUSTAINING MEMBER

CHERRY CHEESE CAKE

1½ packages (33) graham
crackers
⅓ cup sugar
2 sticks margarine
1 8-ounce package cream
cheese
1 teaspoon powdered sugar

1 package lemon Jello
1 cup water, boiling
1 cup sugar
2 teaspoons vanilla
1 can Milnot
1 30-ounce can cherry pie filling

Crumb graham crackers. Add ⅓ cup sugar and 1 stick melted margarine. Mix and press into 9 x 13-inch pan. Melt 1 stick margarine and cream cheese with the powdered sugar. Dissolve Jello in hot water. Add 1 cup sugar and vanilla. Add cheese mixture to the Jello mixture while still warm. Whip Milnot and fold in the Jello mixture. Pour over crust and chill until firm. Spread pie filling over cheese cake. Makes 12 to 15 servings.

FREDA EDDINGTON   SHIPMAN UNIT

CHERRY MARSHMALLOW DESSERT

30 large marshmallows
½ cup milk
1½ cups vanilla wafer
crumbs

¼ cup butter, melted
1 cup heavy cream
1 can cherry pie filling

Melt marshmallows in milk over medium heat. Cool. Combine vanilla wafer crumbs and melted butter. Reserve ¼ cup crumb mixture; press remainder in 9 x 9-inch pan. Whip cream. Fold in marshmallow mixture. Spread over crumbs in pan. Spread pie filling over top. Chill and serve. Makes 6 servings. Note: Cherry pie filling can be replaced by sugared fresh strawberries or 1 can crushed pineapple thickened with cornstarch and cooled.

DOROTHY GREEN   GIRARD NIGHT UNIT

CRANBERRY CASSEROLE

4 cups apples, unpeeled and
chopped
2 cups fresh cranberries
1½ cups sugar
1 stick margarine, melted

1½ cups quick oatmeal
½ cup brown sugar
⅓ cup flour
⅓ cup nuts, chopped

Mix cranberries, apples, and sugar. Spread in a 9 x 13-inch baking dish. In a bowl, mix the margarine, oatmeal, brown sugar, flour, and nuts. Spread over fruit mixture in dish. Bake at 350° for 40 to 45 minutes. Makes 8 to 10 servings.

EVELYN STAYTON   BIRD UNIT

NO BAKE CHEESE CAKE

1 3-ounce package lemon
Jello
1 cup water, boiling
3 cups graham cracker
crumbs
½ cup margarine, melted

1 8-ounce package Philadelphia
cream cheese
1 cup sugar
1 teaspoon vanilla
1 13-ounce can Milnot, stiffly
beaten

Dissolve Jello in boiling water. Chill until thickened. Mix crumbs with melted margarine. Press into bottom of 13 x 9 x 2-inch cake pan, reserving ⅓ cup crumbs. Cream together cream cheese, sugar, and vanilla; add lemon Jello and beat until blended. Fold this mixture into stiffly beaten Milnot. Pour over crust. Sprinkle reserved crumbs over top of cheese cake. Chill thoroughly. Note: Have Milnot icy cold before beating.
EVELYN L. NIEHAUS   MT. OLIVE UNIT

DATE AND APPLESAUCE CAKE

½ cup butter
1 cup light brown sugar
2 eggs
2 teaspoons baking soda
1½ cups applesauce
1 cup dates, chopped
1 cup nuts

1 cup seedless raisins
2 cups flour
½ teaspoon cinnamon
½ teaspoon nutmeg
¼ teaspoon cloves
1 teaspoon vanilla

Cream butter and sugar well. Add eggs. Stir baking soda into applesauce. Mix together dates, nuts, raisins, and flour which has been sifted with the spices. Combine all ingredients and turn into 2 greased 8 x 4½-inch loaf pans. Bake at 325° for 1 hour or longer. Ice with a plain butter icing, if desired. Makes 2 small loaves or 1 large.
JOSEPHINE C. FINNEGAN   BERTHA ELDRED UNIT

DATE PUDDING

3 eggs, slightly beaten
3 tablespoons flour
1 teaspoon baking powder
1 teaspoon vanilla

1 scant cup sugar
1 cup dates
1 cup English walnuts

Use fork to slightly beat eggs. Combine all ingredients and mix well. Spread in a greased 9 x 9-inch pan. Bake at 325° for 35 to 40 minutes until golden brown or a toothpick comes out clean. Do not double recipe. Makes 9 servings.
DONNA SANSON   HONEY POINT UNIT

LEMON CHEESE CAKE

¼ cup butter or margarine
¾ cup bread crumbs, oven
  dried and crushed
¼ cup powdered sugar
4 eggs, beaten
2 cups small curd cottage
  cheese

1 teaspoon lemon rind, grated
1 cup heavy cream
1 cup sugar
1 tablespoon lemon juice
1 tablespoon flour
1 teaspoon vanilla

Spread softened butter or margarine on bottom and sides of 9 or 10-inch pie plate. Mix crumbs and powdered sugar. Set aside ¼ cup crumbs for top. Sprinkle remaining crumbs over butter in plate. Mix remaining ingredients together. Spoon some of filling into crust, then gently pour in remainder. If danger of filling running over, sprinkle some of the reserved crumbs around edge of crust (½ inch). Then pour in remainder. The edge of crumbs will let you fill it really full without it running over. Bake 1 hour at 350°. Makes 6 or 7 servings.

MRS. FRED KRAINZ   BERTHA ELDRED UNIT

FRESH FRUIT VELVET DESSERT

½ cup margarine or butter,
  melted
1 cup flour
¼ cup sugar
½ cup almonds, diced
⅓ cup (3-ounce package)
  lemon gelatin

½ cup sugar
1 cup boiling water
1 cup dairy sour cream
1 cup fresh green grapes, halved
  (or strawberries, raspberries or
  blueberries)

To make crust, roast the almonds lightly in oven or broiler. Combine melted butter, flour, ¼ cup sugar, and almonds in a saucepan. (Mixture will form a ball). Stirring constantly, cook over medium heat for 3 to 5 minutes until mixture is golden and crumbly. Reserve ½ cup crumb mixture for topping. Press remaining crumb mixture into an 8-inch square pan. Refrigerate until completely cooled.

Dissolve gelatin and ½ cup sugar in the boiling water. Add sour cream. Mix with rotary beater until well combined. Refrigerate until thickened but not set, about 1 hour. Fold in fruit. Pour filling into the cooled crust. Chill until firm. Sprinkle reserved crumb mixture over top of filling. Makes 9 servings.

JULIE HEEREN   MONDAY NITERS UNIT

MY GRANDMOTHER'S CUSTARD

3 cups milk
½ cup sugar
4 eggs

1 teaspoon vanilla
Nutmeg, if desired

Heat together the milk and sugar over medium heat until sugar is dissolved, but do not boil. In a bowl with pouring lip, beat eggs until well mixed but not light. Add vanilla. Have hot water ready. Set custard cups into a 9 x 13-inch baking pan. Stir hot milk into beaten eggs, stirring briskly. Pour custard cups ¾ full. Sprinkle a little nutmeg on top, if you like. Pour an inch or a little more of the hot water around the cups in pan. Carefully set pan in preheated 350° oven and bake 10 to 15 minutes or just until custard is set. You can test with narrow blade of knife as you do for custard or pumpkin pie. Remove cups from water immediately. Can be baked in glass casserole; test at 25 minutes baking time.

LELA KLAUS   HONEY POINT UNIT

DISH WATER PUDDING

1 cup flour
1½ teaspoons baking powder
1 teaspoon cinnamon
½ teaspoon cloves
½ teaspoon nutmeg
½ cup brown sugar
½ cup milk

1 tablespoon butter
1 cup dates, chopped, or raisins
½ cup black walnuts, coarsely
   chopped
1½ cups brown sugar
2 cups boiling water
2 tablespoons butter

Sift flour, baking powder, cinnamon, cloves, and nutmeg into a bowl. Add ½ cup brown sugar, milk, and 1 tablespoon butter. Mix well. Add dates and walnuts. Pour into lightly greased 7½ x 12-inch baking dish. In the same mixing bowl used before, put 1½ cup brown sugar, boiling water, and 2 tablespoons butter. Mix well and pour over the batter. (This is the dish water.) Bake at 350° for 50 minutes. The batter rises to the top and the sauce goes to the bottom. Makes 10 servings.

MARIAN GWILLIM   PIASA UNIT

PINK PANTHER

1 No. 2 can crushed
   pineapple
1 No. 2 can cherry pie filling

1 can Eagle Brand milk
1 9-ounce carton Cool Whip
½ cup nuts, chopped

Fold all ingredients together. Pour into 9 x 13-inch pan. Refrigerate overnight. Makes 15 servings.

YOLANDA NEWMAN   BERTHA ELDRED UNIT

FRESH PEACH DUMPLINGS

3 cups flour
1½ teaspoons salt
1¼ cups shortening

1 tablespoon lemon juice
10 to 12 tablespoons ice water
8 fresh peaches

Mix flour and salt; cut in shortening as for pastry. Add lemon juice and water. Blend. Roll dough thin for 8 six-inch squares. Wrap around clean, fresh peach with skin on and stone in. Bake at 425° for 30 minutes. Cool. Remove stone with small spoon. Fill cavity with Hard Sauce. Return to oven long enough to heat sauce. Makes 8 servings.

Hard Sauce:
½ cup butter
1½ cups powdered sugar

Flavoring

Blend ingredients until smooth, flavoring with lemon, almond, or rum extract, using only a few drops.

JANEVA CLARK   CARLINVILLE NIGHT UNIT

PEACH DELIGHT

6 cups fresh peaches
1 cup sugar
3 tablespoons cornstarch
½ cup orange juice

2 tablespoons lemon juice
1 baked 9-inch pie shell or
  graham cracker crust

Mash 1 cup peaches. Blend sugar and cornstarch in a saucepan; stir in orange juice and mashed peaches. Cook over medium heat, stirring constantly, until mixture thickens, about 8 minutes. Boil 1 minute, stirring as it cooks. Remove from heat, stir in lemon juice and cool. Pour half of cooked glaze into pie shell, spreading evenly on bottom and sides, completely covering pie shell. Fill with remaining peaches. Pour remaining glaze over top, completely covering pie. Refrigerate at least 3 hours. Serve with whipped cream on top.

PEARL STARCK   BERTHA ELDRED UNIT

FROZEN PEACHES 'N' CREAM

1½ cups crushed vanilla
wafers, about 36
¼ cup melted butter
2 tablespoons orange juice
1 tablespoon lemon juice

½ pound marshmallows, 20
large, quartered
1 cup fresh peaches or canned,
drained
1 cup whipped cream

Combine crumbs and butter. Pat evenly on sides and bottom of 8-inch square pan. Combine juices, heat to boiling, add marshmallows and stir until dissolved. Let cool. Add peaches and fold in whipped cream. Pour into wafer crust. Freeze 3 or 4 hours or until firm. Cut into squares. Makes 8 to 10 servings.

MRS. JOHN BRUNETTO   GET TOGETHERS UNIT

LEMON FRUIT FREEZE

⅔ cup butter or margarine
⅓ cup sugar
7 cups Rice or Corn Chex
cereal, crushed to 3 cups
1 14-ounce can Eagle Brand
milk

½ cup ReaLemon lemon juice
1 21-ounce can lemon pie filling
1 17-ounce can fruit cocktail, well
drained
2 cups whipped topping

In medium saucepan, melt butter, stir in sugar, then crumbs. Reserving ⅓ cup crumbs for garnish, press remaining crumbs firmly on bottom of 13 x 9-inch baking pan. Bake at 300° for 12 minutes. Cool. In large bowl, mix Eagle Brand milk and lemon juice. Stir in pie filling and fruit cocktail. Pour over crust. Top with whipped topping and reserved crumbs. Freeze for 4 hours. Remove from freezer 20 minutes before serving. If desired, garnish with lemon slices. This will keep in the freezer for up to 3 months. Makes 12 to 15 servings.

EUNICE JACOBS   GILLESPIE NIGHT UNIT

LEMON FLUFF

15¼-ounce can crushed
pineapple
1 cup sugar
2 eggs, well beaten

1 package lemon Jello
1 large can Milnot, chilled
2½ to 3 cups vanilla wafer
crumbs

Drain pineapple. Add sugar and eggs to pineapple juice. Bring to boil. Remove from heat and add lemon Jello. Set aside. Whip Milnot. Fold warm mixture into whipped Milnot. Put vanilla wafer crumbs in bottom of 13 x 9-inch pan, saving a few crumbs for the top. Add pineapple to whipped cream mixture. Pour over the crumbs. Sprinkle crumbs on top. Chill at least 2 hours. Makes 15 servings.

LELA FITZGERALD   HAGAMAN UNIT

DUMP CAKE DESSERT

1 can cherry pie filling
1 16-ounce can pineapple
1 package yellow or white
cake mix

1 cup margarine or butter
Nuts or coconut, if desired
Whipped cream or ice cream

Mix the pie filling and pineapple in a 9 x 13-inch cake pan. Sprinkle cake mix over fruit and drizzle melted butter or margarine over it. Sprinkle on nuts or coconut if a crunchy topping is desired. Bake at 350° for 40 to 50 minutes. Top with whipped cream or ice cream. Note: Any kind of fruit pie filling is good.

HELEN MANSHOLT   GILLESPIE NIGHT UNIT

HEATH BAR DESSERT

36 Ritz crackers, crushed
1 stick margarine, melted
2 packages instant pistachio
pudding
2 cups milk

2 cups vanilla ice cream, slightly
softened
1 9-ounce carton Cool Whip
4 large Heath bars, crushed

Mix together crushed crackers and margarine. Spread on bottom of an 11 x 14-inch pan. Mix pudding, milk, ice cream, and Cool Whip. Pour over crackers. Sprinkle crushed Heath bars over pudding mixture. Chill thoroughly, preferably overnight. Makes 12 servings.

LORRAINE OBERTINO   GET TOGETHERS UNIT

ORANGE DESSERT

2 packages vanilla tapioca
pudding
3 cups cold water

1 package orange Jello
1 can mandarin oranges, drained
1 package Dream Whip, whipped

Cook pudding and water over medium heat, stirring constantly, until mixture comes to a rolling boil. Stir in Jello until dissolved. Chill a short time and add the mandarin oranges. Fold in whipped Dream Whip. Let set overnight in a 9x13-inch pan.

MARIE VINCENT   DO MORE UNIT

LEMON OR CHOCOLATE COOL

1 cup flour
½ cup margarine
2 teaspoons sugar
½ cup nuts, chopped
1 8-ounce package cream
   cheese, softened

1 cup powdered sugar
2 cups Cool Whip
2 packages lemon or chocolate
   pudding mix, instant or regular
3 cups milk
Nuts

Mix first four ingredients. Spread in 9 x 12-inch pan. Bake at 350° for 15 minutes. Cool. Cream the cheese, powdered sugar, and fold in 1 cup Cool Whip. Spread over cooled crust. Mix pudding as per package directions using only 3 cups milk. When pudding is cool, spread over mixture in pan. Top with 1 cup Cool Whip and garnish with nuts. Makes 12 to 15 servings.

MRS. PHILIP BOWMAN   HAGAMAN UNIT

MARY RAMEY, DO MORE UNIT, omits sugar from crust, and uses 2 cups Cool. Whip, and 2 packages lemon instant pudding mix.

MINT DAZZLER DESSERT

2 cups vanilla wafer crumbs
¼ cup butter or margarine,
   melted
½ cup butter
1½ cups powdered sugar,
   sifted
3 eggs, slightly beaten

3 squares unsweetened
   chocolate, melted
1½ cups whipping cream
1 10-ounce package miniature
   marshmallows
½ cup crushed peppermint
   candy

Blend together crumbs and ¼ cup melted butter or margarine. Press firmly into bottom of 9 x 13-inch pan. Cream ½ cup butter and powdered sugar. Add eggs and melted chocolate, beat until light and fluffy. Spoon over crumbs in pan and set in refrigerator while whipping the cream. Fold marshmallows into whipped cream and spread over chocolate layer. Sprinkle with crushed peppermint candy. May be frozen. Remove from freezer ½ hour before serving time. Makes 12 servings.

GENEVA C. ARMOUR   MONDAY NITERS UNIT

LADYFINGERS

3 eggs, separated
½ cup sugar
½ cup cake flour, sifted

½ teaspoon vanilla
2 tablespoons powdered sugar
1 tablespoon sugar

Beat egg yolks and ½ cup sugar in small bowl until light. Gently fold in cake flour and vanilla until smooth. Batter will be thick. Beat egg whites in small bowl just until stiff peaks form. Gently fold in the yolk-sugar mixture until combined. Drop 2 teaspoons batter, side by side, on a lightly greased and floured baking sheet. Shape into an oval finger about 3 inches long and 1 inch wide, using spatula. Repeat until all batter is used. Mix powdered sugar with 1 tablespoon sugar and sprinkle over ladyfingers. Let stand 5 minutes before baking. Bake at 350° for 8 minutes. Cool on wire rack. Makes 5 dozen. To freeze, place in freezer on baking sheet. When frozen, package, seal, label, date, and return to freezer. To serve, let stand in wrapping at room temperature a few minutes.

DORIS RENO   PIASA UNIT

PINEAPPLE FLUFF DESSERT

1½ cups vanilla wafer
  crumbs
¼ cup nuts, chopped
¼ cup butter, melted
1 No. 2 can crushed
  pineapple, undrained

1 3-ounce package lemon gelatin
4 eggs, separated
2 tablespoons butter
¼ teaspoon salt
½ cup sugar

Mix crumbs, nuts, and melted butter. Reserve ¼ cup for topping. Press remainder into bottom of 9 x 13-inch baking dish. Chill. Mix undrained pineapple with gelatin and 4 slightly beaten egg yolks. Cook until thickened. Stir in 2 tablespoons butter. Chill until partially set. Beat 4 egg whites with salt to soft peaks; gradually add sugar, beating to stiff peaks. Fold into pineapple mixture. Pour over crust; sprinkle with reserved crumbs. Chill until set. Makes 12 servings.

EILEEN HAMMANN   GILLESPIE NIGHT UNIT

PLUM KUCHEN

½ cup butter
1 cup sugar
1 egg
½ cup dairy sour cream
¼ teaspoon vanilla
1 cup flour

½ teaspoon baking powder
¼ teaspoon salt
1 pound fresh blue plums, 6 or 8
2 tablespoons sugar
1 teaspoon cinnamon

In mixing bowl, cream butter and sugar. Add egg and beat until fluffy. Stir in sour cream and vanilla. Sift flour, salt, and baking powder together. Fold into batter just until thoroughly moistened. Spread batter in a greased and floured 9-inch square or round pan. Quarter and pit the plums. Arrange attractively on the batter. Sprinkle the cinnamon and 2 tablespoons sugar over plums. Bake at 350° for 1 hour. Serve warm with sweetened whipped cream, if desired. Makes 8 or 9 servings.

WILMA WARGO   GET TOGETHERS UNIT

PLUM PUDDING

1 cup brown sugar
1 cup milk
1 teaspoon cinnamon
1 cup plus 2 tablespoons
   flour
3 teaspoons baking powder

2 tablespoons butter
1 cup raisins
1 teaspoon nutmeg
⅓ teaspoon salt
1½ cups brown sugar
1½ cups boiling water

Mix all ingredients together except the 1½ cups brown sugar and the water. Spread into a well-greased 9 x 13-inch pan. Sprinkle 1½ cups brown sugar over top of batter; pour boiling water over all. Bake at 350° for 30 minutes.

VELMA WAGGONER   PIASA UNIT

QUICK AND EASY DESSERT

36 Ritz crackers
1 stick margarine, melted
2 packages instant pistachio
   pudding

1½ cups milk
1 quart vanilla ice cream
1 9-ounce carton Cool Whip
2 to 3 Heath Bars, crushed

Crush crackers and mix with margarine. Press into 9 x 13-inch pan. Bake at 350° for 8 minutes. Let cool. Mix pudding, milk, and ice cream. Pour over cracker mixture. Spread Cool Whip over top and sprinkle on crushed Heath Bars or butter brickle chips on top. Refrigerate. Makes 18 servings.

VELDA ROESLER   MT. OLIVE UNIT

GRANDMA RHOADS' PLUM PUDDING

2 cups currants
2 cups raisins
1 cup candied citron
½ cup each candied oranges
  and lemon peel
½ pound chopped suet
½ cup flour
3 cups stale bread crumbs
4 eggs, separated
1 cup brown sugar
1 cup blanched, shredded
  almonds

¼ cup molasses
½ cup milk
¼ cup each brandy and sherry
1 teaspoon cinnamon
1 teaspoon nutmeg
½ teaspoon cloves
½ teaspoon soda
1 teaspoon salt
1 tablespoon water

Chop fruit and suet with flour; add crumbs and nuts. The old time housewife lets this mixture stand 36 hours. Beat yolks of eggs until thick and lemon colored. Add to flour and fruit mixture and stir well. Add spices, salt, sugar, molasses, milk, brandy, and sherry. Add soda dissolved in cold water. Mix thoroughly and fold in whites of eggs, beaten until stiff and dry. Fill buttered 2-quart mold ¾ full. Cover and steam over water for 6 hours. Cool. When ready to serve, steam one hour, turn out and serve as wanted. May be frozen or chilled. Makes 8 servings.

Golden Sauce:
1 cup powdered sugar
½ cup butter

3 egg yolks
1 cup whipped cream

Beat egg yolks until thick; gradually beat in sugar. Cook over hot water, beating constantly. Add butter slowly. Cook until mixture coats spoon. Chill. Fold in whipped cream flavored with vanilla.

MILDRED ECKMAN SCOPEL   BERTHA ELDRED UNIT

RAISIN PUDDING

1 cup sugar
1 cup flour
1 cup raisins
2 teaspoons baking powder

½ cup milk
1 teaspoon vanilla
1⅓ cups brown sugar
2 cups boiling water

Mix sugar, flour, raisins, baking powder, milk and vanilla. Pour into greased 7 x 12-inch baking dish. Mix brown sugar and boiling water; pour over top of batter. Bake at 350° for 30 minutes or more until done.

MRS. IVAN JENKINS   GIRARD DAY UNIT

SLOVENIAN PLUM DUMPLINGS

½ teaspoon salt
2 eggs, beaten
1½ cups freshly mashed
    potatoes
¼ cup Cream of Wheat

1½ cups flour
15 Italian blue plums
7½ teaspoons sugar
Cinnamon

Add salt and eggs to mashed potatoes. Combine with Cream of Wheat and flour. Mix and knead. Roll out dough and cut into 15 squares. Wash, halve, and pit plums. Place ½ plum on each square. Fill each plum with ½ teaspoon sugar and a dash of cinnamon. Top with another plum half. Fold corners of dough to center; pinch lightly. Drop gently into boiling, salted water and simmer 20 minutes. Drain well and serve with buttered bread crumbs or Sauce.

Sauce:
½ cup honey
¼ cup butter

1 teaspoon cinnamon

Combine ingredients and heat thoroughly.

ANNA KALASKIE   GET TOGETHERS UNIT

SUET PUDDING

2 cups chopped suet, salted
    to taste
1 cup sugar
1 cup sour milk
2 teaspoons baking soda,
    dissolved in
½ cup boiling water

1 cup molasses
1 cup raisins
2½ cups flour
½ teaspoon nutmeg
1 teaspoon cinnamon

Mix all ingredients thoroughly. Put into greased 8 x 3-inch round mold. Cover. Put mold on rack in larger pan. Steam over water for 3 hours. Serve with Hot Sauce.

Hot Sauce:
2 cups water
¾ cup sugar

2 tablespoons cornstarch
1 teaspoon vanilla

Cook water, sugar, and cornstarch until clear. Add vanilla or rum flavoring. More water may be added for a thinner sauce.

MARIE MATHIAS   CARLINVILLE NIGHT UNIT

ENGLISH PLUM PUDDING

Crumbs from 1 large stale
loaf of bread
3 cups warm milk,
approximately
6 eggs
1½ pounds ground suet
1½ pounds raisins
1½ pounds currants
½ pound mixed candied peel

5 cups sugar
½ teaspoon salt
1½ tablespoons cloves
3 tablespoons cinnamon
1½ tablespoons nutmeg or
allspice
1½ teaspoons ground ginger
6 cups flour

Crumb bread and mix with warm milk. Beat eggs and mix all ingredients together. Grease 1 gallon pan and fill ⅔ full. Tie aluminum foil or waxed paper over top. Set pan in boiling water and boil 8 hours. Note: Recipe will make 6 1-pound coffee cans with 2 pound of batter to each can.

MRS. PAUL N. ODELL   PIASA UNIT

QUICK PUDDING

½ cup brown sugar
½ cup sugar
2½ cups water
2 tablespoons butter
½ cup raisins
½ cup sugar

2 tablespoons butter
½ cup milk
1 cup flour
1 teaspoon cinnamon
3 teaspoons baking powder

To make a sauce, combine brown sugar, ½ cup sugar, water, 2 tablespoons butter, and raisins in a saucepan. Bring to a boil and simmer while making pudding. Cream ½ cup sugar and 2 tablespoons butter; add milk and dry ingredients. Mix well. Pour hot sauce into 2-quart pan. Pour pudding mixture over sauce. Bake at 375° for 30 minutes. Serve hot or cold. Makes 6 servings.

EILEEN NICHOLS   GIRARD NIGHT UNIT

RHUBARB CRISP

1 egg
¾ cup sugar
2 tablespoons flour
3 cups rhubarb, cut up

4 tablespoons butter
⅓ cup brown sugar, packed
⅔ cup flour

Beat egg, stir in sugar and flour. Add rhubarb and blend well. Spoon into a greased 8-inch baking dish. Combine the butter, brown sugar, and flour. Mix until crumbly. Sprinkle over rhubarb. Bake at 350° for 40 minutes. Serve with whipped topping, if desired. Makes 6 servings.

FERN SANDERS   BRUSHY MOUND UNIT

PUMPKIN CAKE ROLL

3 eggs
1 cup sugar
⅔ cup pumpkin
1 teaspoon lemon juice
¾ cup flour
1 teaspoon baking powder

2 teaspoons cinnamon
1 teaspoon ginger
½ teaspoon nutmeg
½ teaspoon salt
1 cup nuts, finely chopped
Powdered sugar

Beat eggs on high speed of mixer for 5 minutes. Gradually beat in sugar. Stir in pumpkin and lemon juice. Stir together flour, baking powder, cinnamon, ginger, nutmeg, and salt. Fold in pumpkin mixture. Spread in greased and floured 15 x 10 x 1-inch pan. Top with nuts. Bake at 375° for 15 minutes. Turn out onto towel sprinkled with powdered sugar. Starting at narrow end, roll towel and cake together. Let cool and unroll. Spread filling over roll. Reroll and chill. Makes 8 servings.

Filling:
1 cup powdered sugar
2 3-ounce packages cream
   cheese

4 tablespoons butter
½ teaspoon vanilla

Mix ingredients together and beat until smooth.
MRS. NORMAN HARMS   MONDAY NITERS UNIT

PUMPKIN TORTE

24 graham crackers, crushed
⅓ cup sugar
½ cup butter
2 eggs, beaten
¾ cup sugar
8 ounces cream cheese
2 cups pumpkin
3 egg yolks
½ cup sugar

½ cup milk
½ teaspoon salt
1 tablespoon cinnamon
1 envelope plain gelatin
¼ cup cold water
3 egg whites
¼ cup sugar
½ pint whipping cream

Mix graham crackers, ⅓ cup sugar, and butter. Press into 9 x 13-inch pan. Mix 2 eggs, ¾ cup sugar, and cream cheese. Pour over crust. Bake 20 minutes at 350°. Cook pumpkin, egg yolks, ½ cup sugar, milk, salt, and cinnamon until mixture thickens. Remove from heat and add gelatin which has been dissolved in cold water. Cool. Beat egg whites, ¼ cup sugar, and fold into pumpkin mixture. Pour over baked, cooled crust. Top with whipped cream.

VELMA SCHOPPE   NILWOOD UNIT

RHUBARB TORTE

1 cup butter
2 cups flour
¼ cup sugar
6 egg yolks
2 cups sugar

7 tablespoons flour
¼ teaspoon salt
1 cup cream
5 cups rhubarb

Mix butter, 2 cups flour and ¼ cup sugar until crumbly. Pat into bottom of a 9 x 13-inch pan. Bake at 350° for 10 minutes. Combine egg yolks, 2 cups sugar, 7 tablespoons flour, salt, and cream. Add to rhubarb. Pour mixture over crust. Bake at 350° for 45 minutes or until custard is set. Spread Meringue on hot dessert. Bake at 325° for 15 minutes. Makes 12 to 15 servings.

Meringue:
6 egg whites
¾ cup sugar

¼ teaspoon salt
½ teaspoon cream of tartar

Add cream of tartar to egg whites. Beat until soft peaks form. Slowly add the sugar and salt, beating until stiff but not dry.

MRS. CLIFFORD BEILSMITH   BRIGHTON EARLY BIRDS UNIT

REFRIGERATOR TORTE

1 cup flour
½ cup butter, softened
½ cup nuts, finely chopped
½ cup powdered sugar
1 8-ounce package cream
  cheese

1 cup powdered sugar
1 9-ounce container Cool Whip
2 3-ounce packages instant
  pudding
2½ cups milk

Mix together as for pie crust the flour, butter, nuts, and ½ cup powdered sugar. Press into bottom of 9 x 13-inch cake pan. Bake at 375° for 10 to 12 minutes until lightly browned. Cool. Cream the cream cheese. Gradually add 1 cup powdered sugar. Beat until light. Fold in ½ container Cool Whip. Spread over cooled crust. Beat instant pudding with milk until thick, 3 or 4 minutes. Spread over cream cheese mixture. Cover with remaining Cool Whip. Refrigerate. Makes 24 servings. Note: Use chocolate, chocolate fudge, butterscotch, or lemon flavor pudding. Vanilla is NOT a good flavor.

MARGIE THOMAE   SHIPMAN UNIT

RACHEL'S CHOCOLATE DESSERT

1 stick margarine
1¼ cups flour
½ cup pecans, chopped
8 ounces Philadelphia cream
 cheese
1 cup powdered sugar, sifted

½ large carton Cool Whip
2 3¾-ounce boxes chocolate pie
 filling
3 cups milk
1 teaspoon vanilla
½ cup nuts, chopped

Blend margarine, flour, and ½ cup pecans until mealy. Press into bottom of 9 x 13-inch pan. Bake at 375° for 20 minutes and let cool. Blend cream cheese, powdered sugar, and Cool Whip until smooth. Spoon onto cooled crust. Refrigerate 1 hour. Mix chocolate pie filling with milk and vanilla. Cook over medium heat until mixture comes to a boil; let cool. Pour over cream mixture. Top with remaining Cool Whip. Sprinkle with ½ cup nuts. Refrigerate.

HELEN HETTICK   SCOTTVILLE UNIT

ICE CREAM DESSERT

3 cups Rice Krispies,
 crushed
½ cup brown sugar
1 cup flaked coconut

⅔ cup nut meats
1 stick margarine, melted
1 can pie filling, your choice
2 quarts ice cream

Mix Rice Krispies, brown sugar, coconut and nuts. Add melted margarine. Pat crumbs into 9 x 13-inch pan, reserving ½ cup crumbs. Spread ice cream over top. Sprinkle with reserved crumbs. Freeze. At serving time, top with pie filling. Makes 18 servings.

VELDA ROESLER   MT. OLIVE UNIT

ICE CREAM CAKE

68 Ritz crackers, crushed
1 stick margarine, melted
4 tablespoons sugar
2 packages instant vanilla
 pudding

2 cups milk
1 quart vanilla ice cream
1 large container non-dairy
 whipped topping

Mix crackers, melted margarine, and sugar together. Pat into 9 x 13-inch pan, saving ½ cup crumbs for topping. Mix pudding with milk. Add ice cream and beat until thick. Pour on crust. Spread whipped topping over ice cream mixture. Sprinkle on reserved crumbs. Freeze until ready to serve.

MARY PLOGGER   MEDORA UNIT

GRANDMA'S FROZEN DESSERT

1 11-ounce package vanilla
  wafers
½ cup butter, melted
⅔ cup crunchy peanut butter
1 8-ounce package cream
  cheese

1 cup milk
2 cups powdered sugar
2 9-ounce cartons Cool Whip
Chocolate syrup

Crush vanilla wafers. Mix with butter and press into bottom of 9 x 13-inch pan. Beat together crunchy peanut butter and cream cheese. Add milk and powdered sugar. Fold in Cool Whip. Pour into pan over crushed wafers. Drizzle chocolate syrup over top and freeze. Makes 12 to 15 servings.

MRS. BONNIE SHELTON   PIASA UNIT

THREE LAYER PRETZEL DESSERT

1½ sticks margarine
3 tablespoons sugar
2 cups broken pretzels,
  crushed to coarse crumbs
1 8-ounce package cream
  cheese
⅞ cup sugar

1 large carton Cool Whip
1 6-ounce package strawberry
  Jello
2 cups boiling water
1 pound carton frozen
  strawberries

Melt margarine, mix with 3 tablespoons sugar and pretzels. Pat into 13½ x 8¾ x 1¾-inch baking dish. Bake at 350° for 10 minutes. Cool. Mix cream cheese with ⅞ cup sugar. Add Cool Whip and spread over cooled crust. Dissolve strawberry Jello in boiling water. Add frozen strawberries, stirring until thawed and Jello is syrupy. Spread over cream cheese mixture and refrigerate. Makes 12 to 15 servings.

MRS. KARL BALL   GIRARD NIGHT UNIT

STRAWBERRY AND CREAM SQUARES

2 packages strawberry Jello
1½ cups boiling water
2 10-ounce packages frozen
  strawberries

1 3½-ounce can crushed
  pineapple
2 large fully ripe bananas, diced
1 cup dairy sour cream

Dissolve Jello in boiling water. Add strawberries, stirring occasionally until thawed. Add pineapple and bananas. Pour half of the mixture into a 9 x 9 x 2-inch pan. When firm, spread sour cream over the layer evenly. Pour remaining Jello mixture over sour cream. Chill until firm. Makes 9 servings.

KATHLEEN HARMS   NILWOOD UNIT

APRICOT ICE

1½ cups sugar
½ quart water

1 16-ounce can apricots
Juice of ½ lemon

Boil sugar and water together a few minutes. Set aside to cool. Put apricots through a sieve or may use blender so they are fine. Add lemon juice. When syrup is cool, add to apricot mixture. Freeze in refrigerator trays for 2 hours or more. Serve with whipped cream. Sponge cake is also good with this. Makes 6 to 8 servings.

MRS. GEORGE E. ADAM   STAUNTON UNIT

HOMEMADE VANILLA ICE CREAM

3 cups sugar
1 quart Half and Half
2 large cans Carnation milk
1 pint whipping cream

1 can Eagle Brand milk
3 tablespoons vanilla
Milk

Mix sugar with Half and Half. Add rest of ingredients except milk and mix thoroughly. Pour into ice cream freezer; fill with milk within 2½ inches from top of container. Makes 1½ gallons ice cream.

MARY FRANCES KEENEY   SCOTTVILLE UNIT

HOMEMADE VANILLA ICE CREAM

6 eggs
3 cups sugar
3 tablespoons vanilla

2 ½-pint cartons whipping cream
2 1-pint cartons Half and Half
Milk

Combine eggs, sugar, and vanilla in large mixing bowl. Beat for 3 minutes on high speed. On low speed, add the whipping cream and Half and Half. Pour mixture into freezer can and add enough milk to proper level. Freeze according to ice cream freezer directions. Makes 1½ gallons.

ROSEMARIE RHODES   MONDAY NITERS UNIT

HOT FUDGE TOPPING

1⅔ cups cream or Carnation
   milk
2 cups sugar

3 squares unsweetened
   chocolate
1 teaspoon vanilla

Cook the cream, sugar and chocolate over low heat for 15 minutes, stirring constantly. Remove from heat and add the vanilla. Beat until smooth.

RUTH TRAVERS   SHIPMAN UNIT

ICE CREAM

5 eggs
1 cup sugar
½ cup white syrup
½ pint whipping cream

1 quart Half and Half
Pinch of salt
4 teaspoons vanilla
Milk

Beat together the eggs and sugar until thick and light yellow in color. Add the syrup, whipping cream, Half and Half, salt and vanilla, and beat into the egg mixture. Pour into freezer container and add milk to fill line. Follow freezer instructions for freezing. Leftovers will freeze without getting icy. Makes enough for 1 gallon freezer.

RUTH DEATHERAGE   BARR UNIT

FRUIT ICE

1 large can crushed
   pineapple
4 mashed bananas
Juice of 3 oranges, or,
1 6-ounce can frozen orange
   juice

Juice of 3 lemons, or 1 6-ounce
   can frozen lemonade
3 cups sugar
1 can Milnot

If desired, chop crushed pineapple finer in blender. Mix all ingredients and pour into ice cream freezer. Finish filling with water to fill line or to cover paddles. Makes 1½ gallons.

MARY FRANCES KEENEY   SCOTTVILLE UNIT

GERMAN CHOCOLATE ICE CREAM

1 cup sugar
¼ cup flour
¼ teaspoon salt
¼ teaspoon cinnamon
1 quart milk

2 4-ounce bars sweet cooking
   chocolate, melted
3 eggs, beaten
1 quart cream or Half and Half
1 cup pecans, chopped

Combine sugar, flour, salt and cinnamon in a heavy saucepan. Gradually add milk. Cook over medium heat until thickened, stirring constantly. Cook 2 minutes. Blend in chocolate. Stir a small amount of hot mixture into eggs; return to cooked mixture. Cook 1 minute. Do not boil. Cool. Stir in cream. Chill. Stir in nuts. Churn freeze. Makes enough for 1 gallon freezer.

MRS. BONNIE SHELTON   PIASA UNIT

PASTRIES

Since the 1860's, coal mines dotted the landscape of Macoupin County and played a very important part in its economy. Deep veins of soft coal brought many people from southeastern Europe to work in the mines. Monterey Mine is one of the latest to be sunk in the county. It produces three million tons of coal per year and employs 625 people. It is the second largest mine, production wise, in Illinois, and is a division of Exxon Coal U.S.A., Inc.

Photographed by Dave Beatty

218

PIE CRUST

1 cup lard   ½ cup water
1 teaspoon salt   2 cups flour

Place lard, salt, and water in bowl. Add flour and mix well. Roll ⅛ inch thick. Bake at 450° for 12 to 15 minutes. Makes 4 shells. Note: Warm pan and moistened rim prevents shrinking. To prevent burned edges, cover edge with 1-inch circle of foil, if needed.

OLIVE BATES   HAGAMAN UNIT

PIE CRUST

4 cups flour   ½ cup Crisco or lard
1 tablespoon sugar   1 tablespoon vinegar
1 teaspoon salt   ½ cup water
2 sticks margarine   1 egg
½ stick butter

Sift dry ingredients. Work in the margarine, butter and lard until mealy. Use pastry blender. Beat egg with vinegar and water for 2 minutes. Add to flour mixture. Stir and shape into ball. Chill in refrigerator 20 minutes before using. May be refrigerated up to one week and used as needed. Makes 2 double crust pies. Bake in 425° oven for 10 minutes.

EVELYN PINTAR   GET TOGETHERS UNIT

FRIED PASTRY

2 eggs   1 teaspoon vanilla
2 tablespoons sugar   1½ cups flour
2 tablespoons cream   Deep fat
   (or evaporated milk)   Powdered sugar
½ teaspoon salt   Cinnamon

Beat eggs until very light. Add sugar, cream, salt, and vanilla. Mix in flour to make dough which can be rolled paper thin. Cut in squares and make a slit in center of each square or cut into strips and tie loose knots. Fry in deep fat heated to 375° until golden brown. Sprinkle with powdered sugar and cinnamon.

VICA MAKUH   GET TOGETHERS UNIT

EASY PIE CRUST

1½ cups flour   ½ cup oil
¾ teaspoon salt   ¼ cup milk
1 teaspoon sugar

Sift flour, salt and sugar into 8-inch pie pan. Make hole in center and add oil and milk. Mix together. Pat into pan with fingers, reserving enough to crumble for top crust. Bake at 400° for about 10 minutes.

DONNA DILL   SCOTTVILLE UNIT

AMAZING COCONUT PIE

2 cups milk   ¼ cup butter or margarine
¾ cup sugar   1½ teaspoons vanilla
½ cup biscuit mix   1 cup coconut
4 eggs

Combine milk, sugar, biscuit mix, eggs, butter, and vanilla in electric blender container. Cover and blend on low speed for 3 minutes. Pour into greased 9-inch pie pan. Let stand about 5 minutes, then sprinkle with coconut. Bake at 350° for 40 minutes. Serve warm or cool. Makes 8 servings.

KATHY BRAY   PIASA UNIT

ANGEL FOOD PIE

4 egg whites   ¼ cup sugar
½ cup sugar   ½ teaspoon vanilla
1 teaspoon vanilla   1 cup nuts
1 cup whipping cream   1 baked pie shell

Beat egg whites until almost stiff. Add ½ cup sugar and 1 teaspoon vanilla. Beat until peaks form. Pour into a baked 9-inch pie shell. Bake 20 minutes at 350°. Let stand until cold. Whip cream, add ¼ cup sugar, and ½ teaspoon vanilla. Grind nuts. Spread cream and nuts on top of pie.

MILDRED B. DAVIS   BIRD UNIT

ANGEL FOOD PIE

1 small can crushed
  pineapple
¾ cup sugar
½ cup water

4 tablespoons cornstarch
¼ cup water
3 egg whites
1 9-inch pie shell, baked

Cook pineapple (with juice), ¾ cup sugar, and ½ cup water for a few minutes. Mix ¼ cup water with cornstarch. Pour into the pineapple mixture. Cook until thick, stirring constantly. Let cool a few minutes. Beat the egg whites and fold into the pineapple mixture. Pour into the baked pie shell. Top with whipped cream. Makes 6 or 8 servings.

MRS. WANDA ELLIOTT   GIRARD DAY UNIT

SOUR CREAM APPLE PIE

1 egg
1 cup sugar
1 cup sour cream
2 tablespoons flour

¼ teaspoon salt
½ teaspoon vanilla
2 cups apples, sliced
9-inch pie shell, unbaked

Beat egg lightly. Add sugar, sour cream, flour, salt, vanilla, and apples. Mix well. Pour into pie shell. Bake 30 minutes or until set in preheated 400° oven.

Topping:
½ cup brown sugar
⅓ cup flour

¼ cup margarine

Combine brown sugar, flour, and margarine. At end of baking period, sprinkle topping over pie. Reduce oven heat to 350° and bake 15 minutes. Makes 6 servings.

MARY BURNETT   SHIPMAN UNIT

ENGLISH APPLE PIE

1 cup flour
2 teaspoons baking powder
1 teaspoon salt
1½ cups sugar

1 teaspoon cinnamon
1 cup pecans
2 cups apples, sliced
2 eggs

Mix together all dry ingredients. Add pecans and sliced apples. Beat eggs and pour over flour mixture. Beat well. Pour into greased 9 x 10-inch pan. Bake at 350° for 45 minutes. Makes 6 servings.

CATHERINE TIRA   GET TOGETHERS UNIT

CHOCOLATE CHEESE PIE

1½ cups graham cracker
  crumbs
¼ cup brown sugar
⅛ teaspoon nutmeg

⅓ cup butter, melted
1 ounce square unsweetened
  chocolate, melted

Combine crumbs, sugar, and nutmeg in bowl. Add butter and chocolate. Mix thoroughly. Press crust mixture into a 9-inch pie plate. Chill until firm.

Filling:
1 6-ounce package
  semi-sweet chocolate chips
1 large package cream
  cheese, softened
½ cup light brown sugar,
  packed

⅛ teaspoon salt
1 teaspoon vanilla
2 eggs, separated
¼ cup light brown sugar, packed
1 cup whipping cream, whipped

Melt chocolate and cool 10 minutes. Blend cream cheese, ½ cup brown sugar, salt, and vanilla in bowl. Beat in egg yolks, one at a time, beating well after each addition. Beat in cooled chocolate, blend well. Beat egg whites in bowl until stiff but not dry. Gradually beat in ¼ cup brown sugar. Beat until stiff and glossy. Fold in whipped cream. Pour into chilled crust. Chill overnight. Makes 8 servings.

VERDA BRUNETTO   GET TOGETHERS UNIT

CRANBERRY-APPLE PIE

1 cup sugar
2 tablespoons flour
½ teaspoon cinnamon
3 cups apples, pared and
  sliced
2 cups cranberries, sliced in
  half

¼ cup currants (optional)
2 tablespoons butter or
  margarine
9-inch unbaked pastry shell and
  top crust

Combine sugar, flour and cinnamon; mix well and set aside. Place half of apple slices in pastry shell; top with half of cranberries and half of currants. Sprinkle half of sugar mixture over fruit. Repeat layers. Dot with butter, and cover with top crust. Bake at 400° for 10 minutes, reduce heat to 350° and bake for 55 more minutes or until done. Makes 8 servings.

HELEN HETTICK   SCOTTVILLE UNIT

CORNMEAL PIE

3 eggs, slightly beaten
2 tablespoons water
1 stick margarine, melted
1 cup sugar
1 cup brown sugar

1 tablespoon flour
1 tablespoon vinegar
1 tablespoon vanilla
2 tablespoons cornmeal
1 9-inch pastry shell, unbaked

Mix all ingredients together. Pour into unbaked pie shell. Bake at 375° about 45 minutes or until brown on top and tests done in center. Makes 6 or 8 servings.

MRS. FRANCIS SKEEN   GIRARD DAY UNIT

CRACKER PIE

6 egg whites
2 teaspoons cream of tartar
2 teaspoons vanilla
1½ cups sugar

2 cups soda crackers, crushed
¾ cup nuts, chopped
2 packages Dream Whip
1 No. 2 can cherry pie filling

Beat egg whites, cream of tartar, and vanilla together until stiff. Gradually beat in sugar. Fold in soda crackers and chopped nuts. Pour into a greased 12 x 9 x 2-inch pan. Bake at 350° for 25 minutes. Cool. Prepare Dream Whip according to directions on package. Top cracker pie with Dream Whip and then with pie filling. Refrigerate. Makes 12 servings.

MRS. ZELMA L. TUCKER   BRIGHTON EARLY BIRDS UNIT

CRANBERRY PIE

½ cup butter
¼ cup shortening
2 eggs
1½ cups sugar

1 cup flour
2 cups fresh cranberries (washed
  and well dried)
½ cup English walnuts, chopped

Melt butter and shortening. Let cool. Beat eggs, add sugar and flour a little at a time to butter and shortening. Stir in cranberries and nuts. Pour into a greased 10-inch pie pan. Bake 40 minutes at 325°.

DONA HUBERT   DANDY DOERS UNIT

PASTRIES

SELF CRUST CUSTARD PIE

¾ cup sugar
3 tablespoons flour
3 eggs
Pinch of salt

1 teaspoon vanilla
3 tablespoons margarine, melted
1 can Milnot
Nutmeg

Mix above ingredients and pour into a greased and floured 9-inch pie pan. Sprinkle with nutmeg. Bake at 350° for 20 minutes or until set. Makes 6 to 8 servings.

MRS. DARRELL (BETTY) MOLEN   JUNIOR HOMEMAKERS UNIT

IMPOSSIBLE PIE

1½ cups flaked coconut
1 13-ounce can Milnot
⅓ cup water
4 eggs
1⅛ cups sugar
½ cup flour

½ teaspoon cream of tartar
½ cup butter or margarine at
  room temperature
1 teaspoon vanilla
Pinch of salt

Butter the bottom of a 10-inch glass pie pan. Spread with coconut. Place all other ingredients in blender container; blend well on high speed or can be beaten with a mixer. Carefully pour mixture over coconut, being sure coconut is moistened. Bake at 350° for approximately 35 to 40 minutes or until lightly browned and firm. Serve at room temperature or chilled. It forms its own crust.

NEVA SKINNER   BIRD UNIT

IMPOSSIBLE PIE

4 eggs
6 tablespoons butter
½ cup flour
½ teaspoon salt

2 cups milk
1 cup sugar
1 teaspoon vanilla
1 cup coconut

Put all ingredients into blender in order given. Blend for 10 seconds at a time—four times. Pour into a buttered and floured 10-inch pie plate. Bake at 350° for 50 to 60 minutes. The pie is done when the top is starting to turn golden.

DONA HUBERT   DANDY DOERS UNIT

IMPOSSIBLE PEANUT BUTTER PIE

3 eggs
6 tablespoons butter or
margarine
½ cup flour
½ teaspoon salt

1 cup light or dark syrup
1 cup sugar
⅓ cup chunky style peanut
butter
½ teaspoon vanilla

Put all ingredients into blender jar. Blend 10 seconds at a time, 3 or 4 times. If flour or other ingredients stick to sides of jar, use rubber spatula to loosen (while blender is stopped). Pour into a buttered and floured 9-inch pie pan. Bake at 350° for 50 minutes or until done. Makes 6 servings.

JO MAXEINER   BERTHA ELDRED UNIT

JEFF DAVIS PIE

3 egg yolks
1 cup sugar
½ cup milk
1 tablespoon butter

1 tablespoon cornstarch
1 teaspoon lemon extract
1 pastry shell, unbaked

Mix all together and pour into unbaked 9-inch pie shell. Bake slowly at 350° until set.

Meringue:
3 egg whites, beaten

3 tablespoons sugar

Beat egg whites until dry. Add sugar, beat until peaks form. Spread on baked pie. Return to oven to brown. Makes 6 to 8 servings.

MRS. IVAN JENKINS   GIRARD DAY UNIT

OHIO LEMON PIE

2 lemons, sliced thin
2 cups sugar

4 eggs, beaten
2 9-inch pie crusts

Slice the lemon, rind and all, as thin as paper. Place in a bowl and mix with the sugar. Let stand 2 hours or more. Line 9-inch pie pan with crust. Add the beaten eggs to lemon mixture. Mix well. Pour into crust. Add top crust which has small vents to let out the steam. Bake at 450° for 15 minutes, then reduce heat to 350° and bake until a silver knife comes out clean.

CHRISTINE SELVO   CARLINVILLE NIGHT UNIT

LEMONADE PIE

Graham Cracker Crust:
1¼ cups graham cracker
  crumbs
¼ cup sugar

¼ cup butter or margarine,
  softened

Combine graham cracker crumbs, butter or margarine, and sugar. Press into a 10-inch pie pan. Bake at 375° for 5 to 8 minutes.

1 3-ounce can frozen pink
  lemonade

1 large carton Cool Whip
1 can Eagle Brand milk

Combine all three ingredients on lowest speed of mixer. Pour into the baked graham cracker crust. Chill in refrigerator overnight. Makes 10 servings.

MAXINE RATTERMAN   HONEY POINT UNIT

KEY BISCAYNE LIME PIE

4 eggs, separated, reserving
  whites
1 14-ounce can sweetened
  condensed milk
½ cup lime juice
2 to 3 teaspoons grated lime
  peel

Few drops green food coloring
1 baked 9-inch pie shell
½ teaspoon cream of tartar
½ cup sugar

Beat egg yolks; stir in milk, lime juice, peel, and food coloring. Beat one egg white until stiff; fold into milk mixture. Turn into pastry shell.

Beat reserved egg whites with cream of tartar until foamy; gradually add sugar, beating until stiff but not dry. Spread meringue on top of pie, sealing to edge. Bake at 350° for 15 minutes or until meringue is golden brown. Cool, then chill before serving. Makes 6 servings.

KIM MANSFIELD   SCOTTVILLE UNIT

PECAN PIE

3 eggs
⅔ cup sugar
1¼ cups Mrs. Butterworth's
  syrup

1 cup pecans, chopped
1 9-inch pie shell, unbaked

Beat all ingredients except pecans with rotary beater. Place nuts in bottom of pie shell and pour mixture over them. Bake at 375° for 40 to 50 minutes. Makes 8 servings.

KATHY SIEGEL   NILWOOD UNIT

MACAROON PIE

3 egg whites
1 cup sugar
1 teaspoon vanilla

½ cup pecans, broken
12 dates, diced
2 soda crackers, crumbled

Beat egg whites until frothy. Add sugar a little at a time, continue beating until stiff and all the sugar is dissolved. Add vanilla and stir. Add pecans. dates, and soda crackers. Mix well. Pour into an 8-inch buttered pan. Bake at 325° for 40 minutes. Makes 6 servings.

MARIE W. PAYNTER   PIASA UNIT

MYSTERY PIE

3 egg whites, beaten
1 cup sugar
1 teaspoon baking powder

20 Ritz crackers, crushed
¾ cup pecans, chopped
Cool Whip

Grease a 9-inch pie pan. Beat egg whites until stiff. Gradually add sugar and baking powder. Fold in crushed crackers and pecans. Bake at 325° for 30 minutes. Cool on rack for 30 minutes. Top with Cool Whip and chill for 4 hours before serving. Makes 6 servings.

IDA MAE LEACH   BIRD UNIT

MISSISSIPPI PECAN PIE

1 cup dark corn syrup
¾ cup sugar
3 eggs, slightly beaten
3 tablespoons butter

1 teaspoon vanilla
1 cup pecans, coarsely broken
1 unbaked pie shell

Boil sugar and syrup together about 2 minutes. Pour slowly over eggs, stirring well. This can be done with the mixer. Add butter, vanilla, and nuts. Turn into a 9-inch pie shell. Bake in 375° oven for 50 minutes or until done. Pie is done when completely puffed across top. Makes 6 to 8 servings.

NORMA KEAGY   POLK UNIT

OATMEAL PIE

1 cup sugar
1 cup corn syrup
½ stick margarine
4 tablespoons canned milk
  or cream
1 teaspoon vanilla

1 cup coconut
1 cup uncooked oats
3 eggs
Dash of salt
1 unbaked deep dish pie shell

Mix all ingredients thoroughly and pour into unbaked pie shell. Bake 30 minutes at 375°. Makes 8 servings.

KATHLEEN JOPLIN   GIRARD NIGHT UNIT

OUT OF THIS WORLD PIE

1 can cherry pie filling
¾ cup sugar
1 large can crushed
  pineapple, undrained
1 tablespoon cornstarch
1 teaspoon red food coloring

1 3-ounce box raspberry Jello
6 bananas, sliced
1 cup pecans, chopped
2 pie shells, baked
Cool Whip or Dream Whip

In saucepan combine cherry pie filling, sugar, pineapple and juice, cornstarch, and food coloring. Cook over low heat until thick. Stir while cooking. Remove from heat. Add Jello and nuts. Cool. Add bananas. Pour into 2 baked pie shells. Top with Cool Whip or Dream Whip. Chill.

CORA MATLOCK   SHIPMAN UNIT

PUMPKIN PIE

3 eggs, slightly beaten
1½ cups pumpkin
1½ teaspoons pumpkin pie
  spice
½ teaspoon salt

1 scant cup sugar
2 tablespoons oil
1 cup milk
1 teaspoon vanilla
1 unbaked pie shell

Beat eggs, add to pumpkin. Add pumpkin pie spice and salt to sugar and then to pumpkin mixture. Add oil, milk, and vanilla. Pour into unbaked 9-inch pie shell. Bake at 425° for 20 minutes. Reduce heat to 325° and bake 45 minutes or until center of pie is done. Makes 6 servings.

ESTHER DOERR   BUNKER HILL UNIT

ELSAH'S NOTABLE PECAN PIE
(From Mississippi town of Elsah, Illinois)

8-ounce package cream
  cheese
⅓ cup sugar
4 eggs
1 teaspoon vanilla
¼ cup sugar

1¼ cups pecans, coarsely
  chopped
1 cup light corn syrup
¼ teaspoon salt
1 teaspoon vanilla
10-inch pie shell, unbaked

In large mixing bowl at medium speed, beat until smooth the cream cheese, 1 egg, ⅓ cup sugar and 1 teaspoon vanilla. Spread over bottom of unbaked pastry shell. Sprinkle with the pecans. In clean bowl at medium speed beat the remaining 3 eggs until frothy. Add corn syrup, salt, and ¼ cup sugar and 1 teaspoon vanilla. Blend and pour gently over pecans. Bake in preheated 375° oven about 40 minutes or until a knife inserted comes out clean. Place on wire rack to cool before cutting. Makes 10 servings.

MRS. LOUIS (EVELYN) LEBRO   SPANISH NEEDLE UNIT

HAWAIIAN PINEAPPLE PIE

3 eggs
1 cup brown sugar, firmly
  packed
½ cup sugar
2 tablespoons butter or
  margarine, melted
1 teaspoon vanilla

½ cup rolled oats, uncooked
½ cup coconut
½ cup white raisins
1 8-ounce can crushed
  pineapple, undrained
1 9-inch pie shell, unbaked

Preheat oven to 350°. In large mixer bowl beat eggs at high speed until lemon colored. Beat in sugars. Add butter and vanilla. Mix well. Stir in oats, raisins, pineapple, and coconut. Mix well. Pour mixture into unbaked pie shell. Bake for 50 to 55 minutes or until filling is set. Cool before serving. Makes 8 servings.

MRS. A. D. ANDERSON   SHAWS POINT UNIT

PUMPKIN PIE

1 cup sugar
1 tablespoon flour
1 teaspoon allspice
1 teaspoon cinnamon
¼ teaspoon ginger

1 egg
1 cup milk
1 cup cooked pumpkin
Pastry for 8-inch pie

Line 8-inch pie pan with pastry. Using mixer, mix all ingredients together until smooth. Pour into unbaked pie shell. Bake at 425° for 10 minutes. Reduce heat to 350° and bake until set. Makes 5 or 6 servings.

MRS. STELLA GROVES   SHAWS POINT UNIT

PUMPKIN PECAN PIE

½ cup brown sugar
½ cup granulated sugar
1 tablespoon flour
½ teaspoon salt
1 teaspoon cinnamon
1¾ cups pumpkin

3 eggs, slightly beaten
1½ cups milk
3 tablespoons chopped pecans
1 teaspoon vanilla
9-inch pastry shell, unbaked

Mix sugars, flour, salt and cinnamon. Add pumpkin, eggs, and milk. Beat well. Heat over low heat until custard begins to thicken. Remove from heat. Add pecans and vanilla. Pour into 9-inch pastry-lined pan. Bake at 450° for 10 minutes. Reduce heat to 325° and continue baking for 45 minutes more or until knife inserted in center comes out clean.

ALENE E. RUYLE   SCOTTVILLE UNIT

RHUBARB CREAM PIE

1 cup cubed rhubarb
1 cup sugar
3 tablespoons flour

½ cup cream
1 tablespoon butter
1 teaspoon lemon juice

Mix ingredients together and pour into prebaked pie shell. Sprinkle with nutmeg. Bake at 425° for 30 minutes.

MRS. JEANETTE BAKER   MONDAY NITERS UNIT

RHUBARB ORANGE CREAM PIE

Pastry for 9-inch pie shell
3 eggs, separated
1¼ cups sugar
¼ cup butter or margarine,
  softened
3 tablespoons frozen orange
  juice concentrate

¼ cup flour
1 teaspoon salt
2½ cups rhubarb cut in ½-inch
  pieces
⅓ cup pecans, chopped
  (optional)

Line 9-inch pie pan with pastry. Make high fluted rim. Beat egg whites until stiff, add ¼ cup sugar gradually. Beat well. Add butter and juice concentrate to egg yolks; beat thoroughly. Add remaining 1 cup of sugar, flour, and salt. Beat well. Add rhubarb to yolk mixture and stir well. Gently fold in meringue. Pour into pastry lined pan. Sprinkle with nuts. Bake on bottom rack in 375° oven for 15 minutes. Reduce heat to 325° and bake 45 to 50 minutes more. Makes 6 or 8 servings.

GWEN BOEHME   MT. OLIVE UNIT

SHAMROCK PIE

Chocolate wafers
1 3-ounce package lime
  gelatin
1¼ cups boiling water
1 tablespoon lemon juice
2 tablespoons creme de
  menthe, or few drops
  green food coloring and
  mint extract

1 8¼-ounce can crushed
  pineapple and syrup
1 cup heavy cream, whipped
½ cup flaked coconut

Arrange single layer of chocolate wafers in bottom of 9-inch pie plate; stand additional wafers around the edge. Fill empty places on bottom with broken wafers. Set aside. Dissolve gelatin in boiling water. Add lemon juice and creme de menthe. Chill until thickened, stirring often. Fold in crushed pineapple. Fold in beaten whipped cream. Turn into chocolate wafer pie shell. Chill until firm. To make shamrock decorations, chop coconut very fine. Shake in jar with few drops green food coloring. Cut out a shamrock shape in a piece of waxed paper large enough to cover pie. Place paper over pie and sprinkle coconut over open shamrock area. Carefully remove paper. Makes 6 to 8 servings.

ALBERTA WILTON   CARLINVILLE NIGHT UNIT

231

STRAWBERRY PIE

1 quart strawberries	1 package strawberry Jello
1 cup water	1 cup sugar
1 tablespoon cornstarch	1 baked pie shell

Put strawberries in a 9-inch baked pie shell. Bring half of the water to a boil. Mix rest of the cool water with cornstarch, then add to boiling water, along with the Jello and sugar. Boil mixture 1 minute. Cool. Pour over berries. Garnish with whipped cream, ice cream, or Cool Whip. This pie may be frozen. Makes 6 servings.

MRS. WILLIAM THOMAS   SOUTH OTTER UNIT

STRAWBERRY GLAZE PIE

1 cup sugar	4 cups strawberries, sliced
1 tablespoon cornstarch	Whipped cream
1 cup water	
1 3-ounce package	
strawberry Jello	

In saucepan, mix sugar, cornstarch, and water. Cook over low heat until thickened. Remove from heat and add Jello. Stir well and let cool. Add strawberries. Pour into baked and cooled 9-inch pie crust. Refrigerate at least 3 hours. Top with whipped cream. Makes 8 servings.

Pie Crust:

1 cup flour	½ teaspoon sugar
½ stick margarine	¼ teaspoon salt
¼ cup Crisco	3 to 4 tablespoons cold water

Blend first 5 ingredients with pastry blender until coarse crumbs. Add cold water. Mix until ball forms. Roll out to fit 9-inch pan. Prick with a fork and bake at 450° for 10 to 12 minutes or until light brown. Cool.

ELDA CREW   CARLINVILLE DAY UNIT

WHITE PIE

2 cups milk
¾ cup sugar
½ cup flour
Pinch salt
1 teaspoon vanilla

Whites of 2 eggs
¼ cup sugar
1 9-inch baked pie shell
Dream Whip
Nuts

Cook milk, ¾ cup sugar, flour, and salt in double boiler until very thick. Add vanilla. Beat egg whites with ¼ cup sugar until stiff. Fold in cooked mixture and pour into baked pie shell. Top with Dream Whip and decorate with nuts. Makes 6 servings.

MARGARET FRIEDMAN   HONEY POINT UNIT

CINNAMON TOAST COBBLER

3½ cups peaches, sliced,
   drain and reserve juice (or
   1 large can)
1 tablespoon cornstarch
¼ teaspoon salt
1 tablespoon lemon juice

¼ cup butter, melted
3 slices rather dry white bread
¼ cup butter, melted
⅓ cup sugar
½ teaspoon cinnamon
¼ teaspoon nutmeg

Mix drained peach juice with cornstarch and salt. Cook slowly, stirring frequently. Add lemon juice and ¼ cup butter. Add peaches and let come to a bubbling boil. Pour peach mixture into an 8 or 9-inch square pan. Set aside. Cut bread slices into 1-inch strips. Dip strips into the ¼ cup melted butter. Cover peach mixture with bread strips. Sprinkle strips with a mixture of the sugar, cinnamon and nutmeg. Bake at 350° for 30 minutes. Makes 8 to 10 servings.

FLORA BURNS   CARLINVILLE DAY UNIT

CHERRY COBBLER

1 1-pound 5-ounce can
   cherry pie filling
½ cup sugar
1 stick margarine, softened
1 cup sifted flour

¼ teaspoon salt
1 teaspoon baking powder
½ cup milk
¾ cup sugar
½ cup water

Pour cherry pie filling into 8 x 8-inch pan. Cream ½ cup sugar and margarine. Sift flour, salt and baking powder together; add to creamed mixture alternately with milk. Spread batter over pie filling. Sprinkle ¾ cup sugar over top; pour water over all. Bake at 400° for 35 to 40 minutes. Other fruit pie fillings may be used.

LELA KLAUS   HONEY POINT UNIT

PEACH COBBLER

3 or 4 cups fresh peaches,
sliced
2 teaspoons lemon peel,
grated
3 tablespoons lemon juice
2 tablespoons quick cooking
tapioca
1½ cups sifted flour

¼ teaspoon salt
2 teaspoons baking powder
⅓ cup butter or margarine
1 egg, beaten
⅓ cup milk
1 cup sugar
½ cup water
2 tablespoons butter

Put peaches in bottom of 2-quart casserole. Sprinkle with lemon peel, juice, and tapioca. Sift together flour, salt and baking powder. Cut in ⅓ cup butter until it forms coarse crumbs. Combine egg and milk, stir in flour mixture, and mix until moist. Spoon over peaches. Combine 1 cup sugar, water, and 2 tablespoons butter. Bring to a boil. Pour over batter immediately. Bake at 375° for 45 minutes. Makes 6 servings.

COMMITTEE

PEACH COBBLER

5 cups peaches, sliced
Juice of ½ lemon
⅓ cup sugar
3 tablespoons butter
¾ cup sugar
½ cup milk

1 cup flour
1 teaspoon baking powder
1 cup sugar
2 teaspoons tapioca
½ teaspoon salt
1 cup cold water

Line an 8 x 12-inch pan with peaches. Sprinkle on lemon juice and ⅓ cup sugar. Cream butter with ¾ cup sugar, add dry ingredients alternately with milk. Pour over fruit. Mix 1 cup sugar, tapioca and salt. Sprinkle over batter. Pour water over all. Bake at 350° for 45 minutes until browned on top. Serve with whipped topping.

MRS. LOUIS GRANDONE   GET TOGETHERS UNIT

QUICK COBBLER

1 stick margarine
1 cup flour
1 cup sugar

1 tablespoon baking powder
⅔ cup milk
3 to 4 cups fresh fruit

Melt margarine in a 13 x 9 x 2-inch cake pan. Mix flour, sugar, baking powder, and milk together. Pour into margarine in pan. Mix. Pour fruit over top. Bake at 375° for 30 to 45 minutes. Makes 15 servings.

MRS. DEAN CLARK   MODELITE UNIT

CAKES

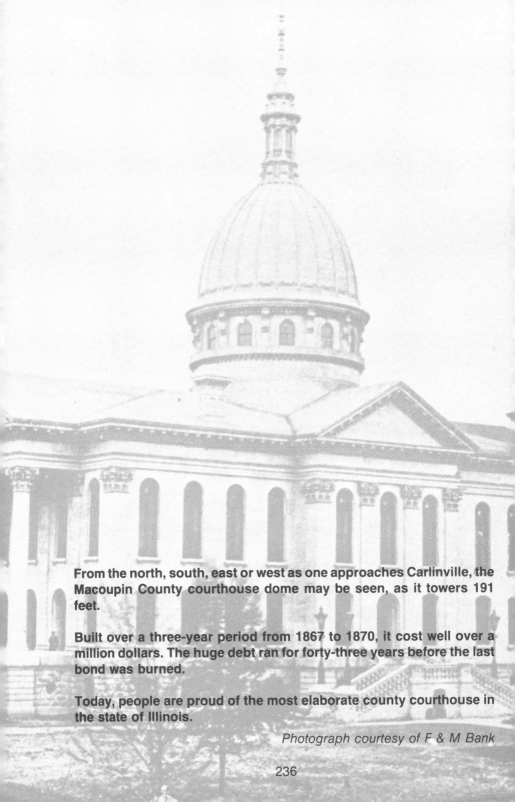

From the north, south, east or west as one approaches Carlinville, the Macoupin County courthouse dome may be seen, as it towers 191 feet.

Built over a three-year period from 1867 to 1870, it cost well over a million dollars. The huge debt ran for forty-three years before the last bond was burned.

Today, people are proud of the most elaborate county courthouse in the state of Illinois.

Photograph courtesy of F & M Bank

APPLE CAKE

1 cup sugar
1 stick margarine
1 cup water
1 cup raisins
1 teaspoon cinnamon

½ teaspoon cloves
2 raw apples, diced
2 cups flour
1 teaspoon baking soda
½ cup nuts

In a saucepan, boil for 3 minutes sugar, margarine, water, raisins, cinnamon, cloves, and apples. Cool. Add flour, baking soda, and nuts. Bake in greased 9 x 11-inch baking pan at 350° for 20 minutes or until tests done. Glaze with powdered sugar icing. Variation: Candied fruit may be added.

BARBARA GREAVES   STITCH AND STIR UNIT

APPLE CAKE

2 eggs
1 teaspoon vanilla
2 cups sugar
1½ cups oil
3 cups flour

1 teaspoon salt
1 teaspoon cinnamon
1 teaspoon baking soda
3 cups apples, chopped

In mixing bowl, stir (by hand, not mixer) eggs, vanilla, and sugar. Add oil and mix well. Fold in flour, salt, cinnamon, and baking soda. Add apples and pour into ungreased 9 x 13 x 2-inch pan. Bake at 300° for 1 hour. Store in loosely covered pan or freeze.

ROSE MARIE VESPER   STAUNTON UNIT

APPLE CAKE

1¾ cups sugar
3 eggs
1 cup oil
2 cups flour
1 teaspoon baking soda

1 teaspoon cinnamon
1 teaspoon salt
2 cups apples, chopped
1 cup nuts, chopped

Mix together sugar, eggs, and oil. Sift together flour, baking soda, cinnamon, salt. Add to sugar mixture. Fold in apples and nuts. Bake in a greased 9 x 12-inch pan at 375° for 45 minutes. Serve with whipped topping while warm. Makes 12 3x3-inch pieces.

ROSETTA PITMAN   PLAINVIEW UNIT

APPLE CAKE

1 cup sugar
2 cups apples, diced
1 egg
1 cup flour, sifted

1½ teaspoons cinnamon
1 teaspoon baking soda
½ cup nuts, chopped

Mix sugar with apples and let stand until sugar is dissolved. Add egg and beat well. Sift dry ingredients together and stir into apple mixture. Add nuts. Pour into 8-inch square pan and bake at 375° for 40 minutes. Serve with Hot Sauce. Makes 9 to 12 servings.

Hot Sauce:
½ cup brown sugar
½ cup sugar
2 tablespoons flour

1 cup water
¼ cup butter or margarine
1 teaspoon vanilla

While cake is baking, prepare sauce. Cook sugars, flour, and water together until clear or transparent. Add butter and vanilla. Stir until butter is melted. Pour over cake while both are hot.

LUCINA LINK   BERTHA ELDRED UNIT

FRESH APPLE CAKE

2 eggs
2 cups sugar
1½ cups oil
2 tablespoons vanilla
1 tablespoon ReaLemon
    lemon juice

3 cups flour
1 teaspoon salt
1½ teaspoons baking soda
1½ cups pecans, chopped
3 cups apples, chopped

Beat eggs, sugar, oil, vanilla, and lemon juice together. Add dry ingredients. Mix well. Add pecans and apples. Place in greased and floured tube or bundt pan and bake at 325° for 1 hour and 30 minutes. Frost.

Icing:
½ cup brown sugar
½ stick margarine

2 tablespoons cream (can use
    Milnot)

Heat ingredients in saucepan until melted. Let cake set a short while, then remove from pan and invert. Pour cooled glaze over top of the cake.

LINDA GWILLIM   STITCH AND STIR UNIT

RAW APPLE CAKE

3 eggs
1½ cups salad oil or
  margarine
2 cups sugar
3 cups flour
¼ cup milk
½ tablespoon cinnamon

2 teaspoons baking soda
1 teaspoon salt
2 teaspoons vanilla
3 cups apples, pared and
  chopped
½ cup pecans or walnuts,
  chopped

Combine ingredients in order listed. Spread in 9 x 13-inch pan or 10-inch tube pan. Bake at 350° for 35 to 40 minutes. Reduce heat to 300° and bake for 10 minutes more. While cake is still warm, add topping.

Topping:
¼ cup butter   1 cup brown sugar
¼ cup milk

Bring ingredients to a boil, cook 2½ minutes. Spread on baked cake.

MRS. JERRY ROYER   DO MORE UNIT

PARTY ANGEL FOOD

1 cup plus 2 tablespoons
  cake flour, sifted
¾ cup sugar
1⅔ cups egg whites
1½ teaspoons cream of tartar
½ teaspoon salt

1 cup sugar
1 teaspoon vanilla
½ teaspoon almond extract
10 maraschino cherries, chopped
½ cup pecans, chopped

Sift cake flour and ¾ cup sugar four times. Combine egg whites, cream of tartar and salt. Beat until egg whites are stiff but not dry. Add 1 cup sugar, 2 tablespoons at a time, mixing well after each addition. Add flour mixture in 4 parts, folding about 15 strokes after each addition. Add vanilla and almond extract. Fold in cherries and pecans. Put into 10-inch tube pan. Pull spatula through batter to break bubbles. Bake at 350° for 45 minutes. Makes 12 servings.

PANSY MILLER   SHAWS POINT UNIT

CHOCOLATE PECAN ANGEL FOOD

1 cup cake flour, sifted
¼ cup cocoa
1 cup plus 2 tablespoons
  powdered sugar
12 large egg whites

Pinch of salt
1 teaspoon cream of tartar
1 teaspoon vanilla
1 cup plus 2 tablespoons sugar
1 cup pecans, chopped

Sift flour, cocoa, and powdered sugar together 3 times. Combine egg whites, salt, cream of tartar, and vanilla in large bowl. Beat until stiff peaks form. Fold in granulated sugar that has been sifted twice. Sift in flour mixture in 4 additions, folding in with large spoon, turning bowl often. Add pecans. Bake in 10-inch tube pan at 375° for 40 minutes. Cool cake upside down in pan, resting on cake rack. Loosen from sides when cool and remove from pan. Makes 15 servings.

RUTH MALHAM   CARLINVILLE DAY UNIT

GREEN ANGEL CAKE

1 package angel food cake
  mix

1 3-ounce package lime Jello

Prepare cake mix as directed on package, folding gelatin into ⅓ of the batter. Alternately spoon batters into ungreased 10-inch tube pan. Zigzag spatula through batters. Bake on lowest rack of oven at 350° for 40 to 45 minutes until cake springs back when lightly pressed. Turn pan upside down over funnel or bottle to cool completely. Remove from pan. Frost and garnish with lime slices, if desired. Chill.

Fluffy Fruit Flavor Frosting:
1 3-ounce package lime Jello
1 cup boiling water

1 9-ounce container Cool Whip

Dissolve Jello in boiling water. Chill until slightly thickened. Blend in Cool Whip. Spread over cake. Makes 10 servings.

MARIE REED   SUSTAINING MEMBER

HEAVENLY ANGEL FOOD CAKE

1½ cups egg whites
¼ cup cold water
½ teaspoon salt
1 teaspoon vanilla

1½ teaspoons cream of tartar
2 cups sugar, sifted
1½ cups cake flour, sifted

Add salt, water, and vanilla to egg whites and beat until foamy. Add cream of tartar and whip until stiff. Sift 1 cup of sugar and all of flour together 3 times. Add remaining 1 cup of sugar to egg whites, 2 tablespoons at a time. Fold in flour and sugar mixture. Bake in angel food tube pan at 350° for 40 minutes.

PEGGY BRUCE   HONEY POINT UNIT

30 MINUTE ANGEL FOOD CAKE

1¼ cups cake flour
1½ cups sugar
1½ cups egg whites

¼ teaspoon salt
1 teaspoon cream of tartar
1 teaspoon flavoring

Sift flour once before measuring. Sift 1 cup sugar with flour several times. Beat egg whites, add salt, beat until frothy. Add cream of tartar and continue beating until stiff but not dry. Beat in remaining sugar and flavoring. Fold in flour and sugar mixture. Bake in angel food cake pan. Preheat oven to 400°. Bake at 375° for 30 minutes.

ROSALIE GRICHNIK   SPANISH NEEDLE UNIT

BANANA CAKE

1½ cups sugar
½ cup butter or margarine
2 eggs
1 cup bananas, mashed

1 teaspoon baking soda
4 tablespoons sour milk
1½ cups flour
Nuts, optional

Cream sugar and butter. Add eggs and bananas. Mix baking soda and sour milk. Add this to butter mixture. Add flour and mix well. Pour into a loaf pan and bake at 350° for 45 to 50 minutes. If using nuts, add before baking.

HESTER B. PARSONS   BRUSHY MOUND UNIT

BANANA TORTE

½ cup butter or margarine
½ cup sugar
4 eggs, separated
1 cup flour, sifted

2 teaspoons baking powder
¼ teaspoon salt
5 tablespoons milk
1 teaspoon vanilla

Cream together butter and sugar. Add egg yolks, beating well after each addition. Add flour to which baking powder and salt have been added, alternately with milk and vanilla, starting and ending with flour mixture. Pour into two 8-inch round lined and greased cake pans. Beat egg whites until they form a peak. Add ½ cup sugar a little at a time, beating continuously, till very stiff. Spread meringue on each cake top, being careful not to disturb cake mixture. Sprinkle with chopped nuts and bake 25 minutes at 350°.

Keep meringue side up when cake is removed from pan. When cakes are cool, slice bananas on one cake top, and cover with cream filling. Place remaining layer on top of lower layer. If desired, decorate with a few pieces of well drained, diced marachino cherries. Make your own cream filling, or use instant.

MRS. EWELL (JOSEPHINE) HARRIS   SUSTAINING MEMBER

BLUE RIBBON BANANA CAKE

¾ cup shortening
1½ cups sugar
1 cup bananas, mashed
½ cup buttermilk
1 teaspoon vanilla
2 eggs

½ teaspoon salt
2 cups cake flour, sifted
1 teaspoon baking soda
1 teaspoon baking powder
½ cup pecans, chopped
1 cup flaked coconut

Cream together shortening and sugar until fluffy. Add mashed bananas, beat 2 minutes. Sift together dry ingredients and add to creamed mixture, along with buttermilk and vanilla. Beat 2 minutes. Stir in nuts and coconut. Pour into 2 greased and floured 9-inch layer pans. Bake at 375° for 25 to 30 minutes.

JEAN KLAUS   HONEY POINT UNIT

BLACK WALNUT CAKE

¾ cup soft shortening
1¼ cups light brown sugar
1 cup sugar
3 eggs
3 cups plus 3 tablespoons
   cake flour, sifted

1 teaspoon baking soda
1 teaspoon salt
1½ cups buttermilk or sour milk
1 cup black walnuts, finely
   chopped
1 teaspoon vanilla

Cream together shortening and sugars until light and fluffy. Add eggs, one at a time, beating well after each addition. Sift together flour, baking soda, and salt. Add flour mixture alternately with buttermilk to creamed mixture. Stir in walnuts and vanilla. Pour batter into 3 9-inch layer pans. Bake at 350° for 35 to 40 minutes.

MRS. HENRY GRYSIEWICZ   STAUNTON UNIT

BROWN SUGAR CHIFFON CAKE

1¾ cups flour
¾ cup sugar
¾ cup brown sugar, packed
3 teaspoons baking powder
1 teaspoon salt
½ cup oil

6 egg yolks
⅔ cup cold milk
2 teaspoons vanilla
6 egg whites
½ teaspoon cream of tartar

Combine first 5 ingredients and make a well in center. Add oil, egg yolks, milk, and vanilla. Beat at medium speed until smooth. Set aside. Combine egg whites and cream of tartar. Beat until very stiff. Gradually pour egg yolk mixture over egg whites, folding in gently with a wire whip. Pour batter into an angel food or tube pan. Bake at 325° for 55 minutes in angel food pan. For tube pan, bake at 350° for 65 minutes. Frost. Makes 16 servings.

Frosting:
1 cup whipping cream
¼ cup brown sugar

½ teaspoon vanilla

Whip ingredients together until stiff.

BEVERLY LEACH   MONDAY NITERS UNIT

BUTTERSCOTCH CAKE

1 box yellow deluxe cake mix
1 package instant
   butterscotch pudding
⅔ cup warm water

½ cup oil
4 eggs
1 cup nuts, chopped

Preheat oven to 350°. Blend all ingredients as listed in large bowl. Beat at medium speed 7 to 10 minutes. Bake in greased and floured 10-inch tube pan for 50 to 55 minutes (test). While cake is warm, punch holes with ice pick all over top of cake. Pour glaze mixture over top of cake. Cool before removing.

Glaze:
Blend ½ cup hot water and 2 teaspoons instant coffee. Add to 2 cups powdered sugar.

COMMITTEE

CARROT PINEAPPLE CAKE

1½ cups flour
1 cup sugar
1 teaspoon baking powder
1 teaspoon baking soda
1 teaspoon ground cinnamon
½ teaspoon salt

⅔ cup cooking oil
2 eggs
1 cup carrots, finely shredded
½ cup crushed pineapple with
   syrup
1 teaspoon vanilla

In large mixing bowl, stir together dry ingredients. Add oil, eggs, carrots, pineapple and vanilla. Mix until all ingredients are moistened. Beat with electric mixer 2 minutes at medium speed. Pour batter into greased and lightly floured 9 x 9 x 2-inch baking pan. Bake at 350° about 35 minutes. Cool and frost.

Frosting:
1 3-ounce package cream
   cheese, softened
4 tablespoons butter or
   margarine, softened

1 teaspoon vanilla
Dash of salt
2½ cups powdered sugar, sifted
½ cup pecans, chopped

Cream together the cream cheese and butter. Beat in vanilla and salt. Gradually add the powdered sugar. Blend well. Stir in pecans.

ADELINE SNEDEKER   PLAINVIEW UNIT

MY SISTER'S CARROT CAKE

2 cups sugar
4 eggs
1½ cups Wesson oil
2 cups carrots, grated

2 cups flour
2 teaspoons baking soda
2 teaspoons cinnamon
1½ cups nuts, chopped

Beat sugar and eggs until fluffy. Add oil and mix. Add carrots, blend thoroughly. Add remaining ingredients and beat 2 minutes. Bake in greased and floured 9 x 13-inch cake pan at 350° for 40 to 45 minutes. Cool completely. Ice with following.

Icing:
½ stick margarine, softened
8 ounces cream cheese,
  softened

1 pound powdered sugar
2 teaspoons vanilla

Beat margarine and cream cheese together. Add vanilla. Add powdered sugar and beat thoroughly. You may have to add small amount of milk if it is too stiff.

BOBBIE FRUEH   JUNIOR HOMEMAKERS UNIT

COCA COLA CAKE

1¾ cups sugar
1 cup margarine, softened
3 tablespoons cocoa
2 eggs
1 teaspoon vanilla
2 cups flour, sifted

¼ teaspoon salt
1 teaspoon baking soda
½ cup buttermilk
1 cup Coca Cola
1½ cups miniature
  marshmallows

Cream sugar and butter; add cocoa, eggs, vanilla. Beat well. Combine flour, salt, baking soda. Mix flour alternately with buttermilk and Coca Cola into creamed mixture. Beat well. Stir in marshmallows. Pour into a greased, floured 9 x 13 x 2-inch pan. Bake at 350° for 40 to 45 minutes. Frost.

Icing:
1 cup pecans
½ cup butter
3 tablespoons cocoa

4 cups powdered sugar
⅓ cup Coca Cola

Brown pecans and butter. Add the cocoa and powdered sugar. (Mixture will be stiff.) Stir in the Coca Cola. Spread on cooled cake.

COMMITTEE

HONOLULU COCONUT CAKE

1 cup butter
2 cups sugar
4 eggs
3 cups flour, sift before
  measuring

4 teaspoons baking powder
1 teaspoon salt
1 cup milk
1 teaspoon vanilla

Cream butter and sugar well. Add eggs, one at a time. Sift dry ingredients three times. Alternately add milk and flour to creamed mixture. Pour into 2 9-inch layer pans. Bake at 350° for 45 minutes. Frost.

Frosting:
¼ cup butter
¼ teaspoon salt
3½ cups powdered sugar
1 small egg

2 tablespoons cream
1 teaspoon vanilla
2 cups coconut

Mix ingredients together well. Frost cake between layers and on top.

MRS. LELA FITZGERALD   HAGAMAN UNIT

ITALIAN CREAM CAKE

1 stick margarine
½ cup vegetable shortening
2 cups sugar
2 cups flour
1 teaspoon baking soda

5 eggs, separated
1 cup buttermilk
1 cup nuts, chopped
1 cup coconut
1 teaspoon vanilla

Cream shortenings and sugar. Sift flour and baking soda. Beat egg yolks. Add egg yolks then flour and buttermilk into creamed mixture, beating well. Stir in nuts, coconut, and vanilla. Fold in 5 beaten egg whites. Pour batter into 3 8-inch cake pans. Bake at 325° for 25 minutes. Cool on racks. Frost with Icing.

Icing:
8 ounces cream cheese
1 stick margarine

1 teaspoon vanilla
1 box powdered sugar

Beat icing ingredients together. Spread over layers then over entire cake. Note: If you like a lighter cake, use half the nuts and coconut.

LOUISE WOODS   BIRD UNIT

COCONUT CAKE

1 package yellow cake mix
1 3-ounce package Jello
  brand instant vanilla
  pudding
1⅓ cups water

4 eggs
¼ cup oil
2 cups Angel Flake coconut
1 cup nuts, chopped

Blend cake mix, pudding mix, water, eggs, and oil in large mixer bowl. Beat at medium speed of electric mixer for 4 minutes. Stir in coconut and nuts. Pour into 3 greased and floured 9-inch layer pans. Bake at 350° for 35 minutes. Cool in pans 15 minutes. Remove from pans and cool completely on racks. Fill between each layer and top with Coconut-Cream Cheese Frosting.

Coconut-Cream Cheese Frosting:
4 tablespoons margarine
2 cups Angel Flake coconut
1 8-ounce package cream
  cheese

2 teaspoons milk
3½ cups powdered sugar, sifted
½ teaspoon vanilla

Melt 2 tablespoons margarine in skillet and add coconut. Stir constantly over low heat until golden brown. Spread coconut on absorbent paper to cool. Cream 2 tablespoons margarine with cream cheese. Add milk, beat in powdered sugar gradually. Blend in vanilla. Stir in 1¾ cups of the coconut. Spread on cake layers, stack all layers, and sprinkle with remaining coconut.

WILMA CLARK   MEDORA UNIT

CROWD CAKE

1 package yellow or white
  cake mix
1 package instant vanilla
  pudding
1 8-ounce package cream
  cheese

1 large container Cool Whip
1 20-ounce can crushed
  pineapple
Coconut
Nuts

Mix cake according to package directions. Pour batter into 15½ x 10½ x 1-inch cookie sheet. Bake at 350° for 20 or 25 minutes. Mix instant pudding with 1 cup milk. Mix and blend well pudding, cream cheese, and Cool Whip. Frost cake. Add topping of crushed pineapple, well drained. Sprinkle coconut and nuts on top to taste. Makes 20 servings.

LILLIAN TETZLAFF   HONEY POINT UNIT

CREME DE MENTHE CAKE

1 box white cake mix   4 tablespoons creme de menthe

Mix cake according to directions on box. Add creme de menthe. Pour into 9 x 13-inch pan. Bake in 350° oven for 45 to 50 minutes or until center springs back when touched lightly with finger. Cool.

Topping:
1 can Hershey's fudge   1 9-ounce carton whipped
  topping (must be   topping
  Hershey's)   4 tablespoons creme de menthe

Spread fudge topping on cool cake. Mix whipped topping with the creme de menthe. Spread over fudge topping. Keep refrigerated.

MRS. ROY WELLER   SOUTH OTTER UNIT

CRUMB CAKE

2 cups flour   Pinch of salt
1½ cups sugar   1 egg
½ cup butter   1 cup buttermilk
½ teaspoon cinnamon   1 teaspoon baking soda

Combine in bowl flour, sugar, butter, cinnamon and salt. Work as for pie crust. Take out ½ cup and reserve for topping. To remainder of flour mixture, add egg, buttermilk, and baking soda. Blend together. Spread in 10 x 13-inch pan. Sprinkle on topping. Bake at 400° for 30 minutes.

SELMA MAKSTELL   GET TOGETHERS UNIT

EASY DESSERT CAKE

1 box strawberry cake mix   3 eggs, beaten
1 can peach pie filling

Mix all ingredients together. Stir thoroughly. Pour into a greased 9 x 13-inch pan. Bake at 350° for 30-35 minutes. Serve with Cool Whip. Makes 12 to 16 servings. Note: Variations—spice cake mix with apple pie filling, chocolate cake mix with cherry pie filling.

VENA HULCHER   GIRARD DAY UNIT

DATE LOAF

4 eggs, separated
1 cup sugar
1 cup flour
2 teaspoons baking powder

2 pounds pitted dates
2 pounds English walnuts
Pinch of salt

Mix egg yolks and sugar to a liquid. Put flour, baking powder, and salt over fruit and nuts. Leave nuts in large pieces. Add egg mixture. Fold in stiffly beaten egg whites. Put into greased 9 x 9-inch pan. Bake at 350° for 45 to 60 minutes.

LORETTA BUTLER   HAGAMAN UNIT

DEVILS FOOD CAKE

1 cup sugar
½ cup shortening
1 egg
1 teaspoon vanilla
2 cups sifted flour

1 teaspoon baking soda
3 tablespoons cocoa
¼ teaspoon salt
1 cup sour milk or buttermilk

Cream together sugar and shortening; add egg and beat well. Add vanilla. Sift flour, baking soda, cocoa, and salt; add alternately with sour milk to creamed mixture. Mix well. Pour into 2 greased 8-inch layer pans. Bake at 350° for 15 to 20 minutes or until toothpick comes out clean. Let layers cool. Frost between layers and on top and sides with Soft Chocolate Icing.

Soft Chocolate Icing:
1 cup sugar
1½ cups milk
2 1-ounce squares bitter
  chocolate

4 tablespoons cold water
3 tablespoons cornstarch
2 tablespoons butter
1 teaspoon vanilla

In saucepan, bring sugar, milk, and chocolate to a boil, stirring constantly. Mix together the cold water and cornstarch. Stir into the chocolate mixture. Cook over low heat until thickened. Remove from heat and add butter and vanilla.

MRS. MARJORY CHISM   HAGAMAN UNIT

DOCTOR BIRD CAKE

3 cups flour, sifted
1 teaspoon baking soda
1 teaspoon cinnamon
2 cups sugar
1 teaspoon salt
2 cups ripe bananas, diced

1 cup cooking oil
3 eggs
1½ teaspoons vanilla
1 8-ounce can crushed
pineapple, undrained
1 cup nut meats, chopped

Sift dry ingredients together. Add the diced bananas along with the oil, eggs, vanilla, and crushed pineapple and juice. Add the chopped nuts. Stir to mix, but do not beat. Pour into a greased and floured 9-inch tube pan. Bake at 350° for 1 hour and 20 minutes.

Note: This is a rich, moist cake that freezes well and is to be served without frosting.

MRS. LEO LOTT   SUSTAINING MEMBER

EGGLESS, MILKLESS, BUTTERLESS CAKE

2 cups sugar
2 cups water
1 cup raisins
⅛ teaspoon salt
⅔ cup lard or shortening
2 teaspoons cinnamon

½ teaspoon cloves
1 teaspoon nutmeg
4 cups flour
2 teaspoons baking soda
½ cup water
2 teaspoons baking powder

Mix the first 8 ingredients in a 2-quart saucepan and put on medium burner. Boil 3 minutes. Set aside and let cool. When the mixture is lukewarm, add flour, baking soda, baking powder, and ½ cup water, adding gradually and mixing well. Pour into greased and floured 13 x 9 x 2-inch pan. Bake at 350° for 30 minutes. Makes 15 servings. Note: May vary by adding nuts, dates, dried fruit. Serve warm with whipped cream or icing. Can also be baked in a loaf pan for 45 minutes.

MRS. MARY SCHWAB   MONDAY NITERS UNIT

APPLESAUCE FRUIT CAKE

1 cup butter
2 cups sugar
2 eggs
2 cups applesauce
2 teaspoon baking soda
4 cups flour
1 tablespoon cinnamon

1 tablespoon allspice
1 teaspoon cloves
1 cup glace fruits
1 cup nuts, chopped
2 cups raisins, soaked and
   drained

Cream together butter and sugar. Add eggs and beat slightly. Mix applesauce with baking soda and add to butter mixture. Combine flour, cinnamon, allspice, and cloves. Stir fruits, nuts, and raisins into flour mixture. Add flour mixture to creamed mixture. Pour into tube pan that has been lined with brown paper cut to fit and greased well. Bake at 300° for 2 hours. Note: Cake can be baked without either the nuts or fruit, if desired.

GAIL SPUDICH   DANDY DOERS UNIT

FRUITCAKE

1 pound mixed candied fruit
1 4-ounce can chopped citron
1 pound pitted dates
½ pound whole candied
   cherries
1 cup raisins
1 cup pecan halves
1 cup walnut halves
4 cups flour, sifted

1 teaspoon salt
 teaspoon ground cinnamon
1 teaspoon ground cloves
½ teaspoon ground nutmeg
1 cup butter
2 cups sugar
4 eggs
1 teaspoon baking soda
1½ cups buttermilk

Prepare 10-inch tube pan by cutting 3 parchment or brown paper liners to fit bottom of pan. Grease each piece of paper with unsalted fat. Top with one layer of waxed paper. Grease all paper and inside of pan generously. Prepare and measure fruit. Leave nuts, cherries, and dates whole. Sift together flour, salt and spices. Use enough of this flour mixture to coat all fruit pieces. Cream butter and sugar; beat in eggs, one at a time. Add soda to remaining flour mixture. Add flour to egg mixture alternately with buttermilk. Mix batter with fruits and nuts. Spoon into prepared tube pan. Bake cake at 300° for 2 hours and 30 minutes. Cool cake out of pan on rack. When cool, baste with orange juice or cider. Wrap in waxed paper, then in foil. Store in covered container in cool place. After two weeks, unwrap and baste again. It is best when cake sets at least three weeks before using.

MAXINE TONSOR   MEDORA UNIT

DARK FRUITCAKE

1 pound seedless raisins	½ teaspoon salt
1¼ cups water	1 teaspoon cinnamon
1½ cups sugar	½ teaspoon cloves
¼ cup shortening	½ teaspoon allspice
2½ cups flour, sifted	1 cup nut meats, chopped
1 teaspoon baking powder	1 package mixed candied fruit
1 tablespoon baking soda	2 eggs

Wash raisins; cook with water and sugar for 5 minutes. Add shortening and cool. Mix and sift dry ingredients together. Add nuts and fruit. Beat eggs until light and fluffy. Add to raisin mixture. Pour over dry ingredients. Bake in greased, paper lined tube or bundt pan in 325° oven for 1 hour and 30 minutes.

WILMA HAMMOND   DO MORE UNIT

GUMDROP FRUIT CAKE

4 cups flour	1 cup pecans
1 teaspoon cinnamon	1 cup shortening
¼ teaspoon cloves	2 eggs
¼ teaspoon nutmeg	1½ cups applesauce
¼ teaspoon salt	1 teaspoon baking soda,
2 cups sugar	dissolved in
1 pound raisins	1 tablespoon hot water
2 pounds large gumdrops	1 teaspoon vanilla
(except black)	

Sift first 5 ingredients together and use part of them to dredge raisins, gumdrops, and pecans. With scissors, cut gumdrops into small pieces. Cream shortening, sugar, and eggs. Add alternately portions of the flour mixture and the applesauce to the creamed mixture. Stir in the baking soda and vanilla, then the raisins, gumdrops, and nuts. Pour into a well greased and floured tube pan. Bake at 275° for 2 hours and 30 minutes or longer until done. Check for doneness by inserting a toothpick in the center. If it comes out clean, cake is done.

FRANCES ANN ROSENTRETER   MONDAY NITERS UNIT

REFRIGERATOR FRUIT CAKE

1 pound graham crackers
1 pound golden raisins
1 quart pecans
¼ pound candied pineapple

¼ pound candied cherries
¼ pound mixed candied fruit
1 5½-ounce can evaporated milk
1 pound marshmallows

Crush graham crackers. Mix graham crackers, fruit and nuts together. Heat can of milk and marshmallows over low heat. Pour over graham cracker and fruit mixture. Mix all together. Line 9 x 12-inch pan with waxed paper. Run cold water over hands so mixture will not stick to hands, and pat cake down in pan. Put in refrigerator. Makes 54 1 x 2-inch pieces.

ROSETTA PITMAN   PLAINVIEW UNIT

GUMDROP CAKE

2 cups carrots, shredded
2⅓ cups water
2½ cups sugar
1 teaspoon allspice
1 teaspoon cinnamon
1 teaspoon cloves
2 tablespoons butter

4 cups flour
3 teaspoons baking soda
2 teaspoons salt
2 cups raisins
1 pound gumdrops, cut into 2 or
  3 pieces
2 cups walnuts, chopped

Combine first 7 ingredients in large saucepan; bring to a boil then simmer for 20 minutes. Cool. Sift dry ingredients into large bowl; add raisins, cut gumdrops, and walnuts. Using hands, break up sticky gumdrops in flour mixture. Add dry ingredients to carrot and spice mixture. Grease 2 5½ x 9½-inch loaf pans with shortening and line with waxed paper. Cut paper to fit pan corners. Fill pans ¾ full. Bake at 325° for 1 to 1½ hours. Remove cakes from pans immediately and remove waxed paper from cakes carefully as gumdrops may pull away from cake. One pound coffee cans may be used or small aluminum loaf pans. Recipe will make 3 small cakes.

DORMA L. CLOSE   SCOTTVILLE UNIT

FUDGE RIBBON CAKE

2 tablespoons butter
1 8-ounce package cream
  cheese
2¼ cups sugar
1 tablespoon cornstarch
3 eggs
2 tablespoons plus 1⅓ cups
  milk

1½ teaspoons vanilla
2 cups flour, sifted
1 teaspoon salt
1 teaspoon baking powder
½ teaspoon baking soda
½ cup butter, softened
4 ounces unsweetened
  chocolate, melted

Cream 2 tablespoons butter with cream cheese, ¼ cup sugar, and cornstarch. Add 1 egg, 2 tablespoons milk, and ½ teaspoon vanilla. Beat at high speed of mixer until smooth and creamy. Set mixture aside. Grease and flour bottom of 13 x 9-inch pan. Combine flour with 2 cups sugar, salt, baking powder, and baking soda in large mixing bowl. Add ½ cup butter and 1 cup milk. Blend well at lowest speed of mixer for about 1½ minutes or 225 strokes by hand. Add ⅓ cup milk, 2 eggs, chocolate, and 1 teaspoon vanilla. Continue beating for 1½ minutes at low speed. Spread half of batter in pan. Spoon cream cheese mixture over batter, spreading carefully to cover. Top with remaining batter, spread to cover. Bake at 350° for 50 to 60 minutes or until cake springs back when touched lightly in center. Cool and frost.

Chocolate Frosting:
¼ cup milk
¼ cup butter
6-ounce package Nestle's
  semi-sweet chocolate
  morsels

1 teaspoon vanilla
2½ cups powdered sugar, sifted

Combine milk and butter in saucepan; bring to a boil. Remove from heat. Blend in chocolate morsels. Stir in vanilla and powdered sugar. Beat until frosting is at spreading consistency. If necessary, thin with a few drops of milk.

ELINOR WALLACE   GIRARD NIGHT UNIT

254

GRAHAM CRACKER AND JELLO CHEESE CAKE

1 package lemon Jello
1 cup water
1 can evaporated milk, chilled
1 8-ounce package cream
  cheese, softened
½ cup sugar

1 teaspoon vanilla
24 graham crackers
1 stick butter or margarine
5 tablespoons sugar
1 teaspoon cinnamon

Dissolve Jello in boiling water and let cool. Whip chilled evaporated milk until thick. Cream the cheese, sugar, and vanilla. Mix together the Jello, whipped milk, and cream cheese mixture. Set aside. To prepare crust, crush graham crackers, add butter or margarine, 5 tablespoons sugar, and cinnamon. Mix well and spread into bottom of 9 x 12-inch pan, reserving 1 tablespoon of mixture for top of cheese cake. Spread cheese mixture over crust. Sprinkle reserved crumbs over top. Chill. Makes 10 servings.

JULIA ARDEN   BERTHA ELDRED UNIT

HEATH BAR BRUNCH CAKE

1 cup brown sugar
½ cup sugar
2 cups flour
1 stick margarine

1 teaspoon vanilla
1 egg, well beaten
1 teaspoon baking soda
1 cup buttermilk

Mix first 5 ingredients together, set aside ½ cup for topping. Add remaining ingredients. Mix well. Pour into greased and floured 9 x 13-inch pan. Sprinkle with topping and cut through.

Topping:
½ cup reserved crumbs
3 Heath bars, crushed while
  still in wrapper

½ cup nuts, chopped

Bake cake with topping in 350° oven for 30 to 35 minutes.

RUBY HOBACK   CARLINVILLE NIGHT UNIT

MRS. JOHN BRUNETTO, GET TOGETHER UNIT uses 8 Heath bars and ¾ cup nuts in topping.

HARVEY WALLBANGER CAKE

1 package yellow cake mix	4 eggs
1 package vanilla instant	¼ cup vodka
pudding	¼ cup Galliano
½ cup cooking oil	¾ cup orange juice

Mix all ingredients together and beat for 4 minutes. Pour batter into well greased and lightly floured bundt pan. Bake at 350° for 45 to 50 minutes. Dust with powdered sugar or frost with orange glaze. Makes 12 servings.

Orange Glaze:

1 cup powdered sugar	1½ tablespoons Galliano
1½ tablespoons vodka	1½ tablespoons orange juice

Mix ingredients together. Drizzle on warm cake. This will soak in.

SALLY ALWARD   SHIPMAN UNIT

CHOCOLATE COCONUT CAKE

1 chocolate cake mix	4 eggs
1 package chocolate instant	¼ cup oil
pudding	2 cups coconut
1⅓ cups water	1 cup nuts, chopped

Blend cake mix, pudding mix, water, eggs, and oil in large bowl. Beat 4 minutes. Stir in coconut and nuts. Pour into 3 greased and floured 8 inch layer pans. Bake at 350° for 30 to 35 minutes. Cool in pans 15 minutes. Frost with recipe below. Makes 16 servings.

Coconut Cream Cheese Frosting:

4 tablespoons margarine	2 teaspoons milk
2 cups coconut	3½ cups powdered sugar
1 8-ounce package cream	½ teaspoon vanilla
cheese	

Melt 2 tablespoons margarine in skillet. Add coconut and stir constantly until golden brown. Spread on paper towels to drain and cool. Cream 2 tablespoons margarine with cream cheese. Add milk. Beat in sugar gradually. Blend in vanilla, stir in 1¾ cups coconut. Frost layers and sprinkle with remaining coconut.

MRS. CHARLES (JEAN) WILLS   BIRD UNIT

DOUBLE CHERRY CHOCOLATE CAKE

1 Pillsbury chocolate fudge
   cake mix
1 package cherry flavored
   gelatin
2 tablespoons salad oil

1 cup water
3 eggs
¼ cup maraschino cherries,
   chopped

Blend in a large mixing bowl cake mix, gelatin, salad oil, and ½ cup water for one minute at low speed. Then beat at medium speed for 2 minutes. Add 2 eggs, one at a time, beating one minute after each addition. Add third egg, cherries, and ½ cup water. Beat at medium speed one minute. Pour into 2 round cake pans or a 9 x 13-inch baking pan, greased and floured. Bake at 350° for 40 to 45 minutes. Cool. Fill and frost with cherry fudge frosting.

Cherry Fudge Frosting:
1 Pillsbury creamy fudge
   frosting mix
Maraschino cherry juice

3 tablespoons cherries, drained
   and chopped
¼ cup nuts, chopped, if desired

Prepare frosting mix as directed on package, substituting maraschino cherry juice for water. Stir in drained cherries and nuts, if desired.

MRS. GRACE POCKLINGTON   NILWOOD UNIT

SOUR CREAM CHOCOLATE CAKE

1¼ cups sugar
1¾ cups cake flour
4 tablespoons cocoa
¼ teaspoon salt
1½ cups sour cream

2 tablespoons butter, melted
2 eggs, well beaten
2 teaspoons baking soda
4 tablespoons boiling water

Sift together sugar, flour, cocoa, and salt. Add sour cream, butter, and eggs. Beat until smooth. Add the baking soda which has been dissolved in the boiling water. Mix well. Bake at 350° for 35 minutes in a well greased and floured 9 x 13-inch pan. Frost with chocolate or seven minute frosting.

THERESA KLAUS   CARLINVILLE NIGHT UNIT

LIGHTENING CAKE

1 cup flour
1 cup sugar
1 teaspoon baking powder
½ teaspoon salt

⅓ cup cooking oil
2 eggs
Milk
1 teaspoon vanilla

Sift flour, sugar, baking powder, and salt into medium size mixing bowl. Measure cooking oil into a measuring cup, add 2 whole eggs. Add enough milk to make 1 cup. Stir into dry ingredients in bowl. Add vanilla. Beat with electric mixer four or five minutes. Pour into greased and floured 8 x 8 x 2-inch baking pan. Bake at 350° for about 30 minutes. Serve warm or cold with chocolate sauce. Makes 9 to 12 servings.

Chocolate Sauce:
1½ cups sugar
5 tablespoons cocoa
3 tablespoons syrup

¾ cup light cream
1 tablespoon butter
1 teaspoon vanilla

Put all ingredients except butter and vanilla into heavy saucepan or iron skillet. Cook over medium heat to soft ball stage. Remove from heat. Stir in butter and vanilla. Note: Cake is also good with fresh strawberries, ice cream or just plain while still warm with butter.

VELMA AMBROSE   SCOTTVILLE UNIT

MY MOTHER'S POTATO CAKE

¾ cup butter or margarine
2 cups sugar
4 eggs, separated
1 teaspoon vanilla
½ cup milk
1 cup warm mashed potatoes

2 cups sifted flour
½ cup cocoa
2 teaspoons baking powder
¼ teaspoon salt
1 cup chopped nuts

Preheat oven to 350°. Cream butter and sugar. Add egg yolks and vanilla and beat until light and fluffy. Add mashed potatoes and mix well. Sift together the dry ingredients and add them alternately with the milk. Mix only until smooth then add nuts. Beat egg whites until stiff and fold into batter. Pour into 2 square 8-inch pans lined with greased wax paper. Bake for 30 to 35 minutes. Cool and frost with your favorite frosting.

MRS. CHARLES WEAVER   SOUTH OTTER UNIT

CHOCOLATE CAKE

1¾ cups sugar	1½ teaspoon baking soda
⅔ cup shortening	½ teaspoon salt
2 eggs	1 cup buttermilk
1 teaspoon vanilla	½ cup cocoa
2½ cups cake flour, sifted	½ cup boiling water

Cream sugar and shortening until fluffy. Add eggs and vanilla. Beat. Sift flour, baking soda, and salt. Add alternately with buttermilk to the creamed mixture. Make a paste of cocoa and water. Let cool and add to batter. Pour into 2 8- or 9-inch layer pans. Bake at 350° for 35 minutes.

JEAN KLAUS   HONEY POINT UNIT

NEVER FAIL CHOCOLATE CUPCAKES

½ cup shortening	1½ cups sifted flour
1 cup sugar	½ cup cocoa
1 egg	½ teaspoon salt
1 teaspoon baking soda	1 teaspoon vanilla
½ cup sour milk	½ cup hot water

Cream shortening and sugar; add egg. Mix baking soda into sour milk and add to creamed mixture. Stir in flour, cocoa, and salt. Add vanilla and hot water, mixing well. Spoon into cupcake liners and bake at 375° for 20 minutes.

MRS. GRANT PITMAN   BIRD UNIT

SWEDISH CAKE

2 cups sugar	1 20-ounce can crushed
2 cups flour	pineapple, undrained
2 teaspoons baking soda	1 teaspoon vanilla
Pinch salt	½ cup pecans
2 eggs	

Mix dry ingredients together; add remaining ingredients and mix by hand. Pour into a greased and floured 9 x 13-inch pan. Bake at 350° for 35 minutes. Makes 18 servings.

MARGY CURTIS   HONEY POINT UNIT

LUSCIOUS DAFFODIL CAKE

2¾ cups sifted cake flour
1½ cups sugar
1 tablespoon baking powder
1 teaspoon salt
½ cup oil
6 eggs, separated

¾ cup cold water
2 teaspoons lemon juice
1 teaspoon grated lemon rind, optional
½ teaspoon cream of tartar

Sift flour, sugar, baking powder and salt together in bowl. Make a well and add in order, the oil, egg yolks, water, lemon juice and rind. Beat with spoon until smooth. Add cream of tartar to egg whites; beat until very, very stiff. Pour egg yolk mixture gradually over whipped whites, carefully folding with rubber scraper just until blended. Do not stir. Pour into 3 ungreased, 9-inch round layer pans. Bake in a very moderate oven, 325°, 25 to 30 minutes, or until the top springs back when touched. Turn each layer upside down on a cake rack; let stand until cold. Run a spatula around the rim of each; turn the layer upside down and remove from pan by gently pressing on the edge of cake with tip of spatula. Frost with seven-minute frosting.

MARIANNA RAMEY   CARLINVILLE NIGHT UNIT

OATMEAL CAKE

1¼ cups boiling water
1 cup quick oats
½ cup shortening
1 cup brown sugar
1 cup sugar
2 eggs, beaten

1 teaspoon cinnamon
1 teaspoon nutmeg
½ teaspoon salt
1½ cups flour
1 teaspoon baking soda

Pour boiling water over oats and let stand 20 minutes. Mix all remaining ingredients together with oats. Pour batter into 13 x 9-inch pan. Bake at 350° for 40 to 45 minutes. Spread topping on hot cake.

Topping:
⅓ cup canned milk
1 cup brown sugar
1 cup coconut

6 tablespoons margarine
½ cup nuts, chopped
1 teaspoon vanilla

Put milk, sugar and margarine in pan. Bring to a boil. Add rest of the ingredients. Spread on hot cake. Broil 5 to 10 minutes. Makes 15 servings.

INEZ ROSS   BARR UNIT

OATMEAL CAKE

1½ cups boiling water
1 cup quick oats
½ cup butter
1 cup brown sugar
1 cup sugar
2 eggs

½ to 1 cup chocolate chips
½ cup nuts
1½ cups flour
1 teaspoon baking soda
1 teaspoon salt
1 tablespoon cocoa

Mix together boiling water, oats, and butter. Let set for 10 minutes. Stir in sugars and eggs. Sift together flour, baking soda, salt, and cocoa. Add to oat mixture. Stir in chocolate chips. Pour into greased 13 x 9 inch pan. Sprinkle nuts and ½ cup of chips over top. Bake at 350° for 40 minutes.

KATHY SIEGEL   NILWOOD UNIT

OLD FASHIONED GINGERBREAD

1½ cups flour, sifted
1½ teaspoons baking soda
¼ teaspoon salt
½ teaspoon cinnamon
½ teaspoon ginger

¼ teaspoon cloves
1 egg
1 cup light syrup
½ cup margarine, melted
½ cup hot water

Sift dry ingredients together, set aside. Beat remaining ingredients together in large bowl until well combined. Gradually add flour mixture, beating until smooth. Turn into greased and floured 9 x 9-inch pan. Bake at 375° for 25 to 30 minutes. Let cool for 10 minutes and turn out. When completely cool, store in aluminum foil. Good with ice cream or apple topping. To reheat, bake at 350° for 15 minutes.

Apple Topping:
1½ cups applesauce
3 tablespoons light brown
    sugar

1½ cups Cool Whip

Combine ingredients well.

MRS. ROGER (DOTTIE) GRUEN   JUNIOR HOMEMAKERS UNIT

PECAN CHRISTMAS CAKE

2 cups butter	1 tablespoon vanilla
2 cups sugar	1½ cups golden raisins
6 eggs	4 cups pecans, chopped
1 tablespoon lemon juice	3 cups flour, sifted
1 teaspoon lemon peel, grated	¼ teaspoon salt
	1 teaspoon baking powder

Cream butter and sugar until fluffy. Beat in eggs, one at a time. Add lemon juice, peel, and vanilla. Mix raisins and ½ cup flour. Sift remaining dry ingredients together. Alternately fold nuts and raisins and dry ingredients into creamed mixture. Spoon into a greased, paper lined, 10-inch tube pan. Bake at 300° for about 1 hour and 50 minutes. Cool, remove from pan. For a sweeter, more moist cake, pour syrup of ¼ cup each orange juice, lemon juice, and a little sugar over the hot cake.

JOYCE JOHNSON   HAGAMAN UNIT

PEACH SKILLET CAKE

1 cup sifted sugar	3 egg yolks, well beaten
4 tablespoons cold water	3 egg whites, beaten stiff
1 teaspoon vanilla	2 cups brown sugar
⅛ teaspoon salt	¾ cup butter
1 cup flour	Peach halves
1½ tablespoons baking powder	

Combine first 7 ingredients; beat well. Fold in egg whites. Dissolve brown sugar in 10-inch iron skillet with butter. Arrange peach halves, hollow side down, in skillet. Cover with batter. Bake at 325° for 35 to 40 minutes. Invert by placing large plate over skillet and turning quickly. Cut like pie and serve with whipped cream or any kind of sauce. Makes 6 servings.

OLLIE CLARK   HAGAMAN UNIT

POUND CAKE

1 pound margarine, softened	6 eggs
1 pound powdered sugar	1 teaspoon vanilla or almond extract
3 cups flour	

In large mixer bowl, beat margarine and powdered sugar together. Add 2 eggs, beat well, then add 1 cup flour and 2 more eggs, beat well. Add last 2 eggs and beat well. Add vanilla or almond extract and last cup of flour. Bake in 10-inch ungreased tube pan for 1 hour and 15 minutes at 350°.

SUE VIECELI   STITCH AND STIR UNIT

PINEAPPLE CAKE

2 cups sugar
2 cups flour
2 teaspoons baking soda

3 eggs
1 No. 2 can crushed pineapple
1 teaspoon vanilla

Combine above ingredients. Put in greased and floured 9 x 13-inch pan. Bake at 350° for 40 minutes. Put on topping.

Topping:
1 cup Pet milk
¾ stick margarine
1½ cups sugar

1 cup flake coconut
1 cup nuts

Heat milk, sugar and margarine to boiling. Add coconut and nuts. Boil 2 minutes. When cake is done, pour topping over cake and bake about 10 minutes more.

MARTHA SNEDEKER   PLAINVIEW UNIT

PINEAPPLE UPSIDE DOWN CAKE

¼ cup margarine
½ cup sugar
1 15½-ounce can crushed
   pineapple, drained, reserve
   juice

3 eggs
1 cup sugar
5 tablespoons pineapple juice
1 cup sifted flour
1 teaspoon baking powder

In 8 x 8 x 2-inch pan, melt margarine over low heat. Add ½ cup sugar and drained pineapple. Stir together and spread evenly. Remove from heat. Separate eggs and beat whites until stiff but not dry; set aside. Using the same beaters, beat yolks until stiff and very light colored, adding 1 cup sugar gradually. Add pineapple juice and then flour and baking powder which have been sifted together. Carefully fold in beaten egg whites and pour batter over pineapple. Bake at 350° for 30 to 40 minutes. Test with toothpick. This will rise to the very top of pan while baking. Remove from pan after 3 to 5 minutes, spreading any pineapple remaining in pan on top. Serve with whipped or ice cream.

DOLORES KLAUS   HONEY POINT UNIT

PINEAPPLE UPSIDE DOWN CAKE

½ cup butter
1 cup brown sugar
1 No. 2 can sliced pineapple
2 tablespoons large whole
  pecans
1 cup cake flour, sifted

1 teaspoon baking powder
⅛ teaspoon salt
3 eggs, separated
1 cup sugar
5 tablespoons pineapple juice

Melt butter in 9 x 9-inch baking pan. Spread brown sugar evenly in pan and arrange pineapple slices on sugar, filling in spaces with pecans. Sift flour, baking powder, and salt together. Beat egg yolks until light, add sugar gradually. Add pineapple juice and sifted flour. Fold in stiffly beaten egg whites. Pour batter over pineapple. Bake at 375° for 30 to 35 minutes. Turn upside down on cake plate when baked. Serve with whipped cream. Makes 8 servings.

IRENE ABBOTT   HAGAMAN UNIT

UNBEATABLE PINEAPPLE CAKE

2 cups flour
1½ cups sugar
¼ teaspoon salt

2 cups crushed pineapple
2 whole eggs
1 teaspoon baking soda

Blend all ingredients with a spoon. Do not beat. Bake in greased and floured 13 x 9 x 2-inch pan at 350° for 35 to 40 minutes. Five minutes after baking, ice cake.

Topping:
1 stick margarine
1 small can evaporated milk
1 teaspoon vanilla

⅔ cup sugar
½ cup coconut
½ cup walnuts, chopped

Combine margarine, milk, vanilla and sugar. Cook 10 minutes. Add coconut and walnuts. Cook 5 more minutes.

MRS. JOHN PARIS   STAUNTON UNIT

POPPY SEED CAKE SUPREME

1 package yellow cake mix
1 3¾-ounce package instant
  vanilla pudding mix
4 eggs

1 cup sour cream
½ cup oil
½ cup cream sherry
⅓ cup poppy seeds

Combine all ingredients, stirring to blend. Beat at medium speed for 5 minutes, scraping sides of bowl frequently. Pour into greased and floured 10-inch bundt pan. Bake at 350° for about 1 hour. Cool in pan 15 minutes. Turn out on wire rack and cool. If desired, glaze with thin powdered sugar icing flavored with cream sherry.

LORRAINE OBERTINO   GET TOGETHERS UNIT

PRUNE CAKE

2 cups sugar
1 cup oil
2 4-ounce jars baby strained
  prunes
1 cup buttermilk
2 cups flour

3 eggs
1 teaspoon salt
1 teaspoon baking soda
1 teaspoon vanilla
1 teaspoon cinnamon
1 cup nuts, very coarsely
  chopped

Combine all ingredients except nuts and mix well. Fold in nuts. Pour into greased and floured tube pan. Bake at 350° for 1 hour or until done. While cake is still warm, spoon topping over cake.

Topping:
1 cup sugar
1 tablespoon corn syrup
¼ teaspoon baking soda

½ cup buttermilk
3 tablespoons butter

Combine all ingredients and cook over low heat, stirring constantly, until it reaches soft ball stage (238°).

LOUISE RIZZIE   GET TOGETHERS UNIT

PUMPKIN CAKE

3 eggs
2 cups sugar
1 cup cooking oil
2 cups flour
2 teaspoons cinnamon

1 teaspoon baking soda
2 teaspoons baking powder
½ teaspoon salt
2 cups pumpkin

Mix all ingredients together well. Pour into a jelly roll pan. Bake at 350° for 25 to 30 minutes. Frost with icing recipe given below.

Icing:
1 3-ounce package cream
   cheese
2 cups powdered sugar

½ cup margarine
1 teaspoon vanilla

Mix ingredients together and spread icing on cake.

PEARL EDWARDS   DO MORE UNIT

RED VELVET CAKE

½ cup shortening
1½ cups sugar
2 eggs
1 teaspoon vanilla
1 teaspoon butter flavoring
3 tablespoons cocoa

1 ounce red food coloring
2 cups sifted cake flour
1 teaspoon salt
1 cup buttermilk
1 teaspoon baking soda
1 tablespoon vinegar

Cream shortening, sugar, eggs, and flavorings. Make a paste of cocoa and food coloring; add to first mixture. Alternately add sifted flour with salt, and buttermilk. Mix baking soda and vinegar; blend into batter. Bake in 3 9 or 10-inch pans lined in bottom with waxed paper at 350° for 25 minutes. Cool on wire racks. Spread between layers, on top and sides with No Cook Icing.

No Cook Icing:
1 pound powdered sugar,
   sifted
1 8-ounce package cream
   cheese
1 tablespoon vanilla

½ teaspoon salt
1 teaspoon butter flavoring
Few drops of milk if needed for
   spreading

Blend ingredients thoroughly. Spread on cooled cake.

MRS. LEONARD GRIFFEL   BRUSHY MOUND UNIT

ROYAL RED VELVET CAKE

Note: It is important to make the icing/filling first. It's success depends on one point—the first mixture must be thoroughly chilled before combining it with the second mixture or the entire contents will curdle.

Icing:
First Mixture—
3 tablespoons flour   1 cup milk

Second Mixture—
1 cup butter at room   1 teaspoon vanilla
   temperature
1 cup sugar

In saucepan, add milk to flour. Cook over low heat, stirring constantly, until thick. Cool. Chill before using. Beat butter, sugar, and vanilla until light and fluffy. Continue beating 15 to 20 minutes. Combine the two mixtures.

Cake:
2 ounces red food coloring   2¼ cups flour
3 tablespoons cocoa   ¼ teaspoon salt
½ cup butter   1 cup buttermilk
1½ cups sugar   1 teaspoon vinegar
2 eggs   1 teaspoon baking soda
1 teaspoon vanilla

Make paste of food coloring and cocoa; set aside. Cream butter and sugar. Add eggs, vanilla, and beat thoroughly. Mix in paste mixture. Sift flour and salt together and add alternately with buttermilk to creamed mixture. Combine vinegar and baking soda. Add to cake batter. Mix at low speed until a velvety mixture results. Pour into 3 greased and floured 8 or 9-inch pans. Bake at 350° for 25 to 30 minutes. Spread prepared icing between layers and on cake.

MRS. LEO WELLING   BRIGHTON EARLY BIRDS UNIT

RAISIN PECAN CAKE

1 pound raisins
1 cup raisin water
½ cup shortening
1 cup sugar
2 eggs
2½ cups flour
1 teaspoon baking powder

1 teaspoon baking soda
½ teaspoon salt
1 teaspoon cloves
1 teaspoon nutmeg
1 teaspoon cinnamon
5½ ounces pecans, chopped

Cover raisins with water and boil for 10 minutes. Drain and cool. Cream sugar and shortening. Add eggs and beat well. Reserve small amount of flour to coat raisins and pecans. Sift flour with remaining dry ingredients. Add dry ingredients to creamed mixture alternately with the raisin water. Fold in raisins and pecans. Pour into ungreased 10-inch tube pan. Bake at 350° for 1 hour. Makes 12 to 15 servings.

MRS. DAVID SCHAFER   BRIGHTON EARLY BIRDS UNIT

RHUBARB CAKE

½ cup shortening
1½ cups brown sugar
1 egg
1 teaspoon vanilla
2 cups flour
1 teaspoon baking soda

½ teaspoon salt
1 cup buttermilk or sour milk
1½ cups raw rhubarb, finely
  sliced
½ cup sugar
1 teaspoon cinnamon

Cream shortening and brown sugar. Add egg and vanilla. Beat. Sift flour, baking soda, and salt together. Add alternately with milk, beating after each addition. Stir in rhubarb. Pour into 13 x 9-inch cake pan. Mix sugar and cinnamon. Sprinkle over top of cake. Bake at 350° for 30 minutes. Makes 15 servings.

MARCIA LLOYD   GIRARD NIGHT UNIT

ICING

1 8-ounce package cream
  cheese
1 stick margarine

1 teaspoon vanilla
1 pound powdered sugar

Beat together cream cheese and margarine at room temperature. Stir in other ingredients until smooth.

HELEN HARTMAN   DO MORE UNIT

SAUSAGE CAKE

1 pound pork sausage,
unseasoned
1½ cups brown sugar
1½ cups sugar
2 eggs, beaten
3 cups sifted flour
1 teaspoon ginger

1 teaspoon baking powder
1 teaspoon pumpkin pie spice
1 teaspoon baking soda
1 cup cold strong coffee
1 cup raisins
1 cup walnuts, chopped

In bowl, combine meat and sugars. Add eggs; mix well. Sift flour, ginger, baking powder, and pumpkin pie spice. In small bowl, stir baking soda into coffee. Add flour mixture and coffee alternately to meat mixture, beating well after each addition. Cover raisins with boiling water for 5 minutes; drain. Add raisins and nuts to batter. Pour into well greased and floured bundt or tube cake pan. Bake at 350° for 1½ hours. Cool 15 minutes before turning out.

KIM MANSFIELD   SCOTTVILLE UNIT

TROPICAL CAKE

1 package yellow cake mix
1 tablespoon sugar

1 tablespoon oil

Mix cake according to package directions adding the oil and sugar. Bake at 350° in greased and floured 10 x 14-inch pan for 30 to 35 minutes or until firm around the edges but still soft in the center. While cake is baking, prepare topping.

Topping:
2 cups brown sugar
1 stick margarine
1 can coconut

1 cup nuts
1 20-ounce can crushed
pineapple, undrained

Mix brown sugar, margarine, pineapple, coconut and nuts. Cook until sugar is dissolved and mixture begins to thicken. Pour over cake, beginning around edges. Bake until a toothpick comes out clean at center of cake. Serve with whipped topping. Makes 15 servings.

DORIS RENO   PIASA UNIT

SPONGE CAKE

4 eggs, separated
1½ cups sugar
2 tablespoons water
1½ cups cake flour, sifted
1 teaspoon baking powder

½ cup cold water
¼ teaspoon cream of tartar
1 teaspoon lemon juice
Grated rind of 1 lemon

Beat 4 egg yolks well; add sugar. Continue to beat egg yolk mixture slowly adding 2 tablespoons water. Sift flour and baking powder together; add to egg yolk mixture alternately with ½ cup cold water. Beat 4 egg whites and cream of tartar until stiff; fold beaten egg whites into batter. Stir in lemon juice and rind. Pour batter into angel food cake pan. Bake at 325° for 45 minutes until brown.

MRS. GEORGE E. ADAM   STAUNTON UNIT

STRAWBERRY SODA CAKE

1 box yellow cake mix
2 small boxes strawberry
   Jello

1¼ cups hot water
1½ cups strawberry soda

Bake cake mix as directed on box. Dissolve the Jello in hot water, add soda. While cake is still warm, poke full of holes with fork. Pour Jello and soda mixture over cake. When cool frost and refrigerate overnight.

Frosting:
1 box vanilla instant pudding
1¼ cups milk

1 small carton Cool Whip

Mix the pudding and milk together until thick. Add the Cool Whip. Spread on cake. Makes 15 servings.

IRENE SCHRAMM   BARR UNIT

SILVER WHITE CAKE

3 cups sugar
1 cup butter
2 cups milk
5 cups flour, sifted

¼ teaspoon salt
4 teaspoons baking powder
1 teaspoon vanilla
6 egg whites, beaten

Cream sugar and butter until very light. Add milk and flour, a little at a time, mixing well. Add last cup of flour with salt and baking powder sifted together. Add vanilla and beaten egg whites, mixing gently. Pour batter into 3 9-inch layer pans which have been greased. Bake at 350° for about 30 minutes or tests done with toothpick.

MRS. IVAN JENKINS   GIRARD DAY UNIT

VANILLA WAFER CRUNCH CAKE

Crust:

½ cup butter
⅓ cup sugar

1 cup pecans, chopped
1½ cup vanilla wafers, crushed

Mix together and pat on bottom of 2 greased loaf pans.

Filling:

1 cup butter
2 cups sugar
4 eggs
2⅔ cups flour

1½ teaspoons baking powder
½ teaspoon salt
1 cup milk
1½ teaspoon vanilla

Cream butter and sugar until fluffy. Add eggs and beat well. Sift flour once, measure and add baking powder, salt and sift again. Add milk, vanilla, and dry ingredients to batter and mix well. Pour on top of crusts, and bake at 350° for 1 hour.

MARGARET LEBETER   MT. OLIVE UNIT

7-UP CAKE

1 package yellow cake mix
1 package instant lemon
  pudding

4 eggs, room temperature
¾ cup oil
10 ounces 7-Up

Mix cake and pudding mixes, eggs, and oil. Add 7-Up. Mix well and pour into greased 9 x 13-inch pan. Bake at 350° for 30 to 40 minutes. Puncture top of warm cake with toothpick and pour Frosting over it. Return to oven for 1 or 2 minutes.

Frosting:

2 cups powdered sugar
⅓ cup lemon juice

1 teaspoon oil

Mix frosting ingredients.

ROBIN MANSHOLT   GILLESPIE NIGHT UNIT

CREAMY FROSTING

½ cup milk
1 egg white
½ cup butter
½ cup margarine

1 cup sugar
1 teaspoon salt
1 teaspoon vanilla
¼ teaspoon almond extract

Scald milk, set aside to cool. Beat egg white until stiff. Combine butter, margarine, sugar, salt, vanilla, and almond extract in small bowl and blend. Add beaten egg white. Stir until blended, then add cool milk. Beat at high speed of mixer until smooth, 5 to 10 minutes, scraping bowl often. If it curdles, just continue beating until smooth. Makes enough for a two layer cake.

EVELYN PINTAR   GET TOGETHERS UNIT

WHITE SNOW FROSTING

1 egg white
¼ cup butter
¼ cup shortening

½ teaspoon coconut extract
½ teaspoon vanilla
2 cups powdered sugar, sifted

Cream together the egg white, butter, shortening, coconut extract, and vanilla. Add the powdered sugar. Beat until light and fluffy. Double this recipe for a layer cake.

JEAN KLAUS   HONEY POINT UNIT

ZUCCHINI CAKE

3 cups zucchini, grated
2¼ cups sugar
1½ cups oil
4 eggs
3 cups flour

2 teaspoons baking powder
1 teaspoon baking soda
1½ teaspoons cinnamon
1 teaspoon salt
1 cup nuts, chopped

Mix zucchini, sugar, oil, and eggs together. Sift dry ingredients together and stir into zucchini mixture. Add nuts. Bake in a well greased and floured 9 x 16-inch pan at 300° for 1 hour and 30 minutes. Cool on rack. Frost. Makes 18 servings.

Icing:
1 3-ounce package cream
   cheese
½ pound margarine

2 cups powdered sugar
1 teaspoon vanilla

Beat ingredients until smooth. Spread on cake.

MRS. EDWARD KOERTGE   BRIGHTON EARLY BIRDS UNIT

ZUCCHINI PINEAPPLE CAKE

3 eggs
2 cups sugar
2 teaspoons vanilla
1 cup cooking oil
2 cups zucchini, grated
3 cups flour

1 teaspoon baking powder
½ cup coconut
1 teaspoon salt
1 teaspoon baking soda
1 cup nuts
1 cup crushed pineapple, drained

Beat eggs until fluffy. Add sugar, vanilla, oil, zucchini. Blend well. Add dry ingredients. Mix well. Stir in pineapple, coconut and nuts. Pour into greased and floured 10 x 15-inch pan. Bake at 325° for 1 hour.

HELEN HARTMAN   DO MORE UNIT

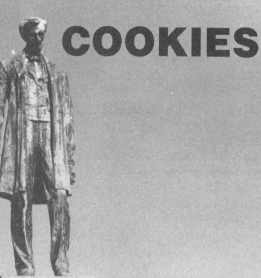

COOKIES

LINCOLN

1809-1865

With main in his hand

Lincoln Monument—Bunker Hill, Illinois was dedicated September 7, 1904.

The inscription on the monument reads:

"In everlasting memory of the
conflict by which the Union
was preserved and in which
they took part, this statue
of Abraham Lincoln was presented
to the Citizens of Bunker Hill
by the soldiers of Company B
1st. Missouri Cavalry
Chas. Clinton Capt.
Abraham Lincoln
16th President
Born Feb. 12, 1809   Died April 15, 1865"

Photographed by Carl Stanton

APPLE BARS

2 cups flour
½ cup sugar
½ teaspoon baking powder
½ teaspoon salt
1 cup butter or margarine
2 egg yolks, beaten

4 medium tart apples, pared,
  cored, and sliced (4 cups)
¼ cup flour
¾ cup sugar
1 teaspoon ground cinnamon
1 egg white, slightly beaten

Combine 2 cups flour, ½ cup sugar, baking powder, and salt; cut in butter or margarine until crumbs are size of small peas. Stir in egg yolks. Divide mixture in half. Press one half over bottom of 13 x 9 x 2-inch pan. Combine apples, remaining flour and sugar, and cinnamon; arrange over bottom crust. Crumble remaining dough over apples. Brush egg white over all. Bake at 350° for 40 to 45 minutes. Cool. Drizzle with powdered sugar icing, if desired. Cut into bars. Makes 12 to 16. Note: May also be made in 15 x 10 x 1-inch pan. Bake for 40 minutes.

KATHY REZNICEK   MONDAY NITERS UNIT

APPLE KOLACHES

2 cups flour, sifted
1 8-ounce package cream
  cheese
1 cup butter or margarine

3 cups red delicious apples,
  pared and finely diced
Cinnamon to taste

To prepare dough, blend together the flour, cream cheese and butter with your fingers until dough forms. Shape into a ball and chill 3 hours or overnight. (After chilling, dough becomes stiff and will need to be worked with moist hands to regain its flexibility.) Mix prepared apples and cinnamon for filling. Roll dough as for pie crust. Cut into 3-inch squares. Place a heaping teaspoon of filling on each square, bring edges together in the middle, and seal. Bake at 400° for 20 to 25 minutes or until golden. Drizzle with glaze.

Glaze:
1 cup powdered sugar
1½ tablespoons milk or water

½ teaspoon vanilla

Combine ingredients and drizzle over warm kolaches.

GAIL SPUDICH   DANDY DOERS UNIT

APPLE BARS

1 cup flour
½ teaspoon salt
½ cup brown sugar
⅓ cup butter or margarine
½ teaspoon cinnamon
1 cup oatmeal

Chopped nuts, if desired
2½ cups apples, peeled and
  sliced
¼ cup sugar
½ teaspoon cinnamon

Combine all ingredients except last three, cutting in oleo or butter. Put half of mixture into 8 x 8 x 2-inch pan and pack tightly. Combine apples, sugar and cinnamon and spread over packed mixture. Top with remaining crumb mixture. Bake at 350° for 40 to 50 minutes or until apples are tender. Makes 9 servings.

MRS. GERALD (NORMA) BOSTON   HONEY POINT UNIT

FRESH APPLE COOKIES

½ cup shortening
1⅓ cups brown sugar
1 egg
½ teaspoon salt
2 cups flour
1 teaspoon baking soda

1 teaspoon cinnamon
½ teaspoon nutmeg
¼ cup milk
1 cup apples, chopped
1 cup raisins
½ cup nuts

Cream shortening and sugar. Add egg and stir together. Add dry ingredients alternately with milk. Stir in apples, nuts, and raisins. Drop by teaspoon onto cookie sheet. Bake at 350° for 10 to 15 minutes. Frost.

Icing:
2 cups powdered sugar
1 teaspoon margarine

½ teaspoon vanilla
3 tablespoons milk

Combine ingredients thoroughly. Spread on cooled cookies.

JOYCE CRUM   BIRD UNIT

ALASKA LOGS

¾ cup flour, sifted
1 cup sugar
1 teaspoon baking powder
¼ teaspoon salt

1 cup dates, chopped
1 cup nuts
3 eggs, well beaten

Sift dry ingredients together. Stir in remaining ingredients. Pour into greased 8 x 8 x 2-inch pan. Bake at 325° for about 40 minutes. Cut in small pieces while warm, shape like logs, and roll in sugar or powdered sugar. Makes about 5 dozen.

RUBY HOBACK   CARLINVILLE NIGHT UNIT

BAKE ALL NIGHT COOKIES

2 egg whites
½ teaspoon cream of tartar
Pinch of salt
⅔ cup sugar
1 teaspoon vanilla

1 teaspoon almond flavoring
1 cup chocolate or butterscotch
  chips
1 cup nuts, chopped (preferably
  pecans)

Preheat oven to 350°. Beat egg whites, cream of tartar, and salt, real stiff. Add sugar gradually and continue beating at low speed. Add flavorings, chips, and nuts, mixing in well by hand. Drop cookies by teaspoon onto foil-lined cookie sheet. Place cookies in preheated oven. Turn off oven and let stand (without opening) at least 5 hours or all night is best. Makes 2 to 3 dozen.

MARGARET GILLER   BARR UNIT

BANANA BARS

1½ cups flour
1 teaspoon baking powder
1 teaspoon salt
1 teaspoon cinnamon
¼ teaspoon nutmeg
⅔ cup sugar

⅔ cup soft butter
2 eggs
1 cup bananas, mashed
1 cup quick oats
½ cup nuts, chopped

Sift first six ingredients together. Add the butter, eggs, and bananas; beat well with spoon. Stir in oats and nuts. Spread in greased 9 x 13-inch pan. Bake at 350° for 20 minutes. When cool, frost with a powdered sugar icing.

MARY JANE THOMAS   MONDAY NITERS UNIT

BANNOCKS (OAT CAKES)

1 cup sifted flour
1 tablespoon sugar
½ teaspoon salt
1 teaspoon baking powder

½ cup butter or margarine
2 cups quick oats
¼ cup milk

Sift flour, sugar, salt, baking powder together. Rub the butter into oats and dry ingredients that have been sifted together (use fingers). Add milk and mix until dough is formed. Roll on floured surface ⅛ inch thick. Cut in pieces about 3 inches square. Place on baking sheet. Bake at 375° for 12 minutes or until lightly browned.

MAE ALLAN   BERTHA ELDRED UNIT

FROSTED BROWNIE BARS

6 tablespoons margarine
1 square unsweetened
   chocolate
1 cup sugar
1 teaspoon vanilla
2 eggs

¾ cup sifted flour
½ teaspoon salt
½ teaspoon baking powder
½ cup nut meats
2 cups miniature marshmallows

Melt margarine and chocolate in saucepan. Remove from heat; add sugar and vanilla, mixing well. Add eggs, beating in one at a time. Sift together flour, salt, and baking powder; add to chocolate mixture and blend well. Stir in nut meats. Spread in greased 11 x 7-inch pan. Bake at 350° for 20 to 25 minutes. Remove from oven and immediately top with marshmallows. Cool. Spread with Frosting. Makes 18.

Frosting:
1 square unsweetened
   chocolate
½ cup brown sugar
¼ cup water

3 tablespoons margarine
1 teaspoon vanilla
¼ teaspoon salt
1½ cups sifted powdered sugar

Heat together the chocolate, brown sugar, and water. Bring to a boil; reduce heat and simmer for 4 minutes. Remove from heat and add margarine. Cool. Stir in vanilla, salt and powdered sugar. Spread over cooled brownies. Note: This recipe not recommended during hot humid weather.

MRS. CHARLES HARP   SHAWS POINT UNIT

LEMON BROWNIES

¾ cup butter
⅓ cup powdered sugar
1½ cups sifted flour
3 eggs, beaten

1½ cups sugar
3 tablespoons flour
2 tablespoons ReaLemon lemon
    juice

Mix butter, powdered sugar and flour until crumbly. Pat mixture into 9 x 13-inch pan. Bake at 350° for 18 minutes. While this is baking, mix slightly the eggs, sugar, flour and lemon juice. Pour over hot baked crust. Bake for approximately 18 more minutes until delicately browned. Cool in pan on rack. Cut in squares. Makes 2 dozen.

MRS. ROBERT BIRK   BRIGHTON EARLY BIRDS UNIT

MOIST BROWNIES

½ cup margarine
1 cup sugar
4 eggs
1 teaspoon vanilla
1 16-ounce can Hershey
    chocolate syrup

1 cup flour
½ teaspoon salt
1 cup nuts, chopped

Cream margarine and sugar; add eggs one at a time, beating well. Add vanilla and chocolate; beat. Add dry ingredients and nuts. Spread in greased 9 x 13-inch pan. Bake at 350° for 25 minutes. Spread with frosting or dust with powdered sugar, if desired. Makes 2 dozen.

DARLENE WOOLFOLK   SCOTTVILLE UNIT

PEANUT BROWNIES

⅓ cup margarine
1 cup sugar
¼ cup brown sugar
2 eggs
½ cup peanut butter

½ teaspoon vanilla
1 cup flour
1 teaspoon baking powder
¼ teaspoon salt
1 cup chocolate bits

Cream butter and sugars until light; add eggs and beat well. Mix in peanut butter and vanilla. Stir together the flour, baking powder, and salt. Add to creamed mixture; blend well. Stir in chocolate bits. Pour into a 9 x 9-inch pan. Bake at 350° for 20 to 25 minutes. Cut into squares when cool. Makes 20 squares.

MRS. HELEN BOWERSOX   GIRARD DAY UNIT

CREAM CHEESE BROWNIES

5 tablespoons butter
1 4-ounce package German
  sweet chocolate
1 3-ounce package cream
  cheese
1 cup sugar
3 eggs

½ cup plus 1 tablespoon flour
1½ teaspoons vanilla
¼ teaspoon salt
½ teaspoon baking powder
½ cup nuts
¼ teaspoon almond extract

Melt over very low heat 3 tablespoons butter or margarine and chocolate. Stir and let cool. Cream 2 tablespoons butter and cream cheese. Gradually add ¼ cup sugar; cream until fluffy. Add 1 egg, 1 tablespoon flour and ½ teaspoon vanilla. Set aside. Beat 2 eggs until light; gradually beat in ¾ cup sugar. Add ½ cup unsifted flour, salt, baking powder. Blend in chocolate mixture, 1 teaspoon vanilla, nuts, and almond extract. Spread half of batter in greased 8 or 9-inch square pan. Top with cream cheese mixture. Spoon remaining batter over top. Run a knife zigzag through batter to make marbled effect. Bake at 350° for 35 to 40 minutes. Let cool. Cut into bars or squares.

TOOTIE GREENWALT   HONEY POINT UNIT

DISAPPEARING MARSHMALLOW BROWNIES

1 cup semi-sweet chocolate
  pieces
¼ cup butter or margarine
¾ cup flour
⅓ cup brown sugar, packed
1 teaspoon baking powder

¼ teaspoon salt
½ teaspoon vanilla
1 egg
1 cup miniature marshmallows
½ cup butterscotch pieces
¼ cup nuts, chopped

Melt chocolate pieces and butter in heavy 3-quart pan over medium heat, stirring constantly. Remove from heat and cool to lukewarm. Lightly spoon flour into measuring cup and level off. Add flour, brown sugar, baking powder, salt, vanilla, and egg to chocolate mixture in saucepan. Mix well. Fold marshmallows, butterscotch pieces, and nuts into chocolate mixture just until combined, about 5 strokes. Spread in greased 8 x 8-inch pan. Bake at 350° for 20 to 25 minutes. Do not over bake. Center will become firm upon cooling. Makes 20.

REGINA DRURY   BERTHA ELDRED UNIT

FUDGE BROWNIES

½ cup sugar
⅓ cup shortening
2 tablespoons water
1 6-ounce package chocolate
   morsels
1 teaspoon vanilla

2 eggs
¾ cup sifted flour
¼ teaspoon baking soda
¼ teaspoon salt
½ cup nuts, coarsely chopped

Preheat oven to 325°. Combine sugar, shortening, and water; bring just to a boil, stirring constantly. Remove from heat. Add chocolate morsels and vanilla; stir until blended. Beat in eggs one at a time. Sift together the flour, baking soda, and salt. Stir flour mixture into chocolate mixture. Add nuts. Spread in greased 9 x 9-inch pan. Bake 25 minutes. Makes 16 squares.

GLADYS OWENS   SHAWS POINT UNIT

CHOCO-NUT DREAM BARS

⅔ cup sugar
1 stick butter or margarine,
   softened
½ teaspoon vanilla
¼ teaspoon salt
1 cup sifted flour

¾ cup sugar
2 eggs
1 teaspoon vanilla
½ teaspoon salt
2 cups nuts, finely chopped

Combine ⅔ cup sugar, butter, ½ teaspoon vanila, and ¼ teaspoon salt. Beat until blended. Gradually stir in flour. Press in bottom of ungreased 9 x 13 x 2-inch pan. Bake at 350° for 12 to 15 minutes. Let cool for 10 minutes. While mixture is cooling, combine remaining ingredients, except nuts, and beat until light. Blend in half of the nuts. Cover the cooled pastry with topping mixture. Return to oven and bake 20 minutes. Frost as recipe below. Sprinkle reserved nuts on top. Makes 32 bars.

Frosting:
½ cup evaporated milk
Dash of salt

1 6-ounce package semi-sweet
   chocolate morsels
1 teaspoon vanilla

Combine milk and salt in saucepan. Bring to a boil over moderate heat. Add chocolate morsels and vanilla; stir until smooth. Let cool until thick enough to spread, about 5 minutes. Spread over bars.

MRS. MILWIDA R. BOYD   BERTHA ELDRED UNIT

BUTTER COOKIES

1 cup (2 sticks) butter or
  margarine
1½ cups sifted powdered
  sugar
1 egg

1 teaspoon vanilla
2½ cups sifted flour
1 teaspoon baking soda
1 teaspoon cream of tartar
¼ teaspoon salt

Cream butter; add sugar gradually, beating until light and fluffy. Add egg and vanilla. Beat well. Sift together dry ingredients and add to creamed mixture, mixing well. Chill dough in refrigerator. Roll dough ⅛-inch thick on lightly floured surface consisting of half powdered sugar and half flour. Cookies will always be crisp. Cut with floured cookie cutter. Place about 2 inches apart on greased baking sheets. Bake at 375° for 8 to 10 minutes or until golden brown. Cool about 1 minute on baking sheet; remove and cool on racks. Makes 6 dozen.

MRS. LEOLA KAMPER   BRIGHTON EARLY BIRDS UNIT

BUCKEYE COOKIES

1 stick margarine
2 cups crunchy peanut butter
1 pound powdered sugar

3 cups Rice Krispies cereal
1 large bag chocolate chips
¼ bar paraffin

Melt margarine. Mix with the peanut butter. Remove from heat; add powdered sugar and Rice Krispies. Blend well. Shape in 1-inch balls and store in refrigerator overnight. Melt chocolate chips and paraffin in double boiler over hot water. Using toothpick, dip each ball in chocolate mixture. Place on waxed paper to set.

MRS. MERLE LONG   GIRARD DAY UNIT

COCONUT MACAROONS

2 cups powdered sugar
2 teaspoons baking powder
3 cups coconut

3 egg whites
1 teaspoon vanilla

Sift powdered sugar and baking powder together; add coconut and mix well. Beat egg whites until very stiff; add vanilla. Fold in coconut mixture. Drop by teaspoon on greased and floured cookie sheet. Bake at 325° until brown. Let cool before removing from cookie sheet.

MRS. WILBUR (ISABEL) SUHLING   SPANISH NEEDLE UNIT

CHOCOLATE COOKIES

1¾ cups sifted flour	1 egg
½ teaspoon baking soda	½ cup milk
½ teaspoon salt	½ cup pecans, chopped
½ cup cocoa	1 teaspoon vanilla
½ cup shortening	36 marshmallows, cut in half
1 cup sugar	Pecan halves

Sift flour, measure, and sift again with baking soda, salt, and cocoa. Cream shortening; add sugar gradually, blending thoroughly. Add egg; beat well. Add flour mixture and milk alternately, beating after each addition. Add nuts and vanilla; mix well. Drop mixture by level teaspoon about 2 inches apart onto well greased cookie sheet. (Cookies will spread). Bake at 350° for 8 minutes. Remove from oven and top with marshmallow half, cut side down. Return to oven and bake 2 minutes, until marshmallows soften. Cool. Frost with Cocoa Frosting and top each cookie with pecan half. Makes 6 dozen.

Cocoa Frosting:

2 cups powdered sugar	3 tablespoons butter, melted
5 tablespoons cocoa	4 tablespoons light cream
Dash of salt	½ teaspoon vanilla

Sift the powdered sugar and measure 2 cups, then mix with cocoa and salt. Add butter, cream, and vanilla; beat until smooth and creamy. Spread on cookies.

MRS. A. E. FRUEH   MEDORA UNIT

CHOCOLATE CREAM DROPS

½ cup butter	½ teaspoon vanilla
½ cup shortening	2 1-ounce squares chocolate,
1 3-ounce package cream	melted and cooled
cheese	2½ cups flour
1½ cups sugar	1½ teaspoons baking powder
1 egg, well beaten	½ teaspoon salt
2 tablespoons milk	½ cup nuts, chopped

Combine all ingredients. Drop by teaspoons onto greased cookie sheet. Bake at 350° for 12 to 15 minutes.

CATHERINE TIRA   GET TOGETHERS UNIT

CARROT COOKIES

2 cups flour	1 egg
2 teaspoons baking powder	1 cup carrots, cooked and
¼ teaspoon salt	mashed
¾ cup sugar	½ teaspoon vanilla
¾ cup shortening	½ cup pecan meats, broken

Mix flour, baking powder, and salt. Cream sugar and shortening; add egg and cooked, mashed carrots. Add to creamed mixture the flour mixture, vanilla, and nut meats. Drop by teaspoon onto greased cookie sheet. Bake at 350° for 18 to 20 minutes. When cool, frost. Makes 5 dozen.

Icing:

1 tablespoon butter or	Juice of 1 large orange
margarine, melted	Powdered sugar

Combine butter and juice. Add enough powdered sugar to thicken to frosting consistency.

ALENE E. RUYLE   SCOTTVILLE UNIT

COCONUT APRICOT STRIPES

½ cup shortening, half butter	1 cup Gold Medal flour, sifted
½ cup powdered sugar	½ cup thick apricot preserves
2 egg yolks	½ cup thick pineapple preserves

Mix shortening, sugar and egg yolks thoroughly. Add sifted flour to sugar mixture. Press and flatten mixture to cover bottom of ungreased 13 x 9½ x 2-inch pan. Bake at 350° for 10 minutes. Remove from oven. Spread with combined preserves. Spread Coconut Meringue over preserves. Return to oven and bake about 20 minutes or until meringue is golden brown. Cool slightly and cut into small bars about 2 x 1-inch. Makes 54 to 60 bars.

Coconut Meringue:

2 egg whites	½ cup flaked coconut
½ cup sugar	

Beat egg whites; gradually add sugar. Beat until stiff and glossy. Fold in flaked coconut.

ELSIE MADER   STAUNTON UNIT

CHINESE CHEWS

¾ cup butter
1 box light brown sugar
1 tablespoon sugar
1 teaspoon vanilla
1½ cups sifted flour

½ teaspoon salt
3 eggs
¾ cup coconut
1 cup pecans

Cream butter and sugars; add vanilla. Sift flour and salt together. Add flour mixture to sugar mixture alternately with each egg, beating well after each addition. Add coconut and pecans. Spread in greased 13½ x 9-inch pan. Bake at 375° for 25 to 35 minutes. Cut in squares and roll in powdered sugar, if desired. Note: One box of brown sugar sounds like a lot, but it is the proper amount to use.

MRS. WILBUR SUHLING   SPANISH NEEDLE UNIT

CHOCOLATE CHIP BARS

¾ cup brown sugar
½ cup margarine
1 egg
1 teaspoon vanilla
1¼ cups flour

½ teaspoon baking soda
½ teaspoon salt
1 6-ounce package chocolate
   chips
½ cup nuts, chopped

Cream sugar and margarine. Beat in egg and vanilla. Stir in dry ingredients. Add chocolate chips and nuts. Pour into 9 x 9-inch pan. Bake at 375° for 12 to 15 minutes. Cool. Cut into bars. Makes 9.
ALDA ARTER   HONEY POINT UNIT

CHOCOLATE CRINKLES

½ cup vegetable oil
4 1-ounce squares
   unsweetened chocolate,
   melted
2 cups sugar
4 eggs

2 teaspoons vanilla
2 cups flour
2 teaspoons baking powder
½ teaspoon salt
1 cup powdered sugar

Mix oil, chocolate, and sugar. Blend in eggs, one at a time, until mixed. Add vanilla. Stir flour, baking powder, and salt into oil mixture. Chill several hours or overnight. Heat oven to 350°. Drop teaspoon of dough into powdered sugar. Shape into balls. Place 2 inches apart on greased cookie sheet. Bake 10 to 12 minutes. Don't over bake. Makes about 6 dozen.

HELEN TIBURZI   GET TOGETHERS UNIT

CRACKER JACK COOKIES

1 cup shortening
1 cup brown sugar
1 cup sugar
2 cups Rice Krispies
2 cups quick oatmeal
2 eggs, beaten

1 teaspoon vanilla
1½ cups flour
1 teaspoon baking powder
1 teaspoon baking soda
1 cup coconut
1 cup nuts, chopped

Cream shortening and sugars. Add Rice Krispies, oatmeal, eggs, and vanilla. Sift flour with baking powder and baking soda. Stir into first mixture. Add coconut and nuts. Drop by teaspoon onto ungreased cookie sheet. Bake at 350° for 12 to 15 minutes. Makes 6 dozen 2½-inch cookies.

VELMA AMBROSE   SCOTTVILLE UNIT

CRISP OR CURLED FRITTERS

3 egg yolks
3 tablespoons cream
½ teaspoon salt
1 tablespoon sugar

6 tablespoons rum
2 cups flour
½ cup powdered sugar

Combine egg yolks, cream, salt, sugar and rum. Mix this into flour and knead until mixture no longer sticks to board. Let stand 20 minutes then roll out ⅛ inch thick. Cut into strips 6 x 1-inch. Tie in loose knot and fry in deep oil until golden brown. Sprinkle with powdered sugar. Serve hot. Makes 6 to 8.

MRS. JOHN PARIS   STAUNTON UNIT

DATE BARS

½ cup boiling water
2 cups dates, chopped
½ cup margarine
1 cup sugar
¾ teaspoon salt
⅛ teaspoon cinnamon

⅛ teaspoon nutmeg
2 eggs
1 cup sifted flour
½ teaspoon baking soda
½ cup nuts, chopped
Powdered sugar

Pour boiling water over chopped dates; let cool. Combine shortening, sugar, salt, cinnamon, nutmeg, and eggs; beat thoroughly. Stir into date mixture. Sift flour and baking soda together; stir into date mixture. Add nuts and blend well. Spread mixture in greased and floured 10 x 10 x ½-inch pan. Bake at 350° for 30 to 40 minutes. Let cool in pan, cut into bars, and roll in powdered sugar. Makes 2 dozen.

MRS. IRVIN SCHUM   SOUTH OTTER UNIT

DISHPAN COOKIES

COOKIES

4 eggs
2 cups sugar
2 cups brown sugar
2 teaspoons vanilla
4 cups cornflakes
1½ cups quick oatmeal

4 cups flour
2 teaspoons baking soda
1 teaspoon salt
2 cups butter, melted
1½ cups nuts, chopped
1½ cups coconut

Beat eggs, one at a time, with sugar. Add brown sugar and vanilla. Stir in cornflakes and oatmeal. Sift flour, baking soda, and salt together. Add to first mixture, mixing well. Stir in melted butter, nuts, and coconut. Roll into balls the size of a small walnut. Place 1½ inches apart on greased cookie sheet. Bake at 350° for 10 minutes. Makes about 100.

MRS. LELAND OERTEL   BRIGHTON EARLY BIRDS UNIT

EASTER RABBIT COOKIES

½ cup butter
1 cup sugar
1 egg, slightly beaten
½ cup milk

3½ cups flour
3 teaspoons baking powder
1 teaspoon salt
1 teaspoon vanilla

Cream the butter; add the sugar. Add egg. Sift flour, baking powder, and salt together. Add to creamed mixture with the milk. Stir in the vanilla. Roll thicker than usual and cut with rabbit cookie cutter or cardboard pattern using a sharp knife. Bake at 375° for 12 minutes until light and brown. Frost. Makes 3 dozen.

Frosting:
1 cup sifted powdered sugar
2 tablespoons cream
Vanilla flavoring

Grated coconut and red hots for
   decoration

Mix frosting ingredients together. Spread on cooled cookies. Sprinkle with grated coconut and put a red hot for the eye.

LOIS KABURICK   HONEY POINT UNIT

FORK COOKIES

1 cup sugar	2 teaspoons cream of tartar
1 cup brown sugar	1 teaspoon baking soda
1 cup Crisco shortening	1 teaspoon vanilla
3 eggs	3 cups sifted flour

Combine sugars, shortening, eggs, cream of tartar, baking soda and vanilla. Add enough flour to make a stiff dough. Pinch off pieces of dough the size of a walnut. Place on greased cookie sheet; press down with a fork. Bake at 450° for 10 to 12 minutes. Makes 5 dozen.

THELMA BOUILLON   HONEY POINT UNIT

FRENCH BARS

2 cups brown sugar	3 cups flour
1 cup shortening	1 teaspoon baking powder
2 eggs	1 teaspoon cinnamon
1 cup hot water	1 cup raisins, if desired
1 teaspoon baking soda	1 cup nuts, if desired

Mix all ingredients together. Pour into 11 x 17 x 1-inch pan. Bake at 350° for 15 minutes. Spread Icing on bars. Makes 24 servings.

Icing:

3 tablespoons brown sugar	½ stick margarine, melted
2 cups powdered sugar	1 teaspoon vanilla
Small amount of milk	

Combine all ingredients thoroughly.

LUCILLE BALLINGER   SHAWS POINT UNIT

GRAHAM CRACKER COOKIES

27 graham cracker sections	½ cup brown sugar, packed
1 stick butter	Pecan nut meats, chopped

Put graham cracker sections into 9 x 13-inch pan. Melt butter in saucepan. Add brown sugar. Boil to dissolve sugar. Spoon over graham crackers. Sprinkle plenty of nut meats over all. Bake at 325° for 8 minutes. Let set to cool. Take out graham cookies when cooled. These are crunchy, very tasty, and easy to do.

MRS. LEA B. HEINZ   BERTHA ELDRED UNIT

BETH'S FRUIT COOKIES

1 cup Crisco or margarine
2 cups brown sugar
2 eggs
3½ cups flour
1 teaspoon baking soda
½ teaspoon salt

½ cup sour milk or buttermilk
1½ cups nuts
2 cups candied cherries
2 cups dates
1 cup raisins

Cream together, shortening and brown sugar. Add eggs, beating well. Sift together flour, baking soda, and salt. Add dry ingredients alternately with buttermilk to creamed mixture. Stir in nuts and fruits. Chill overnight. Drop by teaspoon onto greased cookie sheets. Bake at 325° for 20 to 25 minutes or until firm.

ANN REYNOLDS   HAGAMAN UNIT

FRUIT DROP COOKIES

1 cup margarine
1½ cups light brown sugar
3 eggs
1 teaspoon baking soda
2 tablespoons water

1½ cups raisins or dates
1 cup nuts
3 cups flour
1 teaspoon vanilla

Cream margarine and sugar. Beat in eggs. Dissolve baking soda in water and add to creamed mixture. Add remaining ingredients. Drop by teaspoon onto cookie sheets. Bake at 350° for 10 to 15 minutes. Makes 6 dozen.

DOROTHY STILL   POLK UNIT

GERMAN CHOCOLATE CARAMEL BARS

1 box German chocolate cake
  mix
1 stick butter or margarine,
  melted
⅓ cup milk

1 cup pecans
1 cup chocolate chips
1 bag Kraft caramels, melted with
  2 tablespoons water

Mix cake mix, butter, milk, and pecans together. Pour half of this mixture into 9 x 13-inch pan. Sprinkle chocolate chips over top. Bake at 350° for 8 minutes. Melt caramels with the water. Pour over baked mixture. Pour remaining half of cake mix mixture on top of caramel. Bake for 15 minutes. Cut into bars when cool.

LINDA BAIMA   DANDY DOERS UNIT

HERMITS

1 cup raisins, cooked	2 eggs
2 teaspoons baking soda	3 to 3½ cups flour
1 cup liquid	2 teaspoons cinnamon
1½ cups sugar	2 heaping teaspoons cocoa
½ cup shortening	1 teaspoon vanilla

Cook raisins and drain; reserve liquid and let cool. Add baking soda to cooled, reserved liquid; if needed, add water to make 1 cup liquid. Cream sugar and shortening; add beaten eggs. Add raisins, liquid, and baking soda. Sift flour, cinnamon, and cocoa together. Add to creamed mixture. Add vanilla. Drop by teaspoon onto cookie sheets. Bake at 350° for 10 to 12 minutes. Makes 4 dozen. Note: For shortening, use lard or bacon drippings. Use 3 to 3½ cups flour or enough to make drop cookies.

MRS. ROBERT LITTLE   STITCH AND STIR UNIT

HOLIDAY HERMITS

1 cup shortening, soft	½ teaspoon nutmeg
1 cup sugar	½ cup buttermilk
1 cup brown sugar, firmly	½ cup raisins
packed	½ cup diced mixed candied fruit
2 eggs	and peels
2½ cups sifted flour	½ cup walnuts
½ teaspoon salt	1½ cups rolled oats (quick or old
½ teaspoon baking soda	fashioned), uncooked
1 teaspoon cinnamon	

Beat shortening and sugars together until creamy. Beat in eggs. Sift together flour, salt, baking soda, and spices. Add to creamed mixture alternately with buttermilk, beginning and ending with dry ingredients. Stir in remaining ingredients. Drop by teaspoon onto lightly greased cookie sheets. Bake in preheated 350° oven for 12 to 15 minutes. Makes 6 dozen.

CLARA MAY (MAYME) ARNETT   BIRD UNIT

ICE BOX COOKIES

1 pound margarine (2 cups)
1 cup brown sugar
1 cup sugar
2 eggs

2 teaspoons vanilla
1 teaspoon baking soda
1 teaspoon hot water
5 cups flour

Cream margarine and sugars until light; add eggs, beating well after each addition. Dissolve baking soda in hot water; add to creamed mixture along with the vanilla. Add flour, making a stiff dough. Form into rolls about 1-inch in diameter. Wrap in waxed paper and chill. Slice and bake on greased cookie sheet at 350° for about 8 minutes. Dough may be kept in refrigerator 3 weeks or can be frozen and baked as needed. Leave plain, ice as desired, or push a half nut meat or a few raisins into the top of each slice before baking.

MRS. GERALD EDWARDS   GIRARD DAY UNIT

LEMON-COCONUT SQUARES

1½ cups sifted flour
½ cup brown sugar
½ cup butter or margarine
2 eggs, beaten
1 cup brown sugar, firmly
   packed
1½ cups flaked or shredded
   coconut

1 cup nuts, chopped
2 tablespoons flour
½ teaspoon baking powder
¼ teaspoon salt
½ teaspoon vanilla

Mix together 1½ cups flour, ½ cup brown sugar, and butter; pat into buttered 9 x 13-inch pan. Bake at 275° for 10 minutes. Combine eggs, 1 cup brown sugar, coconut, nuts, 2 tablespoons flour, baking powder, salt and vanilla. Spread on top of baked mixture. Bake at 350° for 20 minutes. While warm, spread with Frosting. Cut into squares. Makes 24 2-inch squares.

Frosting:
1 cup powdered sugar
1 teaspoon butter or
   margarine, melted

Juice of 1 lemon

Combine powdered sugar, melted butter, and lemon juice. Spread on warm baked mixture.

VADA FRANK   PLAINVIEW UNIT

LEBKUCHEN

1⅓ cups strained honey
2 cups light brown sugar
¼ cup water
8 cups flour, approximately
¼ teaspoon cloves
¼ teaspoon nutmeg
1 teaspoon cinnamon

½ teaspoon baking soda
⅛ teaspoon salt
2 eggs
½ pound almonds
¼ pound citron
¼ pound candied orange peel

Boil honey, sugar, and water for 5 minutes. Cool. Sift and measure flour. Add spices, baking soda and salt; sift again. Add to honey mixture. Beat eggs slightly, add to honey-flour mixture. Blanch and sliver almonds. Cut the peel fine. Work almonds, citron, and peel into mixture. Cover and set in cool place to ripen. Roll out ¼-inch thick, adding a little more flour if necessary. Cut in 1 x 3-inch rectangles. Place on greased baking sheet. Bake in preheated 350° oven for about 15 minutes. When cool, cover with Transparent Icing.

Transparent Icing:
1 cup powdered sugar
1 teaspoon lemon juice

5 teaspoons boiling water

Mix ingredients thoroughly.

MARIE DOHM BROWN   NILWOOD UNIT

SOFT MOLASSES COOKIES

2½ cups sifted flour
½ teaspoon ginger
½ teaspoon cinnamon
¼ teaspoon salt
2 teaspoons baking soda
2 tablespoons hot water

½ cup soft shortening
½ cup sugar
½ cup molasses
1 egg
6 tablespoons cold water
½ cup raisins or chopped nuts

Preheat oven to 375°. Sift together first 4 ingredients. Dissolve baking soda in hot water. Mix shortening and next 3 ingredients until creamy. Mix flour mixture alternately with cold water into creamed mixture. Mix in soda and all but a few raisins. Drop by rounded teaspoons 2 inches apart on greased cookie sheet. Sprinkle with remaining raisins. Bake at 375° until done. Makes about 2 dozen.

MARGY CURTIS   HONEY POINT UNIT

LEBKUCHEN (QUANTITY RECIPE)

1½ pints sugar
1 pint lard
2 eggs, beaten
½ gallon sorghum
½ pound citron, cut fine
2 1-pound packages raisins
2 packages currants
1 pound dates, cut fine
1 quart nut meats
Flour (about 5 pounds plus
  6½ cups)

½ cup baking soda
⅓ cup cinnamon
1 tablespoon nutmeg
1 tablespoon cloves
1 tablespoon allspice
1 tablespoon salt
1 pint sour milk or buttermilk
1 tablespoon vanilla
1 tablespoon lemon extract

Cream sugar and lard; add beaten eggs. Add sorghum, citron, raisins, currants (all raisins may be used), dates, and nuts. Sift dry ingredients into 1 quart flour. Add sour milk, vanilla, and lemon extract. Add flour to make a very stiff dough. Mix well. Let stand overnight in cool place. Roll out on floured board; cut. Place on cookie sheet. Bake at 325° for 12 to 13 minutes. Cool and store in tightly covered container. Bake about 3 or 4 weeks before Christmas. Makes 26 dozen.

MRS. ROBERT LITTLE   STITCH AND STIR UNIT

NO BAKE COOKIES

2 cups sugar
1 stick margarine
½ cup milk
2 tablespoons cocoa

2 cups oatmeal
½ cup peanut butter
½ teaspoon vanilla

Heat sugar, margarine, milk, and cocoa in saucepan over medium heat until it boils for 1 minute. Remove from heat. Add oatmeal, peanut butter, and vanilla. Let cool until they hold shape when dropped on waxed paper, or pour into buttered 9 x 9-inch pan, cutting into squares when cool.

ROBIN MANSHOLT   GILLESPIE NIGHT UNIT

MRS. TOM MOULTON, BUNKER HILL UNIT adds ½ cup coconut.

MINIATURE KOLACKY (CRESCENTS CZECHOSLOVAKIA)

1 package yeast
1 cup cream, scalded and
  cooled
½ cup plus ½ teaspoon
  sugar

3 cups flour
⅛ teaspoon salt
1 cup butter, chilled
4 egg yolks
Pinch of mace

Soften yeast in cream; stir in ½ teaspoon sugar and let stand 15 minutes. Blend flour with salt. Cut in butter until mixture resembles coarse meal. Set aside. Beat egg yolks and remaining sugar until thick and lemon colored. Beat in the yeast mixture and mace. Make well in center of flour-butter mixture; add egg mixture and blend well. Chill dough overnight. Place one half the dough on lightly floured surface. Roll ¼-inch thick. Cut dough into triangles. Place Filling in center and roll into crescents. (Filling mixture should be kept in the refrigerator until needed. Dough should be cut into bite-size pieces.) Repeat until all dough is used. Cover and let rise for 10 or 15 minutes. Bake on cookie sheet at 350° for 15 to 20 minutes. Makes 7 dozen.

Filling:
4 egg whites, stiffly beaten
½ cup sugar

1 pound English walnuts, ground

Fold sugar and ground nuts into stiffly beaten egg whites. Note: Dough can also be cut with round cookie cutter. Place Filling on round and either roll or place another round on top.

ERMINIA WENZEL   BERTHA ELDRED

MOUND BARS

2 cups graham cracker
  crumbs
1 stick margarine, melted
¼ cup sugar
2 cups coconut

1 can (14-ounce) Eagle Brand
  milk
1 cup chocolate chips
½ cup peanut butter, plain or
  chunky

Mix crumbs, margarine and sugar. Press into ungreased 9 x 13-inch pan. Mix coconut and milk. Spread over crumbs in pan. Bake at 350° for 15 minutes. Cool. Melt chocolate chips and peanut butter together. Spread on top of baked mixture. Cut into squares. Makes about 75 squares.

JOYCE COOKSEY   MODELITE UNIT

LEMON BARS

1 box lemon cake mix
1 stick butter, melted
1 egg, beaten

8 ounces cream cheese
2 eggs
1 box powdered sugar

Mix together cake mix, melted butter, and beaten egg. Pat into a 9 x 13-inch pan. Cream the cream cheese, eggs, and powdered sugar. Spread over batter in cake pan. Bake at 350° for 30 minutes.

DONNA LANDES   SCOTTVILLE UNIT

MELT AWAY COOKIES

1 cup powdered sugar
2 cups flour
½ teaspoon cream of tartar
½ teaspoon baking soda

1 cup margarine or butter
1 teaspoon vanilla
2 egg yolks

Sift together the powdered sugar, flour, cream of tartar, and baking soda. Cream margarine, vanilla, and egg yolks thoroughly. Add the dry ingredients. Drop by teaspoon onto cookie sheet and press down with glass or fork. Bake at 350° for 10 minutes.

MRS. MARY HEMPHILL   BERTHA ELDRED UNIT

CRUNCHY OAT COOKIES

1 cup whole wheat flour
⅓ cup instant non-fat dry
  milk
¼ cup wheat germ, toasted
¼ cup raw bran
1 teaspoon baking soda
1 teaspoon baking powder
½ teaspoon salt
1 teaspoon cinnamon

¼ teaspoon nutmeg
⅛ teaspoon cloves
1 cup butter
1 cup brown sugar
2 eggs
2 cups old fashioned oats
½ cup walnuts, chopped
½ cup raisins

Stir together first 10 dry ingredients and set aside. Cream butter and brown sugar. Add eggs and beat until fluffy. Gradually add flour mixture, stirring only enough to blend. Stir in oats, walnuts, and raisins. Drop by teaspoon onto ungreased cookie sheet. Bake at 350° for 8 to 10 minutes. Makes 5 dozen.

FRANCES M. CLARK   HAGAMAN UNIT

MINCEMEAT COOKIES

1 cup shortening
1½ cups sugar
3 eggs, beaten
1 9-ounce package
   mincemeat

2 tablespoons grated orange rind
3½ cups sifted flour
½ teaspoon salt
1 teaspoon baking soda

Cream shortening and sugar. Add eggs. Stir in mincemeat, broken in pieces; add remaining ingredients. Drop by small teaspoons 2 inches apart on greased baking sheets. Bake at 400° for 12 minutes. Makes 5 dozen.

MRS. GRANT PITMAN   BIRD UNIT

CHOCOLATE CHIP-OATMEAL COOKIES

1½ cups flour
1 teaspoon baking soda
1 teaspoon salt
1 cup shortening
¾ cup brown sugar
¾ cup sugar

2 eggs
1 6-ounce package chocolate
   chips
1 cup nuts
2 cups oatmeal
1 teaspoon vanilla

Sift flour once; add baking soda, salt, and sift again. Cream shortening; add sugar gradually and cream together until light and fluffy. Add eggs and mix thoroughly. Add flour in two parts and mix well. Add chips, nuts, oatmeal, and vanilla; mix thoroughly. Drop from tablespoon (or teaspoon if smaller cookies are desired) onto ungreased baking sheet approximately 2 inches apart. Bake at 375° for 10 to 12 minutes. Makes 4 dozen.

CHERYLL McNEILLY   MT. OLIVE UNIT

ORANGE BALLS

1 12-ounce box vanilla wafers
1 6-ounce can frozen orange
   juice

1 stick margarine, softened
2 cups powdered sugar
Flaked coconut

Crush vanilla wafers. Let orange juice thaw to mushy stage. Whip orange juice, margarine, and powdered sugar. Add vanilla wafers. Let mixture chill 30 minutes. Mix again. Chill again if sticky. Roll into small balls; roll in coconut. Store in tightly covered container. Ground or chopped nuts may be substituted for coconut. Makes 6 dozen.

LELA KLAUS   HONEY POINT UNIT

OATMEAL CRISPIES

1 cup shortening	1½ cups flour
1 cup brown sugar	1 teaspoon salt
1 cup sugar	1 teaspoon baking soda
2 eggs, well beaten	3 cups rolled oats
1 teaspoon vanilla	½ cup raisins or nut meats

Cream shortening (if margarine or butter is used, add ½ teaspoon salt) and sugars. Add eggs; mix well. Add vanilla. Stir in sifted dry ingredients. Add oats, raisins or nuts. Shape into 2 rolls, wrap in waxed paper and chill for 2 hours or overnight. Slice into 40 pieces and place slices on ungreased cookie sheet. Bake at 350° for 10 minutes or until slightly browned around edges. Makes 40 cookies.

MRS. LOUIS (EVELYN) LEBRO   SPANISH NEEDLE UNIT

OATMEAL COOKIES

2 cups brown sugar	½ teaspoon salt
1 cup margarine	1 teaspoon baking powder
2 eggs	1 teaspoon baking soda
1 teaspoon vanilla	Nuts or coconut, if desired
3 cups quick rolled oats	Powdered sugar
1½ cups flour	

Cream brown sugar and margarine. Add eggs and vanilla. Beat well. Add rolled oats. Sift together flour, salt, baking powder, and baking soda. Add to above mixture. Chill overnight. Roll into balls; dip in powdered sugar. Put on greased cookie sheet and press with a glass. Bake at 350° for 10 minutes. The balls should be the size of a walnut.

THERESA KLAUS   CARLINVILLE NIGHT UNIT

ORANGE SLICE CANDY BARS

1 cup sugar	½ cup nuts
4 eggs	1 pound orange slices, diced
¾ teaspoon baking powder	Powdered sugar
2 cups flour, scant	

Mix sugar and eggs. Add baking powder and flour. Put in nuts and orange slices. Pour into greased 13 x 9 x 2-inch pan. Bake at 350° for 20 minutes or until done. Cut into 2-inch squares. Roll in powdered sugar. Makes 3 dozen.

KAREN HILDEBRAND   GILLESPIE NIGHT UNIT

OATMEAL COOKIES

1 cup raisins
1 cup water
¾ cup shortening
1½ cup sugar
2 eggs
1 teaspoon vanilla
2½ cups flour

½ teaspoon baking powder
1 teaspoon soda
½ teaspoon salt
½ teaspoon cinnamon
½ teaspoon nutmeg
2 cups quick oatmeal
½ cup nuts, chopped

Simmer raisins and water over low heat until raisins are plump. Drain raisin liquid into measuring cup; add enough water to make ½ cup. Cream shortening, sugar, eggs and vanilla; stir in raisin liquid. Sift dry ingredients together; add oatmeal, raisins, and nuts. Gradually add to creamed mixture. Drop by teaspoons onto greased cookie sheets. Bake at 350° for 10 minutes.

MRS. SAM DOOLEY   CARLINVILLE NIGHT UNIT

OATMEAL COOKIES

¾ cup hot water
2 cups oatmeal
2 cups brown sugar
½ cup shortening
2 eggs
2 cups flour
2 teaspoons baking powder

1 teaspoon baking soda
Pinch of salt
2 teaspoons cinnamon
1 teaspoon nutmeg
1 teaspoon vanilla
1 cup raisins
1 cup nut meats

Pour hot water over oats and set aside. Cream sugar and shortening until fluffy; add eggs, beating well after each addition. Sift flour with baking powder, baking soda, salt, and spices. Add flour mixture to creamed mixture alternately with oat mixture and vanilla. Add raisins and nut meats. Drop by teaspoon onto greased cookie sheet. Bake at 350° for 8 to 10 minutes or until lightly browned.

MRS. ELERY WELLER   GIRARD DAY UNIT

POTATO CHIP COOKIES

½ pound butter
½ pound margarine
2 teaspoons vanilla

1 cup sugar
3¾ cups flour
1½ cups potato chips, crushed

Cream butter and margarine until fluffy. Add vanilla and sugar. Beat well. Add flour and beat until well blended. Add crushed potato chips. Drop by teaspoon onto ungreased cookie sheet. Bake at 350° for 13 to 15 minutes.

EVELYN PINTAR   GET TOGETHERS UNIT

PECAN BARS

1 cup flour
¼ cup butter
¼ cup sugar
1 cup brown sugar
2 eggs

½ teaspoon baking powder
2 tablespoons flour
½ cup coconut
½ cup pecans, chopped

Mix 1 cup flour, butter, and sugar as for pie crust; pat into a 9 x 13-inch pan. Bake at 350° for 10 minutes. Mix brown sugar, eggs, baking powder, 2 tablespoons flour, coconut, and chopped pecans together. Spread this mixture over crust as soon as it comes from the oven. Bake again for 20 minutes. Remove from oven and spread with Icing.

Icing:
½ cup brown sugar
3 tablespoons cream or milk
1 teaspoon butter

1 teaspoon vanilla
Powdered sugar

Bring brown sugar and cream to a boil. Add butter and boil 1 minute. Let cool. Stir in enough powdered sugar to make it thick enough to spread. Beat well. Spread over cookie mixture.

ANN REYNOLDS   HAGAMAN UNIT

PEANUT BLOSSOMS

1¾ cup flour
1 teaspoon baking soda
½ teaspoon salt
½ cup shortening
½ cup peanut butter

½ cup sugar
½ cup brown sugar
1 egg
1 teaspoon vanilla
Chocolate kisses

Sift together flour, baking soda, and salt. Set aside. Cream shortening and peanut butter together, gradually adding both sugars and cream well. Add egg and vanilla; beat well. Blend in dry ingredients gradually, mixing thoroughly. Shape into balls and roll in sugar. Place on greased cookie sheets. Bake at 375° for 10 minutes. Remove from oven and top each cookie with a chocolate kiss, pressing down firmly so cookie cracks around edge. Bake 2 to 5 minutes longer until golden brown. Makes 3 dozen.

MRS. ROGER (DOTTIE) GRUEN   JUNIOR HOMEMAKERS UNIT

PEANUT BUTTER COOKIES

½ cup margarine
2 tablespoons shortening
½ cup sugar
½ cup brown sugar, packed
1 egg
½ cup peanut butter

1 teaspoon vanilla
1½ cups flour
¾ teaspoon baking soda
½ teaspoon baking powder
½ teaspoon salt

Cream margarine, shortening, and sugars; beat in egg, peanut butter, and vanilla. Sift together flour, baking soda, baking powder, and salt; add to creamed mixture. Use about 1 teaspoon dough and shape into balls. Place on cookie sheets. Press with fork in criss-cross pattern. Bake at 350° for 12 minutes or until light brown.

MAE ALLAN   BERTHA ELDRED UNIT

PINEAPPLE COOKIES

1 cup shortening (butter and
  margarine mixed)
1 cup sugar
1 cup light brown sugar
2 eggs
1 teaspoon vanilla

1 cup nut meats, chopped
1 cup stewed raisins
4 cups flour
1 teaspoon baking soda
1 8-ounce can (1 cup) crushed
  pineapple

Mix ingredients in order given. Drop onto greased cookie sheet. Bake at 350° for 10 to 12 minutes. Note: Dough should be fairly stiff. If a little more liquid is needed, use the raisin water. I like to use white raisins when available.

MRS. LEO LOTT   SUSTAINING MEMBER

HONEY PUMPKIN COOKIES

¾ cup butter
1½ cups sugar
¼ cup honey
2 eggs
1 cup pumpkin
⅓ cup poppy seed

1 tablespoon milk
2½ cups sifted flour
1 teaspoon baking powder
¾ teaspoon salt
¾ cup nuts, chopped
¾ cup dates, chopped

Cream butter, sugar, and honey. Stir in remaining ingredients. Drop by teaspoon onto greased cookie sheet. Bake in 400° oven for 15 minutes. Makes 4 dozen.

ANN POLO   BRUSHY MOUND UNIT

MY MOTHER'S PIZZELLE

1 pound Imperial margarine,
   at room temperature
4 cups sugar
12 eggs
2 teaspoons vanilla
2 tablespoons lemon juice

Rind of 2 lemons, grated
9 cups flour
2 teaspoons salt
6 teaspoons baking powder
1 teaspoon cinnamon

Beat margarine and sugar until fluffy and light. Beat in eggs, one at a time. Add vanilla and lemon juice. Beat at high speed of mixer for 15 minutes. Mix in lemon rind. Add flour to which has been added salt, baking powder, and cinnamon. Mix until well blended. Chill overnight or 4 or 5 hours. Drop by level tablespoon onto hot pizzelle iron. Bake about 1½ minutes until golden brown. Makes about 20 dozen.

VICA MAKUH   GET TOGETHERS UNIT

FILLED RAISIN BARS

1½ cups raisins
¼ cup brown sugar
1 teaspoon lemon rind
½ teaspoon ginger

½ cup water
1 teaspoon cornstarch
1 tablespoon lemon juice
¼ teaspoon salt

Combine all ingredients in saucepan. Simmer 10 minutes. Let cool. While filling is cooling, prepare dough.

Dough:
½ cup margarine
1 cup sugar
1 egg
1 teaspoon vanilla

2 tablespoons milk
2 cups flour
1 teaspoon salt
1 teaspoon baking powder

Cream margarine, sugar, egg, and vanilla. Blend in milk. Sift flour, salt, and baking powder together; add to creamed mixture. Chill. Spread ⅔ of dough in greased 9-inch pan. Spread cooled filling on it. Roll out remaining dough; cut into strips and criss cross them on top of filling. Bake at 350° for 35 to 40 minutes. Cut into bars when cool.

MRS. LOUIS GRANDONE   GET TOGETHERS UNIT

MOM McCAIN'S PLAIN COOKIES

1 cup butter	3 teaspoons baking powder
1½ cups sugar	⅛ teaspoon baking soda
2 eggs	2 teaspoons nutmeg
4 cups flour	¼ cup sour milk

Cream butter and sugar together. Add eggs, mix well. Sift dry ingredients together and add alternately with sour milk to creamed mixture. Roll out, a small amount at a time, ¼ inch thick; cut with desired cookie cutters. Decorate with colored sugars. Bake at 375° for 10 minutes or until light brown. Cookies may be iced if sugars are not used, or may be left plain. Will keep for several weeks. Makes approximately 4 dozen.

THERESA McCAIN   MT. OLIVE UNIT

PAULS PUMPKIN BARS

4 eggs	2 teaspoons baking powder
1⅔ cup sugar	2 teaspoons ground cinnamon
1 cup cooking oil	1 teaspoon salt
1 16-ounce can pumpkin	1 teaspoon baking soda
2 cups flour	

In mixing bowl, beat together eggs, sugar, oil, and pumpkin until light and fluffy. Sift together flour, baking powder, cinnamon, salt, and baking soda. Add to pumpkin mixture and mix thoroughly. Spread batter in ungreased 15 x 10 x 1-inch baking pan. Bake in 350° oven for 25 to 30 minutes. Cool. Frost with Cream Cheese Icing. Cut in bars. Makes 2 dozen.

Cream Cheese Icing:

1 3-ounce package cream cheese, softened	1 teaspoon vanilla
½ cup butter or margarine, softened	2 cups sifted powdered sugar

Cream together cream cheese and butter or margarine. Stir in vanilla. Add powdered sugar, a little at a time, until mixture is smooth.

BETTY WALTERS   STITCH AND STIR UNIT

RAISIN NUT DROP COOKIES

2 cup raisins, cooked
1 teaspoon baking soda
2 cups sugar
¾ cup shortening
4 eggs, beaten
4 cups flour

4 teaspoons baking powder
1 teaspoon cinnamon
1 teaspoon nutmeg
¾ cup walnuts or pecans,
  chopped
1 teaspoon vanilla

Cook raisins in enough water so you will have 1 cup of raisin juice; add baking soda to juice. Cream sugar and shortening; add beaten eggs. Sift dry ingredients together. Add dry ingredients and raisin juice to creamed mixture. Add cooked raisins, nuts, and vanilla. Drop by teaspoon onto greased cookie sheet. Bake at 400° for 12 to 15 minutes. Makes 8 dozen.

MRS. EDGAR FALTER   BIRD UNIT

RAISIN NUT SQUARES

3 cups flour
1 teaspoon cinnamon
1 teaspoon baking powder
2 cups brown sugar
2 eggs, beaten

1 cup Mazola oil
½ cup raisins
½ cup nuts
1 cup hot water
1 teaspoon baking soda

Sift flour, cinnamon, and baking powder together. Mix together the flour mixture, brown sugar, eggs, oil, raisins, and nuts. Stir baking soda into the hot water. Add to flour mixture. Mix until smooth. Pour into greased and floured 10 x 15-inch baking sheet ½-inch thick. Bake at 375° for 15 minutes. Cool. Ice with powdered sugar and enough water to make a thin glaze. Cut in squares. Makes 20.

GUIDA COFFMAN   BERTHA ELDRED UNIT

SCOTCH SHORT BREAD

½ cup butter (NOT
  margarine)

½ cup sugar
3 cups flour

Cream butter and sugar well. Add flour; knead until all is mixed. Divide into 2 parts. Pat into 8 or 9-inch pie pans. Prick top with fork. Bake at 325° about 30 minutes or until light brown. Cut into bars while warm.

E. ANDERSON   BRUSHY MOUNT UNIT

RANGER COOKIES

1 cup shortening (oil or
  margarine)
1 cup sugar
1 cup brown sugar
2 eggs
1 teaspoon vanilla
2 cups flour

1 teaspoon baking soda
½ teaspoon baking powder
½ teaspoon salt
1 cup oats
1 cup Rice Krispies
1 cup nuts (optional)
1 cup coconut

Cream the first five ingredients in a large bowl. Gradually add flour, baking soda, baking powder, and salt to mixture. Stir in oats. Add rest of ingredients one at a time. Drop by teaspoon onto greased cookie sheet. Bake in preheated 350° oven for 8 to 10 minutes or until light brown. Remove and cool on racks. Makes 4 dozen.

MRS. MARY SCHWAB   MONDAY NITERS UNIT

SNICKER DOODLES

1 cup shortening
1½ cups sugar
2 eggs
2¾ cups flour
1 teaspoon cream of tartar

1 teaspoon baking soda
½ teaspoon salt
1 cup sugar
1 teaspoon cinnamon

Cream together shortening, 1½ cups sugar, and eggs until light and fluffy. Sift together flour, cream of tartar, baking soda, and salt. Add to creamed mixture, mixing well. Roll in small balls then roll in combined 1 cup sugar and cinnamon mixture. Place on greased cookie sheet. Bake at 400° for 8 to 10 minutes.

MRS. OTTO WHITLER   GIRARD DAY UNIT

SPICE BARS

¾ cup margarine
1½ cups brown sugar
2 eggs
¾ cup sour milk
2 cups flour

1 teaspoon cinnamon
¾ teaspoon cloves
Scant ½ teaspoon baking soda
¾ cup raisins (optional)
¼ cup nuts (optional)

Cream margarine and brown sugar until light and fluffy. Add eggs and sour milk. Sift flour with the spices and baking soda. Add to creamed mixture. Stir in nuts and raisins if desired. Spread batter in 11 x 15-inch pan. Bake at 375° for 20 minutes. Good iced with cream cheese or caramel icing.

VERA SCHREITER   CARLINVILLE NIGHT UNIT

SHORT BREAD

1 pound butter (NOT margarine)	1 cup sugar 4 cups flour

Cream butter and sugar (use hands). Add flour gradually and work in. Pat into 9 x 13-inch pan. Prick top with fork. Bake at 325° for 1 hour or until lightly browned. Cut in small pieces while hot. Remove to racks to cool.

MAE ALLAN   BERTHA ELDRED UNIT

TORCHETTI (ITALIAN HORSESHOES)

1 cup flour	4 cups flour
1 cup warm water	Sugar
1 cake or package yeast	
1 pound butter or ½ butter and ½ margarine	

Mix together flour, warm water, and yeast. In another dish, soften butter. Add flour and mix as for pie crust. Add to yeast mixture; mix until it doesn't stick. Set in refrigerator overnight. The next day remove a small amount at a time from the refrigerator and roll out by hand like the size of a pencil. Cut into 6-inch lengths and roll in pan of sugar. Place each roll on cookie sheet and shape like horseshoe. Bake at 375° for 15 to 20 minutes. As ovens vary, check after about 10 minutes as these burn easily.

MRS. MIKE BRUNETTO   SUSTAINING MEMBER

TORCETTI

1 pound margarine	1 package dry yeast
5 cups flour	2 eggs, beaten
½ cup warm milk	1 cup sugar
½ tablespoon sugar	½ teaspoon cinnamon, if desired
½ tablespoon vanilla	

Cut margarine into flour until very fine using a pastry blender. Combine milk, sugar, and vanilla; stir in yeast until dissolved. Add to flour mixture with eggs. Knead lightly, using flour if necessary. Let rise 1 hour or until double in bulk. Divide dough in half. Roll into rectangle a little thicker than pie dough; sprinkle with half of combined sugar and cinnamon, and roll in lightly till sugar mixture sticks to dough. Repeat for rest of dough. Cut with pastry cutter wheel about ½-inch wide and 3 to 4 inches long. Shape like a horseshoe and pinch ends together very lightly. Place on lightly greased cookie sheets. Bake at 375° for 12 to 15 minutes until golden brown.

VICA MAKUH   GET TOGETHERS UNIT

SUGAR COOKIES

1 cup oil
1 cup butter
1 cup sugar
1 cup powdered sugar
1 teaspoon vanilla

2 eggs
4 cups flour
1 teaspoon salt
1 teaspoon baking soda
1 teaspoon cream of tartar

Cream oil, butter, and both sugars. Add vanilla and eggs. Sift flour, salt, baking soda, and cream of tartar (2½ teaspoons baking powder can be used for the baking soda and cream of tartar.) Stir in and blend. Roll a teaspoon of dough into a ball. Dip top half in sugar, press down on ungreased cookie sheet sugar side up. Bake at 350° for 10 to 12 minutes. Makes 4 dozen.

STELLA LOWIS   PIASA UNIT

LUCINA LINK, BERTHA ELDRED UNIT uses no salt, 2 teaspoons vanilla, 4½ cups flour, chills dough several hours before baking, and calls them Amish sugar cookies.

CATHERINE TIRA, GET TOGETHERS UNIT shapes dough into small balls and uses a small glass, covered with a damp cloth, dipped in sugar, to flatten.

SUGAR COOKIES

1½ cups vegetable
  shortening
3 cups light brown sugar
3 eggs
1 teaspoon vanilla
1 teaspoon baking soda

1 cup buttermilk
1 teaspoon baking powder
½ teaspoon salt
1 teaspoon nutmeg or cinnamon
4½ cups flour

Cream shortening; add sugar and beat. Add eggs, one at a time, beating after each addition. Stir in vanilla. Combine baking soda and buttermilk. Sift together baking powder, salt, nutmeg, and flour. Add the buttermilk and flour mixtures alternately to the creamed mixture to make a soft dough. Roll dough on a well floured board ¼-inch thick and cut in rounds with cookie cutter. Place on cookie sheet. Sprinkle with granulated or colored sugar and place a red candied cherry, raisin, or pecan half in center of each cookie. Bake at 425° for 8 minutes. Makes 6 dozen.

MRS. H. K. HALL   BARR UNIT

SPECIAL "K" BARS

½ cup sugar
½ cup dark syrup
⅔ cup peanut butter
1 teaspoon vanilla
3 cups Special K cereal

1 6-ounce package chocolate
chips
1 6-ounce package butterscotch
chips

Combine sugar and syrup. Bring to a boil. Remove from heat and add peanut butter and vanilla. Stir until smooth. Pour over Special K and mix. Spread quickly in buttered 9 x 13-inch pan. Melt chocolate chips and butterscotch chips and spread over cookies in pan. Cut into squares while warm. Makes 2 dozen.

PEGGY BRUCE   HONEY POINT UNIT

SPRINGERLI

5 eggs
2 cups sugar
4 cups flour, more if needed

2 teaspoons baking powder
⅓ teaspoon anise oil

Beat eggs lightly. Add sugar, flour, baking powder, and anise oil. Chill in refrigerator for 1 to 2 hours. Roll out and cut in squares. Let set overnight in cool place. Bake next day at 350° for 10 minutes.

MARY KLAUS   MONDAY NITERS UNIT

TOFFEE-ORANGE BARS

½ cup butter
1 cup sifted flour
2 eggs, beaten
1½ cups brown sugar
1 teaspoon vanilla
2 tablespoons flour

½ teaspoon salt
½ teaspoon baking powder
1 cup California walnuts,
chopped
½ cup flaked coconut

Cut butter into flour until it resembles coarse meal; press into bottom of 13 x 9 x 2-inch pan. Bake at 350° about 15 minutes. Do not brown. Combine eggs, brown sugar, and vanilla. Add 2 tablespoons flour, salt, and baking powder. Stir in nuts and coconut. Spread carefully over baked mixture. Return to oven and bake 25 minutes. Cool. Ice with orange frosting. Makes 24.

BETTY SMITH   MEDORA UNIT

TOFFEE BARS

1 cup butter	1 cup flour
1 cup brown sugar	6 1.05-ounce milk chocolate bars
1 egg yolk	⅔ cup crushed nuts

Preheat oven to 350°. Cream butter, sugar, and egg yolk. Add flour gradually, stirring until well blended. Spread dough in a lightly greased 15½ x 10½ x 1-inch jelly roll pan. Bake for 15 to 20 minutes or until medium brown. Remove from oven. Lay chocolate bars on top; spread when melted. Sprinkle with nuts. Cool and cut into desired size bars or diamonds. Makes 50.

MRS. MELBA K. EICHEN   SHAWS POINT UNIT

TURTLES

½ cup butter	½ cup brown sugar
2 cups flour	⅔ cup butter
1 cup brown sugar	1 cup milk chocolate chips
1 cup pecans	

Cut ½ cup butter into flour and 1 cup brown sugar with pastry blender. Press into ungreased 9 x 13-inch pan. Spread pecans over crust. Boil ½ cup brown sugar and ⅔ cup butter for one-half minute, stirring constantly. Spoon mixture over crust. Bake for 18 minutes at 350°. While hot, sprinkle milk chocolate chips over top. Spread when melted.

LOUISE WOODS   BIRD UNIT

7-Layer Cookie

YUM-YUMS

1 cup graham cracker crumbs	1 small package butterscotch chips
1 stick margarine, melted	1 cup pecans, chopped
1 cup Angel Flake coconut	1 can Eagle Brand milk
1 small package chocolate chips	

Mix together the crumbs, margarine, and pat into an 8 x 12-inch pan. Sprinkle over top the coconut, chocolate chips, and butterscotch chips. Top with chopped pecans. Pour, spreading evenly, the Eagle Brand milk over top. Bake at 350° for 30 to 35 minutes. Cut while warm into squares or bars.

NELLE ELDRED   POLK UNIT

CANDIES

Nature is at it's best during every season as one travels the winding country roads throughout Macoupin county. This secondary road crosses Macoupin Creek—as it courses through Polk township.

Photographed by Ernie Reiher

ALMOND BARK PEANUT BUTTER CANDY

2 pounds white almond bark
1 cup peanut butter
2 cups miniature
  marshmallows

1 12-ounce jar dry-roasted
  peanuts
4 cups Rice Chex

In a 9 x 13-inch pan, melt bark in oven at 300° for 10 minutes. Add peanut butter, marshmallows, nuts and Rice Chex. Drop from spoon onto waxed paper to cool. Makes about 4 dozen.

SALLY ALWARD   SHIPMAN UNIT

CANDY STRAWBERRIES

2 3-ounce packages
  strawberry Jello
1 cup ground nuts
1 cup flake coconut
1 14-ounce can sweetened
  condensed milk

1 teaspoon vanilla
Red sugar, as needed
Slivered almonds
Green food coloring
Green tinted icing

Mix Jello, ground nuts, coconut, milk, and vanilla. Chill one to two hours. Shape into berries, roll in red sugar. Put the slivered almonds in green food coloring to make stems. Put one in each berry. Make leaves with green icing.

MAE STIEHL   MT. OLIVE UNIT

CARAMELS

2 cups sugar
1 cup dark syrup
½ teaspoon salt

3 cups whipping cream
1 teaspoon vanilla
½ cup chopped nuts (optional)

Combine sugar, syrup, salt, and 1 cup of whipping cream. Bring to boil (244°), add another 1 cup of whipping cream. Bring back to 244° then add the third cup of whipping cream. Bring to 248°-250°. Add vanilla and nuts. Pour into 9 x 13-inch pan. Cool, cut, and wrap in waxed paper.

MRS. VICTOR (BERNICE) GRICHNIK   SPANISH NEEDLE UNIT

CARAMELS

1 cup butter or margarine	1 cup light syrup
1 pound brown sugar	1 can sweetened condensed milk
Dash of salt	1 teaspoon vanilla

Melt butter in heavy pan. Add sugar and salt. Stir thoroughly. Stir in syrup, mix well. Gradually add the milk, stirring constantly. Cook and stir over medium heat to firm ball stage (245°)—12 to 15 minutes. Remove from heat, stir in vanilla. Pour into 9 x 9 x 2-inch buttered pan. When cool, cut into squares and wrap in waxed paper.

ELEANOR ROSS   BARR UNIT

CARAMEL POPCORN

Popcorn	2 sticks margarine
2 cups brown sugar (1 cup	½ cup white syrup
white and 1 cup brown	½ teaspoon cream of tartar
sugar may be used)	1 teaspoon baking soda

Pop enough corn for 16 cups. In large saucepan, mix sugar, margarine, syrup, and cream of tartar. Boil for 5 minutes. Add baking soda and stir very good. While foaming, pour over popped corn. Put onto a greased cookie sheet and bake at 250° for 30 minutes, stirring often to keep mixture from running to the bottom. Break apart and stir. Makes about 16 servings.

PAT MILLER   SCOTTVILLE UNIT

CARAMEL CORN

6 quarts popped corn	2 sticks margarine
(unsalted)	1 teaspoon salt
2 cups brown sugar	1 teaspoon water
½ cup white syrup	Flavoring (optional)
1 teaspoon baking soda	Nuts (optional)

Pop corn and place in warm oven while making syrup. Boil brown sugar, syrup, salt, margarine and water for 5 minutes. Remove from heat and add baking soda and flavoring. Pour over warm popped corn and stir well. Spread on cookie sheets. Place in a 200° oven for 1 hour, stirring at 15-minute intervals. Remove from oven and cool. Store in covered container to keep crisp.

STELLA MILLS   SHIPMAN UNIT

OVEN CARAMEL CORN

2 cups brown sugar
2 sticks margarine
½ cup syrup
1 teaspoon salt

½ teaspoon baking soda
1 teaspoon vanilla
8 quarts popped corn (unsalted)

Mix brown sugar, margarine, syrup, and salt; boil five minutes. Remove from heat and add baking soda and vanilla. Beat and pour over corn. Place on two large shallow pans. Place pans in 250° oven and bake one hour; stir every 15 minutes. Will keep in tightly closed plastic container.

DOROTHY McINTYRE   HONEY POINT UNIT

DONNA LANDES, SCOTTVILLE UNIT, uses 6 quarts popped corn.

CRUNCHY PEANUT BRITTLE

3 cups sugar
1 cup water
1 cup light syrup
1 1-pound package raw
   peanuts

½ teaspoon salt
1 tablespoon baking soda
2 tablespoons margarine
1 teaspoon vanilla

In a 3 to 4-quart heavy pan, cook sugar, water and syrup over medium heat to 250°. Add peanuts and salt and cook to 310°. Remove from heat and add soda, margarine and vanilla. Stir until it foams up well. Pour onto a well buttered surface (a marble slab, a well buttered formica counter top, or two large cookie sheets.) As soon as it is cool enough to touch, start at the edge and pull and stretch, working to the center of the candy until all has been pulled to make it thin, crispy, and crunchy.

ROSE MARY HEMBROUGH   BIRD UNIT

DIVINITY

3 cups sugar
¾ cup light syrup
¾ cup water
2 egg whites (unbeaten)

1 3-ounce package Jello
   (strawberry or any flavor)
1 cup chopped pecans
½ cup flaked coconut

Combine sugar, syrup, and water in a heavy pan. Bring to boil, stirring constantly. Reduce heat, continue cooking, stirring occasionally to 252°. Beat egg whites until fluffy, add Jello, beating until it forms peaks. Pour hot syrup in thin streams into egg white mixture, beating constantly. Beat until it loses gloss and holds shape. Fold in nuts and coconut.

MRS. VICTOR (BERNICE) GRICHNIK   SPANISH NEEDLE UNIT

DATE CANDY

2½ cups sugar   ¾ cup milk

Cook to a soft ball stage.

Add:
5 ounces cut up dates

Cook again to soft ball stage. Remove from heat.

Add:
1 cup nuts   **1 tablespoon butter**
1 teaspoon vanilla

Beat well and pour into buttered pan.

MRS. EWELL (JOSEPHINE) HARRIS   SUSTAINING MEMBER

DIVINITY FUDGE

2¼ cups sugar   2 egg whites
½ cup boiling water   1½ teaspoons vanilla
½ cup white corn syrup

Put sugar, water, and syrup in heavy saucepan. Boil to soft ball stage. While it is boiling, beat egg whites until very stiff. Add vanilla and beat more. When syrup is to soft ball stage, pour one-half of it into egg whites and beat again. Boil remainder of syrup to crack stage. Add to egg white mixture and beat again. Drop onto waxed paper. You may add chopped nuts and candied cherries at the last if desired.

WILMA WARGO   GET TOGETHERS UNIT

NEVER FAIL DIVINITY

First Syrup: **Second Syrup:**
1 cup sugar   **2 cups sugar**
⅔ cup water   **1 cup white syrup**
3 egg whites   **½ cup hot water**
                          1 cup chopped nuts
                          1 teaspoon vanilla

Beat egg whites until stiff but not dry. Cook 1 cup of sugar and ⅔ cup water until syrup spins a thread. Pour over egg whites and beat until peaks form. Cook second syrup until it forms a hard ball in cold water. Add to first mixture and beat until it begins to lose its gloss. Add nuts and vanilla. Pour into greased 9 x 13-inch pan or drop by teaspoons onto waxed paper.

MARGARET FRIEDMAN   HONEY POINT UNIT

FUDGE MELTAWAYS

Bottom Layer

½ cup butter
1 1-ounce square
  unsweetened chocolate
¼ cup sugar

1 teaspoon vanilla
1 egg (beaten)
2 cups graham cracker crumbs
1 cup coconut

Melt butter and chocolate in saucepan. Blend sugar, vanilla, egg, graham cracker crumbs, and coconut into chocolate mixture. Mix well and press into ungreased 11½ x 7½ x 1½-inch baking dish or pan. Refrigerate.

Top Layer

¼ cup butter
1 tablespoon milk
2 cups powdered sugar

1 teaspoon vanilla
1½ ounces unsweetened
  chocolate

Mix butter, milk, powdered sugar, and vanilla together. Spread over crumb mixture. Chill. Melt 1½ squares chocolate and spread over chilled filling. Chill. Cut before firm.

Yields: 3 dozen.

THELMA BRUNS   MEDORA UNIT

PEANUT BRITTLE

2 cups sugar
½ cup water
1 cup white syrup
2 cups raw peanuts

1 teaspoon salt
1 tablespoon butter
½ teaspoon vanilla
2 teaspoons baking soda

Cook sugar, water, and syrup. When it reaches a full boil, add the peanuts and salt, stirring all the time. Cook until nuts have popped open or are done. If using a thermometer, cook to hard crack (300°). Remove from heat and stir in butter, vanilla, and baking soda. Pour quickly, while still foaming, into greased pan or other greased surface. Don't stir until foam is gone. Spread thin. When cool enough, pull out, stretching as thin as you can. Start at edge and keep pulling until all is stretched.

MRS. CHARLES THURSBY   BARR UNIT

MRS. VICTOR GRICHNIK, SPANISH NEEDLE UNIT, uses 1 cup of water and 1½ teaspoons baking soda.

QUICK NUT FUDGE

1 pound powdered sugar
½ cup cocoa
¼ teaspoon salt
6 tablespoons butter or
  margarine

4 tablespoons milk
1 tablespoon vanilla
1 cup nuts (chopped)

Combine all ingredients except nuts in top of double boiler. Place over hot water; stir until smooth. Add nuts and mix well. Spread candy in buttered 9 x 15-inch pan. Cool. Cut into squares. Yield: 24 pieces candy.

OPAL ALLEN   SHIPMAN UNIT

HOMEMADE CHOCOLATES

2 sticks margarine or butter
1 cup sweetened condensed
  milk
2½ pounds powdered sugar
½ teaspoon vanilla

12 ounces chocolate chips
1 4-ounce bar sweet chocolate
4 1-ounce squares bitter
  chocolate
¾ bar paraffin wax

Knead well the first four ingredients. Roll into small balls; insert toothpick in top of each. Place on cookie sheets lined with waxed paper. Chill thoroughly. Put in the freezer for a short time. Fondant may be divided before making into balls and nuts or other flavorings added. In double boiler melt the chocolates and paraffin. Dip each ball in chocolate. Place on waxed paper. When cool, remove toothpicks and fill the tiny holes with chocolate mixture.

WILMA HAMMOND   DO MORE UNIT

PEANUT BUTTER BALLS

1 1-pound 2-ounce jar creamy
  peanut butter
1 stick margarine or butter
2½ cups Rice Krispies

1 box powdered sugar
½ bar paraffin
1 small bag chocolate chips

Mix peanut butter and soft butter until well mixed. Add Rice Krispies and mix well. Add powdered sugar; mix well. Make into melon ball-sized balls and put in refrigerator until cold. Melt paraffin and chocolate chips in double boiler. Dip balls in chocolate; drain on waxed paper. Store in refrigerator.

ANNA K. REGLI   POLK UNIT

PEANUT BUTTER CUPS

⅓ pound graham cracker
  crumbs
½ pound butter (softened)

1 cup peanut butter
1 pound powdered sugar
2 cups chocolate chips

Combine crumbs, butter, peanut butter, and powdered sugar. Work together until smooth. Press mixture into 9 x 13-inch pan (or 9 x 9-inch pan for thick candy) that has been buttered. Melt chocolate chips over hot water. Spread over crumb mixture. Refrigerate until firm. Cut into squares.

MARGARET ACKER   CARLINVILLE NIGHT UNIT

REESE PEANUT BUTTER CUPS

3 cups peanut butter
1 cup brown sugar
2 sticks margarine

1½ boxes powdered sugar
⅓ cup paraffin, slivered
2 large packages chocolate chips

Mix together peanut butter, brown sugar, margarine, and powdered sugar. Make into small balls and refrigerate overnight. Melt paraffin and chocolate chips in double boiler. Using toothpicks or pickle fork, dip balls into chocolate. Place on waxed paper. Keep refrigerated.

PAT MILLER   SCOTTVILLE UNIT

PEANUT CRUNCHIES

2 pounds almond bark
2 cups crunchy peanut butter
2 cups Rice Krispies

2 cups miniature marshmallows
2 cups dry roasted peanuts

Melt in a 200° oven the almond bark and peanut butter; takes about 30 minutes. When melted, put into a large mixing bowl and add remaining ingredients. Stir until thoroughly coated. Drop from teaspoon onto waxed paper. Makes about 6 to 7 dozen.

LUCILLE BALLINGER   SHAWS POINT UNIT

PEANUT BUTTER BALLS

4 cups peanut butter
4 cups powdered sugar
1 tablespoon vanilla
1 cup dry milk

½ cup margarine
(for variety add 2 or 3 cups Rice Krispies)

Mix all ingredients until creamy and well blended. Shape into 100 to 120 balls. Refrigerate 1 hour. Dip balls (recipe below) and let stand on waxed paper until dry.

Dip:
1 bar paraffin

1 12-ounce package semi-sweet chocolate morsels

Melt paraffin and chocolate in top of double boiler.

LAVELLA LOWIS   MEDORA UNIT

PECAN DIVINITY ROLLS

Divinity:
2½ cups sugar
⅔ cup light corn syrup
½ cup water
2 egg whites
½ teaspoon vanilla

Caramel
1 cup sugar
½ cup brown sugar
½ cup cream
1 cup milk
(Or 1½ cups Half & Half in place of cream and milk)
¼ cup butter

About 1 quart coarsely chopped pecans

Divinity:
Cook sugar, syrup and water until it reaches the hard crack stage. Pour slowly over 2 egg whites that have been beaten until stiff. Add vanilla. Continue beating until very stiff and cool enough to handle. Form into 6 5-inch rolls and chill.

Caramel:
Cook the caramel ingredients until they form a hard ball. Cool slightly. While still quite warm, dip rolls of divinity into caramel and roll in nuts.

The divinity rolls should be chilled for easy slicing.

LINDA LAMBETH   PIASA UNIT

PLANTATION CRUNCH

1 pound almond bark (white
  chocolate)
2 tablespoons peanut butter
1 cup salted peanuts
  (blanched)

2 cups Captain Crunch cereal (or
  1 cup less than small box)

Melt bark and peanut butter in top of double boiler; stir until smooth. Combine peanuts and cereal; stir into bark-butter mixture until coated. Drop by spoon onto waxed paper and let cool.

MRS. WILLIAM GENETTI   NILWOOD UNIT

TURTLES

1 pound pecan halves
1 can Eagle Brand milk

1 cup white corn syrup
12 bars plain Hershey chocolate

Arrange pecans in groups of four on cookie sheet. Combine milk and syrup. Cook over low heat, stirring to prevent scorching. Cook until caramel colored and thick (230° for 20 to 30 minutes or to soft ball stage.) Spoon caramel onto nuts while still hot. Top with two squares of chocolate bar on each turtle and swirl when chocolate has melted.

GEORGINA V. BLAIR   DO MORE UNIT

MILDRED YING'S FRIED WALNUTS

4 cups walnuts
½ cup sugar

Salad oil
⅛ teaspoon salt

In large saucepan over high heat, heat 6 cups water to boiling; add walnuts and reheat to boiling. Cook 1 minute. Rinse in hot water; drain. Toss walnuts in sugar. In electric skillet heat about 1-inch salad oil to 350°. With a slotted spoon add half of the walnuts to oil. (Sugar crystallizes and makes a glaze.) Fry 5 minutes or until golden, stirring often. With slotted spoon remove cooked walnuts to a coarse sieve over a bowl to drain. Sprinkle with salt; toss lightly to keep nuts from sticking together. Transfer to waxed paper to cool. Fry remaining walnuts. Store in tightly covered container. Makes 4 cups.

DORIS RENO   PIASA UNIT

CANDIES

BARK CANDY
(Microwave)
1 pound confectioners' or candy coating (vanilla, chocolate, butter-scotch, or caramel)
1 cup of any of the following: roasted, salted nuts (unblanched almonds, peanuts, walnuts, pecans, or mixed nuts), sunflower seeds or soya nuts, or raisins

If candy coating is in a solid piece, break into squares. Place in a single layer in a 2-quart casserole. Microwave at Medium (50% power) for 3 to 5 minutes, until pieces are soft, stirring after 3 minutes. Add nuts, seeds, or raisins. Stir until candy coating is smooth and completely melted. Spread on waxed paper to ¼-inch thickness. Cool until hard then break into pieces. Makes about 1¼ pounds.

COMMITTEE

PEANUT BRITTLE
(Microwave)
1 cup raw peanuts
1 cup sugar
½ cup white corn syrup
⅛ teaspoon salt
1 teaspoon butter or margarine
1 teaspoon vanilla
1 teaspoon baking soda

In 1½-quart casserole, stir together peanuts, sugar, syrup, and salt. Cook 8 minutes at High, stirring well after 4 minutes. Stir in butter and vanilla. Cook 2 minutes longer on High. Add baking soda and quickly stir until light and foamy. Immediately pour onto lightly greased baking sheet; spread out thin. When cool, break into small pieces. Store in airtight container. Makes 1 pound.

MARY KLAUS   MONDAY NITERS UNIT

NEVER FAIL FUDGE
(Microwave)
1 pound powdered sugar
½ cup cocoa
½ cup butter or margarine
¼ cup milk
1 teaspoon vanilla
½ cup nuts, finely chopped

Mix sugar and cocoa in 8 x 10-inch utility dish. Drop butter onto sugar mixture in 4 or 5 pieces. Pour in milk. Microwave 2 to 3 minutes on High. Stir lightly and add vanilla and nuts, stirring until nuts are evenly distributed. Spread evenly in dish. Refrigerate 1 hour. Cut into squares. Makes 3 dozen pieces.

LUANNE KOCH   HONEY POINT UNIT

PRESERVING AND CANNING

From this bandstand, local musicians provide residents of Virden and surrounding communities with many hours of listening enjoyment. One of the town's most faithful musicians, Ben Osborn, has played French horn with the band since his return from World War I in 1918.

Records reveal that the Virden Brass Band was organized in 1880. In 1895, a charter was issued to the Virden Concert Band, at which time it became affiliated with the American Federation of Musicians.

Thanks to the support of local contributors, this tradition remains a part of the culture of Virden.

Photographed by Frank Thomas

CHUNK PICKLES

2 gallons cucumbers, sliced
2 gallons water
2 cups dehydrated lime
2 quarts vinegar
9 cups sugar

3 teaspoons salt
1 teaspoon celery seed
1 tablespoon pickling spice
1 tablespoon mustard seed

Select cucumbers of small to medium size. Slice ½ to ¾ inch thick. In 5 gallon container, pour in water and lime; stir well, lime will not dissolve completely. Add cucumbers. Leave cucumbers in lime water for 24 hours. Stir occasionally. Rinse 3 times or enough to remove lime from cucumbers. Combine vinegar, sugar, salt, celery seed, pickling spice, and mustard seed. Heat until sugar dissolves and add cucumbers. Bring to a boil and simmer 35 minutes. Bring to boil; seal in sterilized jars. Makes 14 pints.

MILLIE TURNER   MODELITE UNIT

CRISP PICKLE SLICES

4 quarts medium cucumbers,
    sliced
6 medium onions, sliced
2 green peppers, sliced
3 cloves garlic
⅓ cup coarse salt

5 cups sugar
3 cups cider vinegar
1½ teaspoons turmeric
1½ teaspoons celery seed
2 tablespoons mustard seed

Do not peel cucumbers. Slice thin. Add onions, peppers, and whole garlic cloves. Add salt, cover with cracked ice and mix thoroughly. Let stand 3 hours. Drain well. Combine remaining ingredients and pour over cucumbers. Heat just to a boil. Seal in hot jars. Makes 8 pints.

ZELMA HOPPER   PLAINVIEW UNIT

GOOD PICKLES

Cucumbers
2⅓ cups vinegar
2½ cups sugar
2 tablespoons salt

1 tablespoon celery seed
1 teaspoon turmeric
¾ teaspoon mustard seed

Wash cucumbers and split; pack in jars. Boil remaining ingredients for 5 minutes; pour over cucumbers and seal jars.

VIOLET HOWERTON   PLAINVIEW UNIT

CUCUMBER CELERY RELISH

¾ cup salt
4 cups cold water
4 cups cucumbers, chopped
1 cup green pepper, chopped
3 cups onions, chopped
3 cups celery, chopped

1 4-ounce can pimientos
7 cups sugar
4 cups vinegar
1 teaspoon celery seed
1 tablespoon mustard seed

Dissolve salt in cold water. Pour over vegetables and let stand 4 hours. Squeeze out salt water from vegetables. Combine sugar, vinegar, celery seed, and mustard seed and bring to a boil. Add vegetables to hot syrup and simmer for 10 minutes. Put in jars and seal.

IRENE SCHRAMM   BARR UNIT

FREEZER PICKLES

12 cucumbers, peeled and
   sliced
2 or 3 onions, cut up
2 green peppers, cut up

2 cups vinegar
2 cups sugar
¼ cup salt

Put cucumbers, onions, and peppers into a large bowl. Combine vinegar, sugar and salt; pour over vegetables. Stir well for 10 minutes, then cover and let stand in refrigerator overnight. Put into plastic containers and place in freezer. To use, let thaw in refrigerator all day. These are just as crisp and good as ones freshly made.

SUE VAN NATTAN   STITCH AND STIR UNIT

STICK PICKLES

Cucumbers, medium size, cut
   in sticks
Alum
2¼ cups sugar
2 tablespoons salt

3¼ teaspoons turmeric
2⅓ cups vinegar
1 tablespoon celery seed
¾ teaspoon mustard seed

Place pickle sticks in jars, add pinch of alum on top of each jar. Pour hot syrup over all and seal.

MARIE VINCENT   DO MORE UNIT

LIME SWEET PICKLES

7 pounds medium size
  cucumbers
2 cups lime
2 gallons water
3½ pounds sugar
2 quarts vinegar

1 tablespoon salt
1 tablespoon pickling spice
1 teaspoon whole cloves
1 teaspoon green food coloring
  (optional)

Wash and slice cucumbers. Soak 24 hours in brine made of lime and water. Wash well 3 times in cold water, then add enough water to cover and soak 3 hours. Drain well. Combine remaining ingredients, tying spices in bag. Let cucumbers stand in mixture overnight. Next morning put on stove and simmer 35 minutes. Seal while hot in clean jars.

NANCY SCHIEN   STITCH AND STIR UNIT

BOBBIE FRUEH, JUNIOR HOMEMAKERS UNIT, uses 4½ pounds sugar, 1 teaspoon celery seed, 1 teaspoon mixing pickling spices, and cinnamon bark.

RED CUCUMBER PICKLES

2 gallon medium cucumbers
2 cups lime

8½ quarts water

First day: Wash cucumbers. Peel, remove centers and seeds. Cut into ½-inch slices. Make solution of the lime and water. Cover and soak cucumbers 24 hours in stone jar.

1 cup vinegar
1 ounce red food coloring
1 tablespoon alum
Water
3 cups vinegar

11 cups sugar
12 ounces red hot cinnamon
  candies
8 sticks cinnamon

Second day: Drain cucumbers and rinse well. Soak in clear water for 3 hours. Drain well. Combine 1 cup vinegar, red food coloring, alum, and enough water to cover. Simmer 2 hours. Drain well. Mix 3 cups vinegar, sugar, red hots, and cinnamon. Bring to rolling boil. Pour over cucumbers and let stand 24 hours.

Third day: Drain liquid from cucumbers. Pack cucumbers into sterilized jars. Heat liquid to rolling boil. Pour into jars and seal.

VELMA WAGGONER   PIASA UNIT

SWEET DILL PICKLES

2 jars large dill pickles,
  drained
Garlic cloves
4 cups sugar

2 cups vinegar
2 tablespoons celery seed
1 tablespoon mustard seed

Slice pickles and put in jars with ½ clove garlic to each jar. Combine sugar, vinegar, celery seed, and mustard seed; bring to a boil. Pour over pickles. Pickles will be ready to eat in a few days. Makes 2 quarts.

MRS. ELERY WELLER   GIRARD DAY UNIT

SWEET-SOUR PICKLES

3½ pounds 2½-inch
  cucumbers (about 50)
½ cup granulated pickling
  salt
4 cups boiling water

1½ quarts cider vinegar
2 cups water
1 tablespoon mixed pickling
  spices
3 cups sugar

Wash cucumbers. Slice larger cucumbers into 2½-inch strips. Dissolve pickling salt in boiling water. Pour over cucumbers packed in a stone jar. Cover and let stand until cool. Drain. Combine vinegar, water, pickling spices, and sugar. Bring to a boil and pour over cucumbers. Cover and let stand 24 hours. Bring cucumbers and syrup to a boil. Pack in hot jars within ½ inch of jar top. Adjust lids. Process in boiling water bath 5 minutes. Start timing when water returns to a boil. Makes 5 pints.

MRS. LEO WELLING   BRIGHTON EARLY BIRDS UNIT

WATERMELON RIND PICKLES

20 cups watermelon rind
Boiling water
7 cups sugar

2 cups vinegar
½ teaspoon oil of cinnamon
¼ teaspoon oil of cloves

Cut off outside green part and inside pink part from watermelon rind. Cut into 1-inch cubes. Cover cubes with boiling water and cook until they can be pricked with a fork but not until they are soft. Drain well. Make a syrup of sugar, vinegar and oils. Bring to a boil and pour over rind. Let stand overnight. For the next two mornings drain off syrup, reheat and pour over rind. On the third morning reheat all together and seal in jars. Makes 5 pints of delicious pickles.

MRS. CECIL DENBY   SOUTH OTTER UNIT

ZUCCHINI RELISH

10 cups zucchini, peeled and ground
4 cups onions, ground
5 tablespoons salt
2¼ cups vinegar
2½ cups sugar
1 teaspoon nutmeg

1 teaspoon dry mustard
1 teaspoon turmeric
2 teaspoons celery seed
1 tablespoon corn starch
1 red pepper, chopped fine
1 green pepper, chopped fine

Combine zucchini, onions, and salt; let stand overnight. Drain, rinse in cold water, and drain again. Combine with remaining ingredients. Cook 30 minutes after mixture comes to a boil. Pour into hot sterilized jars and seal. Makes 7 pints.

ALTA FLORINI   BERTHA ELDRED UNIT

DARLENE WOOLFOLK, SCOTTVILLE UNIT, uses 2 green peppers, 2¼ cups vinegar, 5 cups sugar, ½ teaspoon nutmeg, 1 teaspoon cinnamon, ½ teaspoon black pepper, and green food coloring, if desired.

FREEZER SLAW

1 medium head cabbage, shredded
1 teaspoon salt
1 carrot, grated
1 green pepper, chopped

1 cup vinegar
¼ cup water
1 cup sugar
1 teaspoon celery seed
1 teaspoon whole mustard seed

Mix cabbage and salt; let stand 1 hour. While cabbage is standing, make dressing. Combine vinegar, water, sugar, celery seed, and mustard seed. Boil mixture 1 minute, then cool. Squeeze excess water from cabbage and mix with carrot, pepper, and dressing. Fill containers and freeze. Slaw can be refrozen if you have leftovers.

EVELYN FREY   NILWOOD UNIT

MRS. WILLIAM THOMAS, SOUTH OTTER UNIT uses ½ cup water and 2 cups sugar.

SWEET RELISH

4 cups onions, ground
1 medium head cabbage
4 cups green tomatoes
12 green peppers
6 red peppers (1 hot pepper
  optional)
½ cup salt

2 tablespoons mustard seed
6 cups sugar
1 tablespoon celery seed
1½ teaspoons turmeric
4 cups cider vinegar
2 cups water

Coarsely grind vegetables and sprinkle with salt; let stand overnight. Drain, rinse, and drain again. Combine remaining ingredients. Pour vinegar mixture over vegetables. Heat to boil, simmer 3 minutes. Seal in hot jars. Makes 8 pints.

ZELMA HOPPER   PLAINVIEW UNIT

ELDERBERRY JELLY

2 cups prepared elderberry
  juice
2 cups apple juice

4 tablespoons lemon juice
1 box pectin
5 cups sugar

Cut complete head of elderberries; swish berries generously in cold water. Remove berries from heat; using 3 cups of water to a gallon of berries, bring the water to a rolling boil. Mash the berries; strain through a muslin cloth. Bring all juices and sugar to a boil. Add pectin and again bring to a boil. Watch closely. When a clean fork comes out of hot liquid with syrup clinging to spaces between tines, it is done. Skim fruit before pouring into clean hot glasses into which paraffin has been shaved. The paraffin will come to the top and seal the jar. Makes about 5 glasses.

MILDRED P. LEEFERS   SUSTAINING MEMBER

PEAR HONEY

2 cups pears, ground
1 cup crushed pineapple

2 cups sugar
1 tablespoon lemon juice

Combine pears, pineapple, and 1 cup sugar; boil for 5 minutes. Add second cup of sugar and lemon juice. Boil until syrup runs off a spoon into two distinct lines of drops. Pour at once into hot sterilized jars and seal.

ALENE E. RUYLE   SCOTTVILLE UNIT

CANNED PEACHES

Peeled peach halves
¾ to 1 cup sugar for each
  quart

Hot water

Fill each clean, sterilized jar half full of peach halves. Add ¾ to 1 cup sugar depending on how ripe peaches are. Add ½ cup hot (not boiling) water. Finish filling jar with peaches. Add hot water to fill jar within ½ inch of top. Wipe off jars and put on lids. Process in hot water bath for 20 minutes, or 5 minutes at 5 pounds of pressure in pressure cooker. Note: If there is sugar in the jars when you take them from cooker, do not shake. It will disappear in a few days.

STELLA LOWIS   PIASA UNIT

GRAPEFRUIT MARMALADE

1 grapefruit
2 large oranges

2 lemons
Sugar

Wash and dry fruit. Put through grinder, removing only tough centers and seeds before grinding. Measure fruit and put in earthenware bowl. Add 3 times the quantity of water as fruit pulp. Let stand overnight. Next day boil 10 minutes, allow to stand 1 more night. Second day add sugar to fruit, pint for pint. Boil until mixture jells. Pour into jelly glasses.

HELEN (NELLIE) FISHER   BERTHA ELDRED UNIT

PRESERVING AND CANNING

329

QUICK CHILI SAUCE

3 quarts ripe tomatoes,
peeled
3 cups celery, chopped
2 cups onions, chopped
1 cup green pepper, chopped
¼ cup salt

1½ teaspoon pickling spice
1 cup vinegar
2 cups sugar
¼ cup brown sugar
1½ teaspoons black pepper

Chop vegetables and put into a large bowl. Mix in salt and allow to stand overnight. Drain off liquid but do not press. Combine vinegar, sugars and black pepper in sauce pot. Tie pickling spice in a cheesecloth bag. Add the chopped vegetables and spice bag to vinegar mixture. Stir together and cook 15 minutes or until heated thoroughly. Put in hot sterilized jars and seal. No processing is needed. Makes 6 pints.

MRS. LELAND OERTEL   BRIGHTON EARLY BIRDS UNIT

CRYSTALLIZED GREEN TOMATOES

1 cup lime
2 gallons water
7 pounds green tomatoes,
sliced
3 pints vinegar

4½ pounds sugar
7 sticks cinnamon
1 teaspoon celery seed
1 teaspoon allspice
1 tablespoon salt

Combine lime and water. Soak tomatoes in lime water for 24 hours. Wash carefully and soak in clear water for 3 hours. Combine remaining ingredients and bring to boil. Pour over tomatoes while mixture is hot. Let stand for 24 hours. Bring to boil, boil for 25 minutes. Seal in sterilized half pint or pint jars. (These tomatoes are unbelievably crisp and tasty.)

MRS. MELBA K. EICHEN   SHAWS POINT UNIT

DIETETIC

This little red school house stands in the Shipman Community Park. It was built in 1865 and closed in 1947 following consolidation of the rural schools.

The one-room school was prevalent throughout rural Macoupin County when "Home Bureau" was first organized.

Photographed by Jim Frank

CHEESE CAKE PUDDING

2 cups crushed pineapple in
  own juice
1 heaping tablespoon
  corn starch
1 teaspoon vanilla
Small amount of sweetener,
  to taste

1 quart buttermilk
2 teaspoons vanilla
1 teaspoon liquid sweetener
1 teaspoon yellow food color
3 envelopes Knox gelatin
½ cup cold water
Cool Whip (optional)

Mix pineapple, cornstarch, 1 teaspoon vanilla and small amount of sweetener together and heat over medium heat. Stir until thick and clear. Set aside to cool. With mixer, whip buttermilk, vanilla, sweetener, and food coloring until light and foamy. Dissolve gelatin in ½ cup cold water and heat until dissolved. Do not boil. Pour this mixture into whipped ingredients. Beat again. Place in refrigerator until mixture sets, approximately 1 hour. After it has set, add cooled pineapple mixture. Beat at low speed until well mixed. Put into 8 x 8-inch pan and refrigerate overnight. If desired, top each serving with 2 tablespoons Cool Whip. Makes 9 servings.

JENNIE KING   HONEY POINT UNIT

FRUIT JAM

Note: This recipe must be refrigerated. Don't double the recipe because it will be too hard to handle.

2 cups fruit (pineapple, pear,
  peach, apricot, blueberry,
  blackberry, raspberry, or
  strawberry) (unsweetened
  applesauce can also be
  used)

1 teaspoon lemon juice
½ envelope (½ tablespoon)
  unflavored gelatin
½ teaspoon artificial sweetener
  (or more if you want)

Cut up fruit and place in a covered pan over low heat. Do not add water. Check after 5 to 10 minutes. Depending on the juiciness of the fruit, when juice starts to come out, uncover pan and turn heat to medium and keep stirring until fruit is about half cooked and a good amount of liquid has accumulated in pan. Mix lemon juice with some of the fruit juice and dissolve gelatin in it. Stir this into fruit until all is mixed. Do not overcook as it tastes much better slightly undercooked. Add sweetener. Stir. Taste and add more sweetener until it is to your liking. Refrigerate.

COMMITTEE

DIABETIC COOKIES

½ cup dates, chopped
½ teaspoon baking soda
½ cup boiling water
½ cup butter or margarine
2 eggs, well beaten

2 cups flour
1 teaspoon baking powder
15 tablets (¼ grain) saccharin, crushed
½ cup nuts, chopped (optional)

Put dates and baking soda in small bowl; pour boiling water over and let cool. Soften butter with mixer; add eggs, mix well. Add flour, baking powder, and saccharin. Fold in nuts and cooled date mixture. Drop by spoon onto cookie sheet. Bake at 375° for 10 to 12 minutes.

MILLIE TURNER   MODELITE UNIT

SUGAR FREE FRESH APPLESAUCE

6 apples
8 ounces sugar free ginger ale or strawberry soda

¼ teaspoon cinnamon
¼ teaspoon nutmeg
⅛ teaspoon powdered cloves

Peel apples and cut into large pieces. Place in baking dish; pour in soda. Season with cinnamon, nutmeg, and cloves. Bake at 350° for 10 to 15 minutes or until soft. Mash or put through blender. Place in jar and refrigerate. Makes approximately 1 quart. Each ½ cup serving equals 1 fruit exchange.

MARY TAYLOR   BERTHA ELDRED UNIT

DIET SPICE COOKIES

1¼ cups water
⅓ cup margarine
½ teaspoon salt
2½ teaspoons liquid sweetener
½ cup quick oats
½ teaspoon nutmeg

2 teaspoons cinnamon
2 cups raisins
2 eggs
2 cups flour
1 teaspoon baking soda
1 teaspoon baking powder

In saucepan, mix water, margarine, salt, sweetener, oats, spices, and raisins; bring to a boil. Let boil 3 minutes; cool. Add eggs then dry ingredients. Mix well. Drop by teaspoon onto cookie sheet and bake at 350° for 12 to 15 minutes. Or can be baked all at once on cookie sheet and cut into bars. Bake at 350° for 20 to 25 minutes when making bars.

LELA FITZGERALD   HAGAMAN UNIT

OATMEAL RAISIN COOKIES
(Diabetic)

2 tablespoons diet margarine
1 large banana
⅔ cup non fat dry milk
1 teaspoon baking powder
½ teaspoon cream of tartar
1 teaspoon baking soda
1½ teaspoons brown Sweet
  'n Low

1 teaspoon cinnamon
2 tablespoons lemon juice
2 teaspoons vanilla
1½ cups quick rolled oats
4 tablespoons raisins

Melt margarine over low heat. Mash banana in large mixing bowl. Add next 8 ingredients in order given; mix well. Add rolled oats and raisins; mix well. Add melted margarine; mix. Drop by teaspoon onto cookie sheet. Bake at 350° for 11 minutes. Makes about 30 cookies.

MARIAN GWILLIM   PIASA UNIT

ORANGE SHERBET SALAD
(Dietetic)

2 envelopes orange D-Zerta
  gelatin
2 cups boiling water
1 6-ounce can frozen
  unsweetened orange juice
2 small cans Mandarin
  oranges, drained and
  rinsed

1 can diet Shasta orange soda or
  ginger ale
1 cup crushed pineapple in own
  juice

Mix gelatin in boiling water; add frozen orange juice. Drain and rinse oranges. Add soda to gelatin; chill until mixture begins to thicken. Add pineapple and orange sections. Pour into 9 x 13-inch pan and chill until firm. Serve with Cool Whip, if desired. Makes 8 servings. Recipe equals servings with each equaling 1 fruit.

CATHERN BEST   PLAINVIEW UNIT

HONEY BREAD

2 teaspoons salt
½ cup butter or margarine
½ cup honey (molassss or
  maple syrup)

1½ cups very hot water
2 packages dry yeast
1 cup warm water
7 cups unbleached flour

Add salt, butter, and honey to hot water and stir until melted. Dissolve yeast in warm water. Add honey mixture to yeast mixture then add flour. (add 6 cups flour, use 7th cup while kneading.) Knead. Let dough rise 1½ hours. Shape into 2 loaves; place in bread pans. Let rise 1 hour. Bake at 350° for 45 minutes.

COMMITTEE

TROPICANA PIE
(Diabetic)

1 13¼-ounce can crushed unsweetened pineapple, undrained
1½ cups seedless raisins
1 tablespoon lemon juice
1 envelope unflavored gelatin
¼ cup cold water
1 envelope D-Zerta whipped topping
1 cup sour cream
9-inch baked pastry shell

Combine pineapple, raisins, lemon juice in saucepan. Soften gelatin in cold water. Stir into pineapple mixture. Heat to simmer; simmer 5 minutes, stirring often. Place in refrigerator until cool. Prepare whipped topping mix according to package directions. Fold in sour cream immediately. Fold sour cream mixture into pineapple mixture and spoon into baked pastry shell. Cool 1 to 2 hours before serving. Makes 8 to 10 servings.

COMMITTEE

SUGAR-FREE APPLESAUCE COOKIES

1¾ cups cake flour
½ teaspoon salt
1 teaspoon cinnamon
½ teaspoon nutmeg
½ teaspoon cloves
1 teaspoon baking soda
½ cup butter or margarine
1 tablespoon liquid artificial sweetener, or
24 tablets (¼ grain), crushed saccharin
1 egg
1 cup unsweetened applesauce
⅓ cup raisins
1 cup All-Bran

Sift flour, salt, cinnamon, nutmeg, cloves, and baking soda together. Mix butter, liquid sweetener and egg; beat until light and fluffy. Add flour mixture and applesauce alternately; mix well after each addition. Fold in raisins and All-Bran. Drop by level tablespoonfuls onto greased cookie sheet, about 1 inch apart. Bake at 375° for 20 minutes or until golden brown.

COMMITTEE

DIET SNOWBALL COOKIES

2 sticks diet margarine, softened
1 cup diet sugar (Twin sugar)
2 cups flour
1 teaspoon vanilla
1 cup nuts, chopped
Powdered sugar

Cream margarine with sugar; add flour, vanilla and nuts. Roll in balls and bake at 325° for 12 to 15 minutes until lightly brown. After cooled, dip in powdered sugar. Makes 2 dozen. Leave off powdered sugar if for diabetics.

JESSIE RUSSELL   GILLESPIE NIGHT UNIT

This stately home, now the Macoupin County Historical Society Museum, was long-known as the Anderson Mansion. It was built in 1881 by John Anderson, grandson of Colonel James Anderson, who settled in Carlinville in 1834. Located on a sixteen-acre tract on the northwest edge of the city, it was acquired in 1973 from the late Mrs. Jessie Crawford, daughter of John Anderson. Generous fund drives made the acquisition possible.

Appetizers and Beverages

Soups, Stews and Sandwiches

Salads

339

Pastries

Cakes

Preservation and Canning

Dietetic

NOTES

NEED ADDITIONAL COPIES?
Use this handy order form—

MACOUPIN COUNTY,COUNTY H.E.A.
210 North Broad Street
Carlinville, Illinois 62626

Please send me _____ copies of THE HOMEMAKER'S SAMPLE at
$6.50 plus $1.50 handling. (Illinois residents add 5% sales tax).

Enclosed is my check or money order for _____.

NAME_____

ADDRESS_____

CITY_____ STATE _____ ZIP_____

NEED ADDITIONAL COPIES?
Use this handy order form—

MACOUPIN COUNTY,COUNTY H.E.A.
210 North Broad Street
Carlinville, Illinois 62626

Please send me _____ copies of THE HOMEMAKER'S SAMPLE at
$6.50 plus $1.50 handling. (Illinois residents add 5% sales tax).

Enclosed is my check or money order for _____.

NAME_____

ADDRESS_____

CITY_____ STATE _____ ZIP_____

NEED ADDITIONAL COPIES?
Use this handy order form—

MACOUPIN COUNTY,COUNTY H.E.A.
210 North Broad Street
Carlinville, Illinois 62626

Please send me _____ copies of THE HOMEMAKER'S SAMPLE at
$6.50 plus $1.50 handling. (Illinois residents add 5% sales tax).

Enclosed is my check or money order for _____.

NAME_____

ADDRESS_____

CITY_____ STATE _____ ZIP_____

Re-OrderAdditionalCopies